A Way to Move

Also in the CrossCurrents series

Attending to the Margins
Writing, Researching, and Teaching on the Front Lines

Coming of Age
The Advanced Writing Curriculum

Coming to Class
Pedagogy and the Social Class of Teachers

Composition, Pedagogy, and the Scholarship of Teaching

The Dissertation & the Discipline
Reinventing Composition Studies

Feminist Empirical Research
Emerging Perspectives on Qualitative and Teacher Research

Foregrounding Ethical Awareness in Composition and English Studies

Getting Restless
Rethinking Revision in Writing Instruction

Good Intentions
Writing Center Work for Postmodern Times

Grading in the Post-Process Classroom
From Theory to Practice

Gypsy Academics and Mother-Teachers
Gender, Contingent Labor, and Writing Instruction

Kitchen Cooks, Plate Twirlers, and Troubadours
Writing Program Administrators Tell Their Stories

Know and Tell
A Writing Pedagogy of Disclosure, Genre, and Membership

Life-Affirming Acts

Miss Grundy Doesn't Teach Here Anymore
Popular Culture and the Composition Classroom

The Mythology of Voice

Outbursts in Academe
Multiculturalism and Other Sources of Conflict

The Politics of Writing Centers

Race, Rhetoric, and Composition

Resituating Writing
Constructing and Administering Writing Programs

Textual Orientations
Lesbian and Gay Students and the Making of Discourse Communities

Writing in an Alien World
Basic Writing and the Struggle for Equality in Higher Education

A Way to Move

Rhetorics of Emotion & Composition Studies

Edited by Dale Jacobs
& Laura R. Micciche

Foreword by Peter Elbow
Afterword by Lynn Worsham

CrossCurrents
New Perspectives in Rhetoric and Composition
CHARLES I. SCHUSTER, SERIES EDITOR

Boynton/Cook Publishers
HEINEMANN
Portsmouth, NH

Boynton/Cook Publishers, Inc.
A subsidiary of Reed Elsevier, Inc.
361 Hanover Street
Portsmouth, NH 03801–3912
www.boyntoncook.com

Offices and agents throughout the world

Library of Congress Cataloging-in-Publication Data
A way to move : rhetorics of emotion and composition studies / edited by
Dale Jacobs and Laura R. Micciche.
p. cm.— (CrossCurrents)
ISBN 0-86709-533-4 (pbk. : alk. paper)
1. English language—Rhetoric—Study and teaching—Psychological aspects.
2. Report writing—Study and teaching (Higher)—Psychological aspects.
3. Emotions—Study and teaching (Higher). 4. College students—Psychology.
5. Emotions. I. Jacobs, Dale, 1966–. II. Micciche, Laura R. III. Series:
CrossCurrents (Portsmouth, N.H.).

PE1404.W39 2003
808'.042'019—dc21 2003008632

Editor: Charles I. Schuster
Production service: bookworks
Production coordinator: Lynne Reed
Cover design: Joni Doherty
Typesetter: Kim Arney Mulcahy
Manufacturing: Steve Bernier

Printed in the United States of America on acid-free paper
07 06 05 04 03 DA 1 2 3 4 5

Contents

Foreword

Peter Elbow

Have you ever had someone try to change your emotions or tell you that you were having the wrong feelings? Or, worse yet, tell you that you were mistaken about what feelings you were having? The essays in this book remind us that, in a real sense, civilization, culture, government, and education have been one long project in schooling the emotions. When culture, institutions, and family try to control and tame our emotions, it's often in the interests of keeping the peace ("We'll just have to skip ice cream and cake unless you all calm down!"). But does emotional schooling and peacekeeping *always* serve the interests of power? This is a wonderfully complicated question that these essays raise but do not answer; they complicate this theme by insisting on saying: "Let's face it. We too, as teachers and as persons trying to build a fairer society, are also in the business of trying to school the emotions."

There's another theme of complication that I'm grateful for in these essays—a theme that's always perplexed me: Emotions are so stupid!/Emotions are so smart! When we do something stupid (like choosing the obviously wrong food or action or person), emotions were usually in the driver's seat. For a number of decades, scholars have stressed how lived experience, like emotion, is prey to the shaping power of cultural forces—how our experiencing and our feeling and our bodies are "written" by larger influences. Fair enough, useful enough; but misleading if we stop there (just as it is misleading to pretend that individuals are entirely free agents). Lived experience—like our emotions and like our bodies—can function as wedges whereby we resist or "write back" against what is trying to write us. Emotions often yield good insights and intuitions that are only much later confirmed by thinking and evidence. When we ignore emotions and go only for logical thinking, we are liable to miss crucial things—not just in us but in the world.

I'm grateful also, then, for this second theme of complication. It would have been nice if the authors had given answers to these complexities: How can I tell if a feeling is smart or stupid? How do we decide what counts as bad manipulation and good manipulation? But at this stage, "It's very complicated" is the best answer we have. Yet at least one simple answer is clear: We get in trouble if we write off emotions or fail to take them seriously or don't allow them a central role in our thinking about writing and teaching.

I'm particularly interested in one emotional complication that's central to us all as language teachers: people tend to have conflicting feelings about correctness in language. On the one hand, many people seem to have remarkably intense feelings of repugnance at what they perceive as "bad language." There's often a surprising dimension of anger or hate in the way many people describe language that violates (!) what they experience as "correct," "standard," or "natural." I think these feelings reflect the effort and price people have expended in learning—or even just trying to learn—to "do things the right way"—in short, to be civilized. But because of this very same struggle, we often see (and even feel in ourselves?) the impulse to resist civilization—to do things the wrong way. Why does it please people to spell things wrong on purpose (often on glaring neon signs: "E-Z Wash" "Sheer Cuts")? Why do so many people feel the urge to wear baseball caps backwards? I'm not surprised, therefore, to learn from Geneva Smitherman's various works how much language from Black English the mainstream white culture has picked up—when always white people have been taught that this is "wrong English." Do we not see many young people today accelerating the borrowings from African American Vernacular English (AAVE)? Turning to the classroom, I would ask us to think further about the many mistakes that we see so often in students' final drafts. I don't think they are just the result of laziness or ignorance. I believe many students hand in papers with a feeling I've sometimes detected in myself: "If you won't take me the way I am, then too bad for you."

As these essays testify in various ways to the power and importance of the emotions, they reveal the *weakness of critical thinking* when it comes to changing emotions. This theme brings up a special interest of mine: the need for what I call "the believing game" or "methodological believing" (1973; 1986) as a *supplement* to critical thinking. The believing game is the disciplined practice of taking competing views and not just listening to them and refraining from arguing with them, but making an actual effort to believe them in order to see what could possibly be right in them. Yet any belief attained this way is only temporary, since you then move on to try to believe the next view. Critical thinking or what I call the doubting game yields a mirror image of this process. It is the disciplined effort to seek out bad reasoning, contradictions, and other weaknesses in order to determine which views are best. Critical thinking may be fine for seeing flaws in other people's views, but it's not as good at helping us see flaws in our own views. We have an *emotional* connection to our own views. Indeed, critical thinking is often counterproductive when it helps people *fend off* views that run counter to their own—views so often held in place by emotion.

The believing game invites *thinking with feelings* (though it doesn't require it). Pure thinking helps us see flaws, but most of us have difficulty really entering into someone else's view—a view at odds with our own—without feelings. The believing game harnesses in both speakers and listeners by asking holders of minority or dissenting opinions to answer questions like these: "What events and experiences in your life led you to have this view or this way of looking at the world? What does it feel like to have your view? What do you see from your position? How do you experience things from where you sit?" Others must listen and not argue back, unless they can say things that help flesh out or back up that way of thinking or seeing things. Feelings may not be the main thing about the believing game, but in the context of this book, I want to emphasize how the believing game invites the harnessing of feelings for the sake of better thinking.

Acknowledgments

We wish to thank our contributors for their dedication to this project and their patience during the drafting and revising stages. In every case, the contributors responded to our revision suggestions with thoughtfulness, often prompting us to clarify and better articulate our thinking to one another. We also thank those who submitted proposals, but whose words are not presented in this volume, for their ideas helped us to conceive this book in its final form. Thanks as well to the staff at Document Services at the University of Windsor for all their help with manuscript preparation. Without the support and guidance of Charles Schuster, Lisa Luedeke, Eric Chalek, and the wonderful group of people at Boynton/Cook, this volume would not have been possible. Finally, we're grateful for the opportunity to work collaboratively on this book—an opportunity that allowed us to deepen and expand our intellectual lives as well as our friendship with one another.

Introduction

Rhetoric, Editing, and Emotion

The drafting of this book happened in the shadow of the terrorist attacks on September 11, 2001, in New York City and Washington, D.C. Not only did these attacks change the world, but they also changed our classrooms by generating a rhetoric of panic and fear that required immediate response. For instance, at Laura's institution, East Carolina University, many faculty dedicated class time to discussion of the attacks and their aftermath. Prayer vigils were held on campus and the atmosphere of the classroom and the campus was unmistakably altered by questions about safety and the United States' entrance into a "war on terror" with no discernible end in sight. Students in Laura's first-year writing class expressed a deeply felt ambivalence about the unfolding events. On the one hand, some students, powerfully moved by impassioned displays of patriotism across the country, believed strongly that the United States had no choice but to defend itself through the declaration of war. On the other hand, students expressed fear and uncertainty about sending their friends and family members to fight in a war characterized by an elusive enemy and an unclear goal.

For Dale's students at the University of Windsor in Canada, situated in the shadow of the Ambassador Bridge to the United States, the attacks evoked general anxiety and dread, which was further complicated by the school's proximity to the border. In the months that followed the attacks, the border became a symbol of anxiety in both Canada and the United States; people from both countries who had daily crossed over for work or school found themselves continually in the midst of security and surveillance such as we have never seen. Not only were students worried about what the events might mean for their futures, but they also worried about whether or not they could even get to the university or whether or not their parents would be able to get to work, illustrating the way the attacks altered lives at the most intimate, daily level. This sense of foreboding and uncertainty, which characterized students' concerns about their immediate and distant living conditions, formed an emotional tone that marked and at times interrupted the daily work of teaching. At both of our institutions, students and faculty articulated an emotioned discourse in the classroom for which neither seemed prepared nor adequately equipped to address. This is undoubtedly a dramatic instance of how emotion shapes our classrooms—one that makes the emotional context of teaching explicit and undeniable.

The extremity of this situation is certainly not a part of the "regular" emotion work that teachers and administrators of writing generally confront, but it does present us with an example of how emotion affects our work in real, experiential terms. More regular forms of emotion work, as our contributors compellingly demonstrate, include the daily work of building relationships with students and colleagues, reading and responding to student texts, constructing and implementing conceptions of rhetoric that shape curricular design and research practices, excavating rhetorical history in the service of contemporary contexts and purposes, and administering writing programs. The thirteen essays assembled here are grouped into three (overlapping) sections: Theorizing Emotion, Classroom Emotions, and Academic Workplace Emotions. The first section develops theories of emotion that work out of classical rhetoric, feminist studies, and cognitive neuroscience. Contributors demonstrate how these theoretical frameworks might productively inform our conceptions of teaching and research. Section Two explores the specific ways in which emotion shapes and is shaped by our teaching practices. Each essay weaves theoretical discussions of emotion with contextualized studies of classroom practices. The final section focuses on the relation between emotion and our professional roles as teachers and administrators. Here, contributors extend materialist critiques of Composition Studies by describing our professional labor in terms of its emotional value rather than focusing only on economic value, as recent studies tend to do. The organization of *A Way to Move* aims to move the reader from general to specific—from discussions of theoretical traditions that give shape to contemporary emotion studies to discussions of the specific ways that these theories are relevant to our work as teachers and administrators in Composition Studies.

A Way to Move: Rhetorics of Emotion and Composition Studies seeks to articulate and challenge the way we think about emotion. That is, in addition to its conventional understanding as a term that denotes expression of feeling, or affective response to a situation, we want to suggest that emotion also enables and disables change. In particular, we are interested in emotion's capacity to construct a culture of movement in opposition to one of ossification, and in thinking about emotion as a central ingredient in the act of persuasion that has the potential to move our discipline in new directions. Our interest in emotion and its connection with a culture of movement emerges from a set of questions that animate the conception and evolution of this book: How does emotion shape the work of teachers and administrators in Composition Studies? How are we schooled to use emotion in our professional lives? What is the place of emotion, for example, in our various professional relationships—with students, colleagues, research subjects, administrators, and/or advisees? Our collection poses these and other questions that seek to develop a discourse of the emotions by which compositionists might begin to name and interpret the affective dimensions of their work. These essays make visible the way emotion structures and is structured by our various professional locations in classrooms, English departments, and universities. The contributors uncover and elaborate intersections between rhetorics of emotion and Composition Studies in order to reflect critically on how emotion concepts are embedded in the social and institutional fabric of our work. More specifically, contributors both theorize emotion and suggest implications for our daily practices in teaching and administration.

As is probably clear by now, a key term for us is *move*. We take, as our starting point, the Latin root of emotion, *motere*, which means "to move," suggesting that a tendency to act is implicit in every emotion. Movement, or repositioning oneself in the face of ever-changing situations, is a central goal of both classical and contemporary rhetorical theory. Effective rhetoric is dynamic rather than static; effective rhetoric moves us towards new ways of knowing and creates avenues for social change. In our book, linking emotion with movement underscores the rhetorical nature of emotion as a mode of articulation by which thought and action are moved, or are always in flux, and are a source for moving others. We agree with Donald Bryant who, in "Rhetoric: Its Functions and Its Scope," contends that "Rhetoric as distinct from the learnings which it uses is dynamic; it is concerned with movement. It *does* rather than *is*. It is method rather than matter. It is chiefly involved with bringing about a condition, rather than discovering or testing a condition" (1994, 281). "Move" as in "movement" suggests progress toward something like a more substantive understanding of emotion emerging from the tradition of classical rhetoric, as Ellen Quandahl explains so cogently in her chapter. Movement also gestures toward a sense of collective identity and social contestation central to movements for change that produce shifts in thinking and seeing; such thinking, within an institutional context, is evidenced in chapters by William Wright and Brad Peters. Movement evokes physical acts and embodied emotion, as Mary Ann Cain eloquently demonstrates in her participant-observer study of a movement artist working with youth from northeastern Indiana. The pedagogical possibilities entailed in the concept and act of movement are demonstrated in Donna Strickland and Ilene Crawford's essay. The authors urge composition teachers toward an altered pedagogy of correctness, one that is aware of the way emotion and whiteness are tied up together, often creating a schooling of racial difference as well as one of nonstandard language dialects. As can be seen in these examples, movement is a key term that helps us to re-vision the ways in which emotion intersects with disciplinary practices and theories by highlighting the relationship between affect and rhetoric.

As our subtitle indicates, *rhetorics* of emotion also figure prominently in our conception of this book. In keeping with the expansive scope of rhetorical studies, our contributors foreground multiple, interdisciplinary *articulations* of emotion that draw from psychology, cultural anthropology, feminism, political theory, critical pedagogy, and theories of social change. Susan Kirtley's articulation of emotion, for example, draws on the classical rhetorical tradition through her reading of Diotima, while Tom Kerr's conception of emotion has its basis in the realm of cognitive neuroscience. The contributors also concentrate on multiple *sites*—classrooms and administrative posts—where a discourse of emotion can help to apprehend, examine, and critique the nature of our work. To this end, Wendy Ryden explores the rhetoric of politeness that informs many classrooms, while Mara Holt, Leon Anderson, and Albert Rouzie examine how emotion work is structured within writing program administration. We also seek to examine multiple *constructions* of emotion, suggesting that emotions have a history specific to cultural and social contexts. Two such constructions of emotions can be seen in Janet Bean's work on emotion and working class students' narratives and in Piper Murray's essay on how teachers are conditioned to respond to their own feelings of frustration when approaching student writing. Finally, the volume includes multiple *modes* for thinking through emotion and Composition Studies, as seen in Alice Gillam's theorizing of her experience as a writing program administrator or Gretchen Flesher Moon's examination of emotion in contemporary composition textbooks. As contributors move between these multiple articulations, sites, constructions, and modes, they foreground the rhetorical nature of emotion and highlight important links between rhetoric and emotion that inform this volume.

Setting the Stage for *A Way to Move*

One of the most useful ideas for us has been that emotion is not only individually experienced, but is also socially experienced and constructed. In "Understanding Emotions: Some Interdisciplinary Considerations" (1988), Shula Sommers explains that "Emotions reflect, among other things, knowledge of the valuations of a community, concepts of social relationships as well as attitudes and beliefs held in common by members of a community. It follows that an individual's emotions are embedded in the social framework in which an individual functions and that analyses of emotions cannot ignore social phenomena" (26). Sommers suggests that emotion is schooled through cultural institutions such as the family, the media, and all levels of the educational system. Emotions may also be understood as evidence of one's position in social relations and as a form of social action. In their introduction to *Language and the Politics of Emotion*, Catherine A. Lutz and Lila Abu-Lughod claim that emotional discourse is "a form of social action that creates effects in the world" (1990, 12). They focus on discourses of emotion, rather than emotion itself, to show how "emotional discourses are commentaries on the practices essential to social relations" (19). Included in their articulation is the idea that emotion is embodied in experiences that involve the whole person. Drawing from the work of Pierre Bourdieu, Lutz and Abu-Lughod write: "To learn how, when, where, and by whom emotions ought to be enacted is to learn a set of body techniques including facial expressions, postures, and gestures" (12). Emotional dispositions, in this understanding, are created in multiple contexts. While family is certainly a central one, cultural training around gender, race, class, and other identity markers also schools the emotions.

This point is clarified in Peter Lyman's "The Politics of Anger" (1981), where he examines the "socialization of anger" as a key element of "moral training of the good citizen" (62). As other feminists have argued, anger and other unruly emotions are threats to the social order precisely because they are responses to social subordination that are marked by irrationality. Irrationality, as Catherine A. Lutz explains in "Engendered Emotion," is the central term that has defined emotion for centuries. Like the female, Lutz argues, emotion has been viewed as "something natural rather than cultural, irrational rather than rational, . . . physical rather than mental or intellectual" and so on (1990, 69). She examines the emphasis on "emotional control" as evidence in our culture of the "danger of both women and their emotionality" (71). Her work, coupled with that of feminists such as Elizabeth V. Spelman and Sandra Bartky, provides a strong basis from which to problematize gendered constructions of emotion, "natural" distinctions between acceptable and unacceptable emotions, and assumptions about appropriate emotions. Alison Jaggar (1989b) has further questioned the distinction between acceptable and unacceptable emotions, arguing that emotions seen as threatening or unacceptable to the dominant culture can also be used as a spur for social change. Jaggar labels these types of emotions as "outlaw emotions." She writes,

> When unconventional emotional responses are experienced by isolated individuals, those concerned may be confused, unable to name their experience; they may even doubt their own sanity. . . . When certain emotions are shared or validated by others, however, the basis exists for forming a subculture defined by perceptions, norms, and values. By constituting the basis for such a subculture, outlaw emotions may be politically (because epistemologically) subversive. (144)

A Way to Move attempts to build on this idea by extending the feminist critique of emotion as irrational and dangerous and by conceiving emotion as a basis for professional and social action. Feminist revisions of emotion are particularly useful for us as we seek to articulate *rhetorics* of emotion that, among other things, challenge naturalized, feminized conceptions of emotion as frivolous, or dangerous, excess. If we instead view emotion as connected to our rational and ethical lives, we open a space of possibility for reimagining our approaches to teaching, research, and administration.

This sense of possibility assumes that emotion can function as a galvanizing force to create social and institutional movement. Here we engage the spirit of critical pedagogy as embodied by educators like Myles Horton and Paulo Freire. Much of the dynamic thrust of critical pedagogy is summed up by Myles Horton, a labor and civil rights activist who founded the Highlander Folk School in the early 1930s: "I'm less interested in methodology or techniques than I am in a *process* that involves the total person, involves vision, involves total realities . . . if I had to put a finger on what I consider a good education, a good *radical* education, it wouldn't be anything about methods or techniques. It would be loving people first" (Bell *et al.* 1990, 176). Or, as Freire says in the same book, "Knowing for me is not a neutral act, not only from the political point of view, but from the point of view of my body, my sensual body. It is full of feelings, of emotions, of taste" (23). Both see the project of education for a critical democracy as engaged not only in the rational or the ethical, but wholly wrapped up with the emotional part of being human. By reclaiming the place of emotion in education, *A Way to Move* works (usually indirectly) out of Horton and Freire's ideas in order to assess and transform how we perform and conceptualize our work, and how we conduct ourselves as professionals in Composition Studies.

Our volume also builds on initial efforts in Composition Studies to introduce emotion into our disciplinary conversations. The most sustained analysis of emotion in the field, Lynn Worsham's "Going Postal" (1998), focuses on pedagogic violence implied in teaching and learning practices (also see Worsham 2002). She discusses "the way violence addresses and educates emotion and inculcates an affective relation to the world" (216). Like Worsham, we view emotion as socially and historically constructed and bodily lived, a view that makes it possible to consider how we might "unlearn" emotional violence (216). Her major claim is that, if we are committed to social change, "then the work of decolonization must occur at the affective level, not only to reconstitute the emotional life of the individual but also, and more importantly, to restructure the feeling or mood that characterizes an age" (216). Our volume builds on this idea by arguing that Composition's familiar claims for creating equity in the discipline and in classrooms may be expanded through analyses of emotion at multiple levels, including analyses of the institutional structures that circumscribe our activities as teachers and administrators. While Worsham is focused on emotion as a pedagogy of violence reinforced through different forms of schooling (including cultural schooling), our book focuses on the many different ways that emotionality—including but not limited to emotional violence—constitutes an important aspect of our work lives. To put it another way, we contend that the personal and the professional are always interconnected, making the commonplace idea that emotion is solely "personal" an untenable and insufficient claim because it fails to consider the way emotion refuses to be contained in our "personal" lives. In short, we believe it is necessary to move our disciplinary thinking forward by identifying the relation between emotion and our work, analyzing the implications of this relation, and formulating interventions that would meaningfully insert emotion into the rhetoric of the discipline.

Furthering the Conversation: Editing as Intellectual and Emotional Practice

In "Call Me Horatio: Negotiating Between Cognition and Affect in Composition" (1998), Richard Fulkerson argues the following about edited collections:

> It is axiomatic that any collection of writings by 15 or more separate authors will be uneven in quality. But that is scarcely an adequate criticism of the sorts of collections we now see regularly. They are created either by editors' inviting other writers whom they believe to have some interest in an issue to contribute a piece, or worse yet, by issuing a general 'call for papers' on the proposed topic in a scholarly journal or, increasingly, via the internet. And although sometimes the pieces take alternate perspectives on issues, and thus 'talk to each other,' ordinarily the writers do not read the other submissions and may have no idea about repetitions, contradictions, or other interactions. Short, unified, single volumes by single authors . . . ought, I think, to become the basic stand-alone publications in our field. (114–15)

Obviously the book you are holding is not a unified volume by a single author. In fact, we argue that the contributors' focus on multiple *articulations*, *sites*, *constructions*, and *modes* is one of the main strengths of *A Way to Move*. Perhaps because of the collaborative nature of our editing practices, we have, from the beginning, seen this project as a conversation about emotion to which we hoped to add our voices and from which we hoped to learn. To that end, we have attempted to foster an interchange of ideas and have paid close attention to the process of editing, to what happens when you attempt, in book form, to facilitate a segment of an ongoing conversation. When done well, we think edited collections make possible a lively conversation that is better created in fifteen or so voices than in one, especially when the area of focus is relatively underdeveloped in a discipline. The dynamic potential of edited collections emerges for us out of our sense that intellectual exchange and disciplinary knowledge-building is a collective effort that benefits from a diverse range of perspectives and approaches. This range includes, but is not limited to, single-authored texts that focus sustained attention on a given subject, as well as edited collections that present multiple voices and perspectives alongside one another, ideally creating an animated picture of the whole that is not otherwise possible. The multiple voices that inform this volume have helped to create a complex and layered examination of emotion that would have been impossible in a single, unified voice.

Since we believe that the process involved in editing collections determines the shape of the final product, a word about our process is perhaps in order here.

Our conversation about emotion began when we were colleagues at East Carolina University, where Laura still teaches, and continued after Dale moved to the University of Windsor. Part of the strength of that interchange was, and continues to be, the different entrance points that each of us had to the study of emotion—Laura through feminist theory and Dale through critical pedagogies. In the spring of 1999, we put together a panel entitled "Pedagogy and Emotion" for the 2000 Conference on College Composition and Communication in Minneapolis. As we prepared for that conference, Laura had the idea for a collection of essays on the relationship between emotion and Composition Studies and asked Dale if he would like to coedit with her. It was a natural extension of the conversations we had been having in each other's offices for the past year. In Minneapolis, Charles Schuster heard about the proposed volume and offered enthusiastic support, making us promise that he would be able to have the first look at the finished proposal. The conversation had enlarged to three and we began to feel that it was a conversation in which others might want to participate. Confirming Fulkerson's suspicions about the way edited collections get assembled, we issued a call for papers in the summer of 2000, advertising our projected volume in *College English*, *College Composition and Communication*, *Rhetoric Review*, *JAC: Journal of Advanced Composition*, and the *PMLA*. In addition, and "worse yet," as Fulkerson might say, we distributed our call for papers on the H-Rhetor listserv and the WPA-List. We then met to select proposals at the National Council of Teachers of English conference in Milwaukee in the fall of 2000. As we read through over forty excellent submissions, we began to see three natural groupings of essays that would be able to speak to one another, groupings that gave shape to our projected volume.

In order to make the evolving shape of the volume visible to the contributors, we posted the in-progress essays on a website and encouraged everyone involved in the project to read each other's work. To further extend the web of connections within the volume, we invited Peter Elbow to write a Foreword and Lynn Worsham to write an Afterword. As we read multiple drafts of each contributor's chapter, we attempted, through our comments, to strengthen the links between essays in the volume (sometimes referring authors to chapters drafted by other contributors) and to cross-disciplinary scholarship on emotion. During this stage of the process, we became aware of how editing, especially the act of providing feedback and direction for revision, entails its own kind of emotion work. As we crafted letters to each contributor detailing our revision suggestions, we found ourselves checking with one another on the appropriateness of our tone and word choice, often wondering whether our criticism would be received as constructive. The following kinds of questions tacitly guided our practice: How do we say what we mean without either couching it in ambiguous, confusing rhetoric that strives to be overly supportive at the expense of directness, or disrespecting the writer's process of working through ideas? How do we ask a writer to change the tone of an essay, a request that effectively alters the emotional attitude of the piece? How are we schooling emotion through our editing practices? Looking back, it strikes us that editing involves a good deal of emotion management, for as an editor you work with others' ideas and words, establishing an intimacy with the other that is not so unlike the experience of working with student writers.

As coeditors, we also had our own intellectual and emotional relationship to manage. This became clear, for example, when we sat down to write the prospectus together, having no prior experience writing collaboratively with one another. While Dale had grown accustomed to the challenges and rewards of collaborative writing as a result of his training in graduate school, Laura was more comfortable with the solitary writing practices that had served her well up until this point. As she attempted to discipline every word that Dale wrote, charged emotions rose to the surface, leading to a difficult conversation about what it means to write together. This incident brought home to us, in very concrete terms, the complex relationship between writing and emotion, and the ways in which emotion informs our professional identities and interactions, not to mention our personal relationships. Emotion was suffused throughout our collaboration, as this volume argues it is through all our work as compositionists. Through the process of drafting the prospectus, we both came to understand that collaborative writing requires a certain amount of faith in one another and in the process, it requires a willingness to enter into the language choices and meaning commitments of an other, it requires a belief in writing as an ongoing process of inquiry that involves movement between different ideas, voices, traditions, and habits of thought. As we set about the difficult emotion work of functioning as coeditors, we realize now that we were also thinking through the process of facilitating the conversation that a multivoiced collection entails. Editing (especially coediting) is demanding intellectual and emotional work when one allows it to be, and like most work that asks a lot of us, it can be extremely rewarding and exciting because it places us at the center of a conversation that, with any luck, productively and smartly moves in many different directions, enriching and deepening and sometimes even revising the original idea.

As the above comments suggest, editing can call attention to relationships of power that are usually unspoken and sometimes uncomfortable. In her chapter on the relations between researcher and participant in this volume, Mary Ann Cain instructively writes that

> Repositioning researchers as those who exchange language (and knowledge) with their subjects opens into questions of how such relationships are already a site of overtaking and/or resisting another's language uses. In this view, research is also pedagogy, as language is exchanged between researcher and subjects. Current assumptions about neutrality, however, conceal the pedagogical aspects of research. As a result, our knowledge of what forms emotions actually do take in such inquiry, how they are used in social control, and their potential for re-formation through mutual exchange, is unavailable; it is simply "unthinkable."

Cain's comments, though written for a different context, help us to articulate the way editing establishes power relationships. For instance, the editors (and, beyond them, the press itself) have final say over what they want a chapter to do and say, a position that can lead to "overtaking and/or resisting another's language uses" for the sake of the overall vision of the edited collection or, less respectfully, because another's language challenges, subverts, or somehow calls into question the editors' positions in the discourse. While such questioning would ideally be seen as a strength that provides a productive tension in an edited collection, surely this does not always characterize an editor's reading of the matter, for editors are not objective, disinterested parties. In this sense, editorial work can certainly be seen as a form of "social control," to borrow Cain's phrasing, where meaning and emotion are disciplined by a rigid conception of an *imagined*—as opposed to an *evolving*—collection of essays. If editing practices are not built upon a basis of "mutual exchange" between writer and editor, thereby opening a space where meanings can be negotiated, then it's not difficult to see how editing can become a streamlining activity that closes down new meanings. As you might guess, we have tried to approach editing as a process of intellectual discovery, a process that opens meanings, creating a layered text that values and exemplifies a range of approaches to the question of how emotion shapes the work of compositionists. That said, we were continually reimmersed in the emotionality of editing as we had to make hard decisions about cutting and reducing essays during the editorial process of shaping this book. In writing this reflection on our editing experience, we hope to make "thinkable" the way that editing is an intellectual *and* emotional practice, requiring a strong knowledge base and tools for negotiating the difficult work of editing the words of others. Because our field produces a large number of edited collections, we hope there will be more discussion about the material reality of doing this kind of work and about the implications of "edited knowledge" for the present and future of composition as a discipline.

In closing, we see *A Way to Move* as one segment of a much larger conversation and hope that it will prompt further work on the relation between Composition Studies and emotion. For starters, we believe that more work needs to be done in the following areas: racialized emotion and teaching writing; the emotionality of teaching multiculturalism; connections between the postcolonial and emotion theory; emotion expression in the academy and generational differences; graduate student mentoring and the place of emotion; and links between professional identity and emotion. These important issues are inadequately represented in this volume, but they are not invisible to or forgotten by us. We imagine that the thinking presented in *A Way to Move* offers entrance points into discussions about these and other topics, movement outward and forward that would indeed characterize the spirit of this volume.

Dale Jacobs
Laura R. Micciche

Chapter One

A Feeling For Aristotle
Emotion in the Sphere of Ethics

Ellen Quandahl

[V]irtues have to do with actions and emotions.
—Aristotle, *Nicomachean Ethics*

Among the important developments in Composition Studies in the past decade has been the examination of writing pedagogies—classroom practices and how they are theorized, and the work of teachers with students—in the light of broader research on pedagogy as *paideia*, the whole social education of members of a culture (Worsham 1998, 221). This broader research, engaging both the ideological and the unconscious, could be said to examine structures and processes that are "beyond reason"—that is, beyond deliberate thinking and discussion about classroom styles and lessons. Scholars in fields as different as political science, history, and anthropology have shown that the primary other of reason—emotion—is not merely an individual or natural phenomenon, but is rather culturally and historically shaped, and closely linked with discourse. Such research shows the powerful affective dimension of becoming culturally competent. And it suggests that the forms of education, both formal schooling and the experiences of life in a culture, address humans in ways that shape what is said to be deeply "within," offering not only knowledge, perspective, and strategies of reason, but also the very forms of emotion.

In what follows, I argue that Aristotle is an indispensable predecessor for acknowledging and working with rather than against emotion in rhetorical education. For here is a patient observer and analyst of culture who gives emotion a significant place in living well generally, in ethics and in politics. My reading of Aristotle also highlights the character of much recent Composition literature as a deeply ethical project, concerned with the schooling of conduct as one strand of social flourishing or dysfunction, and taking a keen interest in the conditions and training of the individual and social psyche—that which in the past has been called moral psychology.

This linking of rhetoric with ethics and moral psychology is historically long-standing. For, as we know, the *Rhetoric* offers the first comprehensive psychology and survey of the emotions, and positions rhetoric as a branch of ethics and politics, to which the whole body of Aristotle's work is centrally devoted. As John M. Cooper has suggested, Aristotle's approach to ethics was deeply rooted in "the study of the psychological conditions required—the sorts of desires, the attitudes to self and others, the states of mind and feeling, the kind of knowledge and insight required—if one is to lead the best life that is humanly possible" (1999, x). What I wish to show is that not only the account of emotions in the *Rhetoric*, but also its location in the domain of ethics is significant for what it reveals about current themes—and silences—in pedagogy.

This project may at first glance seem an odd one, since scholarly tradition links Aristotle with the view that sharply separates reason and emotion, promoting rationality as the center of morality, and making emotion incompatible with the rational ideal (Homiak 1993). There is ample evidence for this reading. As well, it is easy to cite passages in which Aristotle says clearly that women, slaves and non-Greeks are inferior to citizen males in their powers of reasoning and capacity for virtue, and ask whether such thinking infects or contaminates the whole body of work (Jarratt and Reynolds 1994, 44; Groenhout 1998, 172). However, reading the texts of Aristotle, one discovers, ironically, that while he does indeed suggest that the human "soul" consists of rational and irrational parts, he is not altogether certain that they are separate, "like parts of the body or any other divisible thing, or whether they are only logically separable though in reality indivisible, as convex and concave are in the circumference of a circle" (*Nicomachean Ethics* 1102a).[1] Feminist scholars have shown that Aristotle holds not only that the "non-rational" part is fully human, but that it is necessary in cultivating a full and ethical life (Koziak 2000; Achtenberg 1996). Others see Aristotle as an exemplar of the view that emotions are not only *not* fully separate from reason, but involve reason or cognition—and thus also language—in crucial ways (Walker 2000; Nussbaum 1994; Cooper 1999). All see Aristotle as an important *resource* for understanding emotion in political, social, everyday life. These writers also undertake what I would call a radical recontextualizing, demonstrating that the *Rhetoric* is part of a vast project and range of observation and reflection by Aristotle about how a person and a society can live well and flourish. It is by keeping in view this range of work and its goal that one arrives at a feeling for Aristotle.

Emotions in an Ethical Sphere

First of all, in looking at *where* Aristotle talks about the emotions, one has to notice that it is not "the official work on 'psychology,' the *De Anima*" that offers helpful material, but rather the works on ethics and the *Rhetoric* (Frede 1996, 258). So in Aristotle there is a significant connection and interplay of emotion with ethics as well as persuasion. Indeed, here is the intriguing idea that the very conceptualizing of emotion belongs in the ethical sphere, which is also a political one. One also has to notice that reading passages in the ethical works can feel, for moderns, more like reading psychologies, with their accounts of the affective powers and their roles in human relations, than like reading ethics. Why is this? Perhaps the greatest surprise about the *Ethics*, for readers today, is the "astonishing absence" of talk about rules (MacIntyre 1984, 150). Aristotle does have a great deal to say about virtues, but these are not principles. Rather, he says again and again, "the virtues have to do with actions and emotions" (*NE* 1104b). Equally surprising is that ethics is a study within the field of politics, and politics is the study of the good, both for the individual and the state.[2] As he investigates what the good is in this interdependent sphere, Aristotle focuses on *action* and *living well*, for the aim of politics is the highest good attainable by action, and that is happiness. Here happiness means doing well, or living well over time (*NE* 1095a and 1098a). So politics—and its subfield, ethics—is above all a practical study, not unlike literacy studies, with a broad goal for students' equal and full participation in the society (New London Group 1996, 60).

How does Aristotle link ethics and emotions? What sort of ethics is this? The answers to these questions ought to be of great interest, given the recent concern among compositionists with the ethics of teaching writing, with teaching ethics in the writing classroom, and with the role of emotion in rhetoric research (Gale *et al.* 1999; Spigelman 2001; Bizzell 2000). Four propositions will give a feeling for such answers, reminding us at the same time that Aristotle's *Rhetoric* is not a programmatic handbook, but one piece of a broad meditation on what citizen leaders need to know. I use these propositions to sum up a range of philosophy, and hope to give just enough detail to show that Aristotle's thinking about emotion is extensive and generative. Indeed, as Jeffrey Walker has shown, his "preferences" for reason and the facts of a case "could not contain the implications of his own account of *pathos*" (2000, 92).

1. "Thumos" is a social force. Scholars have discovered a crucial hinge between emotions and ethics/politics in a Greek word associated with spiritedness, and also with heart, or the seat or capacity for emotions, *thumos*. This is a term recently brought to the attention of writing teachers by Walker, in a splendid article on the persuasive figure of speech and writing that Aristotle calls the enthymeme, or rhetorical syllogism. Walker shows that the root word of this term is *thumos*, "often linked to both the production and the reception of passional thought and eloquent, persuasive discourse" (1994, 49). Despite the recent research arguing that Aristotle separates persuasion through enthymeme from persuasion through *pathos* (Gaines 2000), it appears that the passions are embedded *within* this critical concept of Aristotle's rhetoric. There is now a body of research tracking *thumos* and its relation to speech in Greek thought, suggesting that this heart-word ought to become a key term for rhetoric. Barbara Koziak has shown that *thumos* affords a range of representations for women in Homer, and presents dramatically different senses in Plato and Aristotle. She reminds us of a conundrum in Plato—that, on the one hand, in his mythic, tripartite psychology, reason tames and controls the emotional part, but on the other hand, Plato analogizes philosophy with eros, so that knowing involves desire.[3]

Koziak and others recognize that Aristotle fully opens this door, giving a significant place to emotion in moral conduct. This has to do with his understanding of human sociality. Alisdair MacIntyre makes the point that for Aristotle, "friendship, company and a [political community] are essential components of humanity" (1984, 135). Importantly, socialness is rooted not only in the human capacity for speech (*Politics* 1253a), but also in the capacity to be moved, the term for which is *oreixis*, usually translated as desire.[4] It is wonderful to discover the great rationalist saying that "thought alone moves nothing" (*NE* 1139a); thought requires desire in deciding and acting.

To pause over a technical but important distinction, Aristotle distinguishes the desiring *capacity* from the specific emotions and also from the condition in which we are in relation to the emotions (*NE* 1105b). He divides the capacity of desire into three kinds, one of which is named by the heart-word, *thumos.* In working out what it is that this desire desires, Koziak turns to specific emotion instances in the *Rhetoric*. Readers may well be familiar with Aristotle's definition: "The emotions [*pathe*] are those things through which, by undergoing change, people come to differ in their judgments and which are accompanied by pain and pleasure" (1378a.1.8). But Aristotle presses on to say something less frequently noticed, that he will discuss the emotions under several headings: "I mean, for example, in speaking of anger, what is their *state of mind* when people are angry and against *whom* are they usually angry, and for what sorts of *reasons. . ."* What is notable here is something perfectly rhetorical—the situatedness and particularity of the emotions. Koziak argues that the emotions of the *Rhetoric* are "desires for a certain state of social relations" (2000, 96). The capacity to feel these emotions, then, could also be called a social capacity.

If Koziak is right, this rich insight embeds several key ideas born out in the *Ethics*. One is that the very existence and experience of emotions depends upon social conditions (Jaggar 1989, 135). This is perfectly in keeping with Aristotle's suggestion that the capacity to be moved is given to us by nature but not by nature developed (*NE* 1103a). As we will see, in the *Ethics* he is very clear in showing that the dispositions, or how people are disposed to be moved, their habits of emotion and action, *develop* through both learning and action.

I take it, then, that the survey of emotions in the *Rhetoric* could be said to examine already developed ways in which people are moved in social situations. In other words, these emotions are what Aristotle observes, and it is no surprise that some of his observations seem unusual to us, since our emotions are schooled in an utterly different time and place. If, however, we take this observing as a pedagogical move, we begin to see the importance, for Aristotle, of seeing how people feel and in what situations, to the education of orators and citizens and to concerns about what political regime will be best. This point is a significant gloss on the idea of happiness or living well as an aim of ethics and politics.

2. Virtue is the disposition to act and feel. I have already noted that Aristotle distinguishes the capacity to be moved from the character or disposition in relation to emotions. His language on this point is unfamiliar and suggestive, for it turns out that human character or disposition—"how we are" in relation to the emotions—is a definition of *virtue* (*NE* 1105b–1106a). As almost every philosopher writing about the *Ethics* notes, virtues, for Aristotle, are dispositions toward *praxis* and *pathos*, toward acting and being acted upon, doing and feeling.[5] For general readers, this is perhaps another great surprise of the *Ethics*. These are not William Bennett's virtues.

Rather, "Excellence . . . is that state of character which enables [a person] to be called *eudaimon*" (Urmson 1980, 160), in other words, to live a life of happiness or well-being. When Aristotle explains his ideas about this state of happiness, he speaks of *ergon*, or the characteristic function or work of the human. A being's function allows it to be itself. For humans, this "consists in an activity of the soul in conformity with the rational principle" (NE 1098a). Interestingly, this rationality is linked with—indeed for some scholars *is*—one of the forms of desire (*boulesis*): being able to desire what is good, to take an interest in what is better and worse (Broadie 1991, 107). This rational desire, or desiring rationality, requires emotions, which are learned together with the moral sense through social activity.

As Kosman beautifully puts it, for Aristotle, "a virtue is not [merely] chosen—think how easy the moral life would then be!" (1980, 111). In other words, virtues are dispositions—that is, characteristics or habits (*hexeis*) of feeling and action that develop through activities. Thus the name for moral virtue (*ethike* or habit) is related to *ethos* (*NE* 1103a). Feminist Alison Jaggar is perfectly Aristotelian, then, when she describes emotions as "dispositional rather than episodic" and as "habitual responses that we may have more or less difficulty in breaking" (1989b, 133, 136). And, again, the moral dispositions—which we may more accurately call moral/emotional dispositions—are not "implanted in us by nature," but enacted. Unlike seeing or hearing, which "we first possess and then use," the virtues are things that "we acquire by first having put them into action" (*NE* 1103a). An important related point is that Aristotle is unwilling to call an action virtuous unless the doer knows and cares about what she is doing (*NE* 1105a). Jaggar also provides a useful amplification and helps to draw out the linkage between emotion and ethics when she describes the relation of emotions and values. She suggests that "values presuppose emotions," and that "if we had no emotional responses to the world, it is inconceivable that we should ever come to value one state of affairs more highly than another" (1989b, 137). The virtues, then, are acquired through the complex practices of moral life, and they depend upon the capacity to feel, *to be affected.*

3. Emotions and virtues are rhetorical. For modern readers, a curious refrain in the *Ethics* concerns having feelings in the right way: "we can experience fear, confidence, desire, anger, pity and generally any kind of pleasure or pain either too much or too little, and in either case not properly. But to experience all this at the right time, toward the right objects, toward the right people, for the right reason, and in the right manner—that is the median and the best course" (1106b). It would be worrisome if Aristotle were telling people which joys or pains were the correct ones to feel, for we have excellent contemporary research that shows how dominant regimes work partly by determining the acceptable emotions.[6] Equally worrisome would be a theory that always counseled the intermediate or middling amount of emotion, an Aristotle who prefers the milquetoast to the impassioned person. But it would be a mistake to see this work as being a set of *rules* for emotion. Rather, I suggest that Aristotle offers a view of both the emotions and the virtues as profoundly rhetorical.

Rhetoricians have been clear that the realm of rhetoric comprises the messy areas in which judgments must be made even where there is not a precise science of inquiry and where nonexperts have to address complex issues. The *Ethics* echoes this view (*NE* 1104a), but also adds a new dimension to this notion of the contingent. For it is clear that the issue is more than a matter of the *kind* of knowledge that is available, of Aristotle's having broken the Platonic equating of virtue and knowing. Aristotle also opposes the view that the good person is so because of imperviousness to the contingencies of life. Nussbaum argues that Aristotle's view of the emotions rests on this very critical notion: "the ascription of significant worth to items [and people] in the world outside of the agent, items that he or she does not fully control" (1994, 91). She thus distinguishes Aristotle from Socrates and from the Hellenistic philosophers, who hold that to value such externals is counter to virtuous self-sufficiency. For Aristotle, the passions are components of judgment and motivators of correct action (Nussbaum 1994, 390–92). She cites, for example, Aristotle's comment that not to feel anger in certain situations is a deficiency, that people whose anger is not aroused when their loved ones are insulted seem to have no feelings, and concludes that anger is an important motivator for defending people that are beloved (1994, 95).

4. Emotions comprise judgment and affect. If indeed emotions motivate actions that involve a moral component, they must also be closely tied with language, weaving together both affect and judgment. This view, called "cognitivist" in contemporary philosophy, holds that emotions are "forms of intentional awareness containing a view of their object" (Nussbaum 1994, 80). This contemporary language highlights Aristotle's understanding that an emotion depends on the way one views a situation, and that it is bound up with beliefs, which, as Nussbaum suggests, are its precondition. Aristotle's analysis shows that pity, for example, involves the belief that the one pitied is undeserving of what has befallen her, that the one who pities is similarly vulnerable, and that the things suffered really are significant. In other words, the experience of an emotion is bound up in a fairly "complex series of reflections" (Nussbaum 1994, 86–87). Even the pain and pleasure of emotions *derive* from these and are directed at these. In other words, emotion is not a simple phenomenon of the individual body, but a complex phenomenon of attention, body, belief, and judgment that can both contribute to argument and deliberation and be influenced by them.

Summing up the idea that emotions include conceptualization, evaluation, and something very like decision, Cooper points out that the feeling of an emotion includes for Aristotle three central elements: distress or pleasure, its cause by the way things seem to one, and the social dimension that we have already seen—desire for some behavior in response or change in the social situation (1999, 422). He points out that for Aristotle the distinction between reasoning and *thumos* has nothing to do with the ordinary modern distinction between reason as "the faculty of concept formation" and desire as a "concept-free faculty of urges." Rather, he suggests that "the very same terms in which reason thinks about the circumstances of action and about the relative values of things in the world in general, are also employed by" *thumos* (244–45). This drives home the point we have already seen, that Aristotle does not fully separate the workings of the reasoning and desiring capacities. This argument clearly challenges traditional notions of what *reason* itself might mean.

But it would be unwise to leave it at that, without acknowledging the contemporary debate over "cognitivist" views. On the central point itself, that emotions involve some kind of cognitive or language-mediated content, Aristotle and many contemporary theorists are in agreement, seeing emotion as in some sense involving affect and judgment (Worsham 1998, 216). The difficulty lies in the idea that the judgment can be evaluated as appropriate and reasonable or inappropriate and unjustified (Spelman 1989, 265). It is said that such a view reestablishes the hierarchy of reason over emotion, undercutting emotion's role as a force in ethical action. Taking this idea into the modern workplace, Worsham, for example, argues, "Cognitivism . . . capitalizes on the fact that those in subordinate positions can and must be taught, especially in school and workplace, that emotional responses (such as anger, rage, or bitterness) are always inappropriate and unjustified personal responses" (1998, 224–25). Two feminist approaches to this work are relevant to Aristotle.

Abu-Lughod and Lutz have noted that, in modernity, it is only recently that the commonplace view of emotions as "things internal, irrational, and natural" has been challenged (1990, 2). In their review of the strands of this scholarship, they include work that focuses specifically on the linkage of emotion and language, suggesting that "emotion gets its meaning and force from its location and performance in the public realm of discourse" (7). But they show that it is not this linkage that opens the door for the ideology of emotional suppression and control, but the commonplace view that understands emotions as primarily about internal states rather than about social life. For, when emotion is seen in this quite ordinary way, it is also seen as something needing to be kept in check, even dangerous. Indeed Lutz argues that "*Because* emotion is construed as relatively chaotic, irrational and antisocial, its existence vindicates authority and legitimates the need for control" (1990, 87, my emphasis).

In another very important response, feminist Elizabeth Spelman takes up a passage from Aristotle that we have already noted (though in slightly different translation): "[anyone] who does not get angry when there is reason to be angry, or does not get angry in the right way at the right time and with the right people, is a dolt." Starting here, Spelman's interest is in thinking about how ideas about the appropriateness of emotions is tied to ideas about "the moral and political dimensions of our relations to each other" (1989, 263). She uses the passage to show that if "cognitivism" is taken to mean that emotions are rescued from irrationality or lack of dignity by the control of reason, then "control" has not been fully understood. For perceptions or judgments about a situation will as readily "result in one's *becoming* angry" as in ceasing to be angry. Indeed, as Aristotle shows, in some circumstances, when one does not become angry, one is "a 'dolt,' or someone without self-respect, or a bad friend" (268). Thus, without romanticizing or essentializing the emotions, Spelman suggests that emotions are "revelatory of important parts of our lives as moral agents" (270).

Finally, these four propositions demonstrate that for Aristotle the emotions have their life in a social world that is their precondition and in which they bind the individual. Social culture educates emotions by setting the scene in which they are enacted and become dispositions. This means that the development of the emotional capacity is simultaneously a development of ethical commitments, and, conversely, that a development of ethical commitments is simultaneously a development of the emotional capacity. If this is so, and if individual and cultural character equate with dispositions to act and feel, we can begin to see that emotion contributes significantly to orientation, judgment, and action. The nexus of judgment-emotions explored by Aristotle suggests that both pains and pleasures are thoroughly connected to and indicative of people's dispositions and enacting of what they believe to be right, true, appropriate, and good—in short, of what we today see as "disciplined" life. Our contemporary research shows that this is the only kind of life available to us, given both conscious training of dispositions and the silent but massively productive shaping of feeling by circumstance, history, family, institutions, and so on. As Sandra Bartky puts it very poignantly, emotions "cling to the disciplines" (1998, 23), which conspire to shape people's sense of what is better and worse. The evidence of this, that emotions have their vitality in an ethical sphere, is everywhere in ordinary life. Yet reflection on this fact and implications for analyses of institutional practices do not regularly follow.

Emotion in the Pedagogical Sphere

At the start of this essay, I noted the interest today in pedagogy understood as the whole social education of members of a culture, with classroom practices as a subset of this larger field. One of the most ambitious contemporary studies to explore this theme, with special attention to emotion, is Lynn Worsham's "Going Postal: Pedagogic Violence and the Schooling of Emotion," an article that undertakes—as Aristotle would—an expansive review of current opinion. Worsham surveys theories about the psychic and social dramas that bring humans into the order of culture, and about recent school pedagogies designed to empower, and to work with and through desire. She makes clear the idea that drives this collection, that the working day, including schooling, produces "an affective relation to the world, to oneself and to others" (219). The worry that shapes her article, that dominant pedagogy hampers people's abilities to name and interpret affective lives (222–23), is closely linked to her definition of emotion, which will by now appear both familiar and different: "the tight braid of affect and judgment, socially and historically constructed and bodily lived, through which the symbolic takes hold of and binds the individual, in complex and contradictory ways, to the social order and its structure of meanings" (216). This definition highlights the complex, often alienating operations of social power in producing affective frameworks, accounts of which distinguish and separate Aristotle from contemporary theory. This current research enables Worsham's argument that Composition pedagogies—now which routinely claim to empower students—have been naïve, often by variously focusing on individual passions and experiences as fundamental. Nevertheless, reading this work alongside Aristotle, one is struck by the ethical or "eudaimonist" quality of this essay and the pedagogies it reviews—their dedication to individual and social flourishing. One is also struck by the thundering silence in the latter on the place of *pathos* or a theory of pathos in writing instruction, which can hardly, then, be called rhetorical.

What if we were to consider whether Aristotle implies a way to move—in research and classroom practice—on these complex issues? As Gretchen Flesher Moon shows in this volume, the representations of Aristotle in current handbooks give a negative answer, since they treat emotions but glancingly, as the inferior, not quite respectable of the three *pisteis* or "proofs" named in the *Rhetoric*, and link ethics with reason and *logos*. However, in an important move that sums up the emotional/ethical axis that I have been developing, scholars show that the "pisteis" may be more usefully understood as "faiths" or "trusts" (Lain Entralgo 1970, 176). Indeed, "Being-persuaded. . .is *trusting* or a form of trusting, and in that sense it is a specific type of pathos" (Walker 2000, 84).[7] People's good reasons have the force of "goodness" because goodness combines thought and feeling. It is scarcely yet imaginable how this insight ought to alter writing pedagogies, for it establishes that the effect of language on hearers and readers is very centrally bound up with their faith, including its connotations of a moral sense, in how things are. Rhetoricians may recognize this faith as similar to Kenneth Burke's nonreligious use of the term *piety*, designating "the sense of what properly goes with what." Burke's term indicates not only a "complex interpretive network" that could be addressed by good reasons, but also the powerful affective force of that network, given its rootedness in the linguistic experiences of social groups (1984, 74–75).

How might such insights be put to use? Aristotle offers no educational program. Indeed, he describes his *Rhetoric* in contrast to handbooks, and he offers only spare remarks on education in general, in the *Politics*. There, his observations about emotion are carried into his review of political regimes, which have emotional consequences (*Pols.* 1295b). This is a crucial insight, and one now being born out in writing research. Famously, Aristotle proposes a very broad paideia that includes intellectual and political culture, and also education in emotional/ethical dispositions (*Pols.* 1263b; Lord 1996, 275). Most likely, tragedy provided some part of this emotional education, for in watching it, people "do not learn rules of conduct, but patterns of [action and emotion], or what can happen when we feel in this way, at that time, toward this person, on account of this reason" (Koziak 2000, 146).

My reading of this material is that deliberate emotional education, then, ought to include deep thought about how institutions teach and manage emotion, and broad opportunities to learn and reflect on what happens when people *feel* in particular situations. On this first point, Composition now has a developing body of research that analyzes the embedding of our teaching institutions within larger cultural forces, and some quite specific studies of the emotional distress to students caused by particular pedagogies (Porter 2001; Johnson 2001). When it articulates ethical commitments, as Worsham does, in and through an examination of the ways in which social structures are solidified by the emotional ties that they foster and rely on, this work is fully rhetorical in the sense I have been examining. We also have very promising work showing the role of both emotions and experiences in scholars' and students' relationship to research (Bizzell 2000, 13). But the field is still silent on how emotion might figure in a rhetorical pedagogy because the current work on ethics in Composition has not yet deeply considered the emotional dimension articulated, in their differing ways, by Aristotle and Worsham.

While Aristotle offered no program of education, he did offer the *Rhetoric* for a specific group of citizen leaders. It is a book addressing what they needed to know about how language achieved its effects in the kinds of discourses in which they engaged. It includes information about how people *feel* in situations. Our students write vastly different kinds of discourses, far removed from these. But if it is true, as Worsham suggests, that current culture comprises much emotional miseducation; if habits of feeling and action are socially developed and enacted; and if being moved by language is taken to mean both developing and trusting an orientation, then surely effective readers and writers will need information about these issues. While we have yet to imagine such a pedagogy, I suggest that there are three promising areas to develop: (1) information about and opportunities to analyze the linking of social scenes, feelings, and the moral sense, (2) opportunities to observe repertoires of feeling represented in language, and (3) discursive tasks that teach and require an understanding of the ethical role of feeling in judgment. For our access to emotion, finally, is in language. Emotion does not occur "naturally" or beyond the boundaries of the social, nor is there a pure knowledge that can shape or refute it. It is bound up with the language in which we see, and which is given to us to see, particular situations and their demands. Given that we have only *doxa* by which to engage these, our study of the moral/emotions must be centered in discourse. It is language study that allows us to see what happens when people feel this way, about this person, in this situation.

Notes

1. Translation by Martin Ostwald, 1962. All subsequent references are to this translation, and will be noted by the abbreviation *NE*.

2. This linkage is also suggested in the *Rhetoric*, where Aristotle says, "rhetoric is a certain kind of offshoot of dialectic and of ethical studies (which it is just to call politics)" (1365a). Trans. Kennedy, 1991. Subsequent references are to this edition.

3. Koziak 2000, 78–79; Achtenberg, 1996; Jaggar, 1989; and Hall 1998, all call attention to this dimension of Plato's philosophy.

4. Cooper 1999, 240–242; Koziak 2000, 93; Nussbaum 1994, 81.

5. See Urmson, 1980, 159; Kosman 1980, 104; Macintyre 1984, 149.

6. Jaggar has described "outlaw" emotions experienced by subalterns and often revealing "coercion, cruelty, injustice or danger" (1989b, 145). Peter Stearns (1986) documents changes in both emotions and emotional standards in American workplaces and even links them to management practices.

7. Jarratt (2002, 20) also establishes connections between Peitho, ancient goddess of persuasion, and individual and communal desires, arguing that "it is because one can feel desire, can yearn for a different future, a just response to a past act, a fair valuation of a leader, that one can persuade and be persuaded." See also, Kenneth Burke 1969, 51–52.

Chapter Two

The Feeling of What Happens in Departments of English

Tom Kerr

In *The Feeling of What Happens: Body and Emotion in the Making of Consciousness* (1999), cognitive neuroscientist Antonio Damasio uses the expression "the feeling of what happens" to indicate the primacy of the body and emotion in the emergence and maintenance of consciousness. This essay is about the corresponding primacy of the body and emotion in English department culture and what cognitive neuroscience can tell us about it.[1] *What happens*, as I appropriate Damasio's phrase in my title, refers to the constitutive activities and relationships that form a specific culture, in our case departments of English, and *the feeling of* refers to the affective dimensions of those activities and relationships, which change, I maintain, from culture to culture, group to group. I assume that form and function of a culture or subculture constitute, in every instance, its specific identity. In our case, a shared trait among members of departments of English is an abiding interest in, if not fascination with, processes of literary interpretation and/or production, as well as with language and writing in general. Second, and inextricably linked to the *function* of departments of English is a member's susceptibility to the *form*—to the prevailing ideological framework, including founding assumptions, values, beliefs—within which interpretation and production occur. While it is impossible to say just how many individuals share the first trait or to describe a prevailing ideological framework that would satisfactorily account for every individual's experience in the group "English department," the existence of the group alone suggests *ipso facto* that the trait is shared by a critical mass of individuals and that some form of ideological cohesion exists. I assume here, in other words, that motives for joining the group are finite. I also assume that certain qualitative aspects of the feeling of what happens in departments of English, while perhaps not entirely unique, are at least characteristic of the culture, and may be attributed to what I will call for now the academic suppression of pathos—suppression captured, for instance, in the following claim made by an English professor to a graduate student in emotional distress due in large part to the pressures of graduate school: "I'm not very good at these things," he said. "That's why I read books."

While the distinction between "functional" and "dysfunctional" family or other systems is a blunt one, I have often heard the latter term applied to interpersonal relations in departments of English, where I have spent the past fifteen years of my working life. I've also heard the term *dysfunctional* (never *functional*) applied to individuals and entire departments. The distinction is the tip of an epistemological iceberg. Functional, of course, denotes communication and associated behavior between individuals and among groups that is clear, direct, honest, open, respectful, dialogic, productive, and mutually agreeable. Dysfunctional, on the other hand, names communication or behavior that fails at one or several of these points, and includes the potential of "acting out," as when a person substitutes indirect, aggressive, or even offensive behavior/communication for the open, honest, direct sort. As far as categorical distinctions go, these would seem to have sufficient descriptive value to have secured a place in the vernacular of English department culture. Like the expression *touchy-feely*, shorthand in English departments for any post-1960s pedagogy or discourse that takes up self- and interpersonal expression as a proper object of academic discourse, the term *dysfunctional* may be regarded as an ideological marker, a portmanteau loaded with significance.

At the literal level, the term as applied to social relations in departments of English simply indicates a communication breakdown of one kind or another, and may or may not be intended to disparage. For example, "The committee is dysfunctional" might mean that people on the committee are not able to communicate with each other effectively. Or, "Professor Z's behavior is completely dysfunctional" might indicate that Professor Z is not communicating clearly or respectfully with his/her colleagues. At the figurative level, however, the use of such a blunt term signifies an epistemological *aporia*, a failure of understanding. Calling a committee or a colleague's behavior dysfunctional effectively extends the "dysfunction," mystifying rather than clarifying the relations in question. As applied to complex social groups and/or individuals, the term "dysfunctional"—despite its quasi-clinical veneer—functions in most if not all cases as a pejorative term, and it stems from the same cultural reflex that gives us "touch-feely," whose explanatory value is equally nil. This reductive reflex, what amounts to an articulated cultural prohibition of *direct* emotional language and behavior, derives from academic culture's traditional values, particularly its privileging of mind over body, artifact over experience, thought over emotion. And since—as is now well established in the fields of neurobiology and cognitive neuroscience—language, thought, and writing begin and end with emotion, our failure in English adequately to theorize the emotions, to contend with them directly, as *symbolic phenomena rooted in the body,* is all the more remarkable. The failure results both from difficulties inherent in the ongoing scientific investigation of the neurological underpinnings of human emotion, thought, and language, and of a cultural regime ironically predicated in many respects on the suppression of emotion, wherein poems, stories, and essays quite often stand in for direct involvement with others, "text" functioning not unlike an actor's understudy—not the actor, *in corpore*, but enough like her to put on the show.

In the discussion that follows, I turn to Antonio Damasio's neurobiological theory of consciousness for how it might help us meditate differently on the feeling of what happens in departments of English. It is my contention that until our disciplinary understanding encompasses not only the expressive and psychological but also the biological and political dimensions of emotion, we are bound to reproduce certain oppressive cultural patterns and practices, not the least of which is the self-defeating propagation of shame, as sown by the evasive professor cited above, that defy our discipline's own best intentions and make our working lives nastier and more brutish than they might be otherwise.

Academic Neglect of the Emotions

Rhetorical study since Aristotle has regarded the emotions as proper objects of study, but until very recently that study has, with a few exceptions, been retarded not only by scientific but also disciplinary constraints. In Composition Studies, Alice G. Brand, drawing on psychology and biology, has for years been building an interdisciplinary bridge between thought, emotion, and writing (see Brand 1980, 1989, 2000; Brand and Graves 1994), and Lynn Worsham and others, drawing on philosophy and critical theory, have extended rhetoric's purview of the emotions to include analyses of their *nonessentialist*, sociopolitical dimensions (Worsham 1992–93). Still, in the bulk of our scholarship and, more to the point, in the daily goings-on of our working lives, emotion, unlike language, is frequently treated as the proper subject of psychology or the sacrosanct substance of personality and/or character, as the implicit, taboo ground upon which explicit, public rituals of creative and analytical expression take place. For instance, we do not in our course descriptions or mission statements promise to engage deeply and/or critique (or evaluate) the *emotions* of our students or colleagues, but the constant interpretation, production, and exchange of text amounts to no less. We freely license ourselves to talk with our students and among ourselves about "text" and its analogues—interpretation, writing, voice, and experience—and we do so unapologetically. We argue endlessly, for example, about the extent to which texts and students are socially constructed and about what kinds of texts, "expressive" or "social epistemic," students *ought* to produce in writing classes and how we *ought* to regard them. We conference privately with students about their linguistic *choices*. We grade texts to establish exchange value, rarely admitting to the widely held feeling among students that *they*, not merely their *texts*, are being judged (see Faigley 1992). As texts themselves, grades shield us and our students from the direct emotional force of our judgments. At conferences, in journals, and through the tenure review process, we critique the writing of our colleagues openly, constructively or otherwise, but are more apt than not to duck and cover when someone wants to talk about "feelings" candidly, in a public departmental forum such as a committee or departmental meeting. It is perhaps noteworthy, as well, that email has become for many in our field a convenient way to respond *textually* to others who have stirred strong emotions in them, and long, emotionally complex email exchanges regarding workplace encounters are not uncommon.

Thus we embrace texts. But what formal means—shared conceptual paradigms, methods, means of evaluation, terministic screens—have we developed to talk about the abundance of feeling that *always already* accompanies the "text" (or the grade) and the complex social relations, in classrooms, in committees, in the offices and hallways of our departments, in which the text is embedded? When it comes time to talk about how one feels about our work, we are most often left to our own devices, private conversations with allies (if we're lucky), venting at home with friends and family (if we have friends and family), professional therapy (if we value it), and other external sources (if they exist). When we want to deal with feelings, in other words, we close doors, talk in whispers, "take it outside"—every person for him- or herself—or, perhaps, fire off a disembodied email. And yet, what Brand observes of the writing classroom may also be said of English departments, material conditions notwithstanding: "when things are stalled . . . it is because of emotion. When things go well, it also because of emotion" (Brand 2000, 216). The feeling of what happens, whether addressed directly or not, profoundly affects *what* happens.

Body as Text, Emotion as Sign

It is imperative that we understand emotion quite explicitly as *symbolic* communication, as a highly inflected semiotic system—a rhetoric of the body, if you will—that relies on signs and representations at both the molecular (interior, biochemical) and molar (exterior, behavioral) levels of the organism. Indeed, emotions involve all manner of neural mapping and prelinguistic representation, and operate in two different economies, one encompassing both the organism and its environment and the other restricted to the organism itself. In the first, an emotion or set of emotions produces a specific reaction to the inducing situation: the emotion "tells us" whether to run, become immobile, attack, or engage in some pleasurable activity (Damasio 53–54). When other people or animals are part of the inducing situation, it is their emotions, whether expressed in language or not, to which our emotions are responding. Sometimes language is adequate to the representational task, sometimes—as when one is "angry beyond words" or "at a loss for words," left speechless by an act or spectacle—it is not. And we are all familiar with situations wherein language fails miserably to represent all the emotions in play, but where communication is nonetheless successful (i.e., one gets the point). Communication, in other words, *is* emotional, is "touchy-feely."

As for the second economy, emotional communication regulates the internal states of our organism, "providing increased blood flow to arteries in the legs so that muscles receive extra oxygen and glucose, in the case of a flight reaction, or changing heart and breathing rhythms," in the case, say, of presenting a paper before an audience (54). Emotions not only signal our intentions and reactions to others, they also tell our own bodies what to do and when to do it. In this perspective, naming complex behaviors or patterns of communication as "dysfunctional" rather than, say, understanding them as a purposeful response to internal and external stimuli is to grossly misinterpret the text, in a manner that we would consider unconscionable, even unethical, if the text were mere words on paper. Imagine a literary scholar dismissing *Ulysses* as "chaotic." In Damasio's five-part neurobiological definition of emotion we get an inkling of the Joycean, biological complexity behind the scenes of *our* scenes—intellectual, political, and emotional:

1. Emotions are complicated collections of chemical and neural responses, forming a pattern; all emotions have some kind of regulatory role to play, leading in one way or another to the creation of circumstances advantageous to the organism exhibiting the phenomenon; emotions are *about* the life of an organism, its body to be precise, and their role is to assist the organism in maintaining life.
2. Notwithstanding the reality that learning and culture alter the expression of the emotions and give emotions new meanings, emotions are biologically determined processes, depending on innately set brain devices, laid down by a long evolutionary history.
3. The devices which produce emotions occupy a fairly restricted ensemble of subcortical regions, beginning at the level of the brain stem and moving up to the higher brain; the devices are part of a set of structures that both regulate and represent body states.
4. All the devices can be engaged automatically, without conscious deliberation; the considerable amount of individual variation and the fact that culture plays a role in shaping some inducers does not deny the fundamental stereotypicity, automaticity, and regulatory purpose of the emotions.
5. All emotions use the body as their theater (internal milieu, visceral, vestibular and musculoskeletal systems), but emotions also affect the mode of operation of numerous brain circuits: the variety of the emotional responses is responsible for profound changes in both the body landscape and the brain landscape. The collection of these changes constitutes the substrate for the neural patterns which eventually become feelings of emotion. (51–52)

In such a physiological anatomy of emotion, one can see why expressions like "touchy-feely" or "dysfunctional" fail miserably as descriptors of emotional phenomena and related behavior, which is designed, in all its variations, to "assist the organism in maintaining life." Emotion can never be "dysfunctional": inappropriate, counterproductive, destructive, even violent, yes; dysfunctional, no.

The Political Biology of Emotion

When a colleague huffs and puffs and walks angrily out of a meeting, his or her behavior is not only functional, it is also representational, and can therefore be "read" and responded to as such—as an expression, ultimately, of biological processes that begin and end with "text" (whereby a sign in the form of a statement or series of statements triggers anger and a sign in the form of an act makes the anger visible). Those who are walked out on will, in their turn, respond in distinctly functional ways, no matter whether they call after the person, ignore the act, or speculate conspiratorially as to cause. The circumstances producing particular emotional responses may be exceedingly complex, but the responses themselves are neither inscrutable nor dysfunctional; indeed, they are political, and there is no reason we should not interpret such responses, such scenes, with as much alacrity and sophistication, theoretical and methodological, as we interpret a poem, a play, an essay, or any other text.

In Damasio's theory, the intermediary between the physiological processes of emotion and social behavior, including the act of interpretation, is consciousness, a neurobiological system in which feelings of emotion (sensing emotion) and knowledge of emotion (apprehending emotion) come into play. As he explains, "we only know that we feel an emotion when we sense that emotion is sensed as happening in our organism" (279). Emotions in themselves are impersonal; it is the feeling of those emotions as belonging to us and, consequently knowing they belong to us, that makes them personal. Consciousness for Damasio is thus not distinct from, but rather an effect of, or coextensive with, emotion (127). This is a crucial distinction for writers, literary critics, and teachers. It gives new theoretical weight to the "felt sense" Sondra Perl talks about in relationship to the composing process and helps us collapse, once and for all, false dichotomies between reason and emotion, mind and body, text and person. She writes, "When writers are given a topic, the topic itself evokes a felt sense in them. This topic calls forth images, words, ideas, and vague fuzzy feelings that are anchored in the writer's body. What is elicited, then, is not solely the product of a mind but of a mind alive in a living, sensing body" (Perl 1994, 151). Biologically, emotion makes consciousness possible, and consciousness translates emotions into feelings, from which spring language and reason. Language, in other words, is epiphenomenal—an emotional effect, just as Nietzsche presciently argued long ago in "On Truth and Lying in the Extramoral Sense," where he observed that "the origin of language is not a logical process, and the whole material in and with which the man of truth, the scientists, the philosopher, works and builds, stems, if not from a never-never land, in any case not from the essence of things" (Nietzsche 1989, 249).

Of course, the mere mention of biology ("the essence of things") in the humanities often raises legitimate concerns about essentialist and/or reductive arguments, arguments that inhibit or threaten to inhibit the range of the imagination, as Edmond Wilson's sociobiological theory of human culture was initially impugned by some for doing (1978), or lead to ugly, racist conclusions, such as those reached by Richard J. Herrnstein and Charles Murray in *The Bell Curve: Intelligence and Class Structure in American Life* (1996). It is important to note, therefore, that Damasio's biological theory of consciousness does not obviate culture; indeed, his theory offers a biological explanation for why people across cultures are both the same *and* different. It is, according to Damasio, not the biological systems that are different, but rather the *inducers* of emotions that vary: "Regardless of the degree of biological presetting of the emotional machinery, development and culture superpose the following influences on the preset devices: first, they shape what constitutes an adequate inducer of a given emotion; second, they shape some aspects of the expression of the emotion; and third, they shape the cognition and behavior which follows the deployment of an emotion" (57). These observations are important to the present discussion for two reasons. First, the concept of inducer as something more than blunt stimulus, as an initial condition that shapes the response of a system or an organism, allows us to understand how different cultures and subcultures produce different patterns of biological response and behavior. This idea lends credence to my conviction that there does exist a distinct feeling of what happens in departments of English, and the sequential emotion-feeling-thought chain offers a concrete structure for analysis of this otherwise intangible feeling of what happens.

Second, one obstacle to further elaborating the role of emotions in English departments is a constitutional resistance to the notion that "in spite of the infinite variations to be found across cultures, among individuals, and over the course of a life span, we can predict with some success that certain stimuli will produce certain emotions (That is why we say to a colleague, 'Go tell her that; she will be so happy to hear it')" (Damasio, 54). Writers and those who study writers and their texts rightly tend to cherish the singular, the one of a kind, Pope's oft' been thought but ne'er so well expressed, and deplore clichés. But emotions, which are repeated in continuous feedback loops designed to keep the organism alive and functioning as effectively as possible, are as *redundant* as it gets. Can one hate clichés and love emotions? One way to despise the pedestrian, clichéd nature of emotion is fiercely to embrace individualistic expression and behavior, not just over and above group dynamics and communal relations, but in spite of them. Eccentric behavior, whether constructive or destructive, is often regarded as a prerogative and privilege, the expression of a strong-willed individual, of individualism, of nonconformity—an *a priori* good. The emotional waves a wildly eccentric person may cause in the workplace are thus frequently regarded as inevitable, inscrutable, beyond the group's purview. One hopes, for instance, that X or Y will stop behaving in ways that many members of the group find disruptive or offensive, but direct, formal discussion of the individual's or group's emotional dynamic is verboten, for that would be tantamount to group therapy and/or an invasion of the individual's right to privacy. Above all else, the cultural myth holds that emotions are nothing if not private, even when we are faced with mountains of evidence to the contrary.

Shame and Ideology

By describing the neurobiological processes through which one becomes conscious of oneself and others—and by demonstrating how emotion is constructed in the organism's interaction with self and other—cognitive neuroscience helps us understand precisely how emotions and feelings are public *and* political, a fact that becomes most apparent when emotions become both the object and means of ideological manipulation. At the most basic level, such manipulation may take the form of political fear-mongering, as when politicians build support for war or prison construction by playing on public fears and the desire to punish. But ideological manipulation of emotion takes on much finer hues and textures as well; the systemic, culturally sanctioned suppression of the emotions that one finds in departments of English serves as a good example. In addition to the obvious effects on interpersonal and group dynamics, such suppression—whatever the immediate cause (e.g., ignorance, avoidance, or willful neglect)—carries dire political consequences. When feelings are seen either as excessive or irrelevant, when the body, in other words, is discounted, as I have argued elsewhere to be the case in academic discourse and culture (Kerr 1996), shame—that is "the self regarding the self with the withering and unforgiving eye of contempt" (Karen 1992, 43)—becomes pervasive, an instrument of ideological control.

At the individual level, a certain kind of shame is easy enough to comprehend. When a person *feels* angry, sad, frustrated, embarrassed, or afraid, for instance, ignoring, dismissing, or mocking the feeling often triggers shame, to greater or lesser degrees and with consequences that depend on an individual's constitution and previous experience with shame and related emotions. One may be shamed by having strong feelings that seem inappropriate or excessive precisely to the extent they are not acknowledged by those with whom they are experienced, and differential power relations exacerbate such shame. Take tenure politics, for example. Published associate and full professors are generally responsible for setting the bar and encouraging/pressuring assistant professors to publish before they perish. Mostly in casual conversation, but also via department and college handbooks, and through display cases and other venues for showcasing published work, expectations are set, consequences for failing to meet these are spelled out, and a great deal of value is attributed to publication. If an assistant professor is in a groove, on track to meet or exceed expectations, there is little occasion for shame. A conversation about the importance of publishing in the department between one or more tenured faculty members and the assistant professor may very well work to support and facilitate her work. If, on the other hand, an assistant professor finds herself struggling to publish and is therefore facing an uncertain tenure review, strong feelings such as fear, frustration, helplessness, or anger are likely to be present during the same conversation. When such feelings are ignored—and I submit to you that they are systematically ignored—shame is the most likely result, and shame, wherein "the self regard[s] the self with the withering and unforgiving eye of contempt," is a poor motivator when it comes to writing, creative or otherwise. Depending on a number of variables, the hapless assistant professor may come to feel small and insignificant when standing beside her *published* colleagues. When left unattended ("let's hope she gets something published soon"), the feeling may fulfill its own prophecy (i.e., she does not publish) and, at the same time, serve a specific ideological function, i.e., the maintenance of an existing hierarchy. While shame itself is a life-regulating emotion, like all other emotions, it can quickly degenerate when it exceeds beneficial tolerances or falls out of balance. As sociologist Thomas Scheff observes, "shame is normal . . . like breathing air: it's necessary. Personalities and civilizations coexist, even thrive, with normal shame. But unacknowledged shame is a pathogen. It kills" (qtd. in Karen 1992, 52).

At the cultural (versus individual) level, shame can be harder to apprehend. As Jean Paul Sartre (1948) correctly observed, one feels shame only in relation to another who makes or knows the rules—the ideological standard—by which a person is judged, and so it depends on a relational, cultural, *institutional* context. Both Plato and Aristotle understood this perfectly well; the former argued that students in order to learn must first be reduced to a state of shame (Plato 1952, 508c), the latter noted that "once we are on a given level, it makes us ashamed not to be as well educated, say, as the rest are; and similarly, with respect to all else (Aristotle 1932, 113). When the "rest" is an institution, or an academic department in which emotion *as pathos* has been historically suppressed, one cannot escape the ideological structure of shame. Either as undergraduates, or as graduate students and T.A.s, or as adjunct instructors, or as assistant, associate, or full professors, most of us have experienced one sort or another of institutional shame (though we may not have called it that), or at least witnessed shame-based behavior around us (though we have not recognized it as such). How many times, for instance, have you heard a student say, "This paper isn't very good," as, eyes averted, he or she hands it in. Or how often have you heard yourself or other writers belittle their work, or bemoan the fact that they can never seem to do enough—read enough, write enough, publish enough? How many people have you known who, apparently capable writers and thinkers with a robust interest in teaching and writing, have ultimately excluded themselves or been excluded from the group, the culture, as a result of feeling inadequate, ashamed? What other avoidance behavior have you witnessed: students and/or colleagues making quick turns in the hall, ducking into stairwells, students skipping classes after receiving a low grade? Such phenomena, of which the personal stakes are often very high, cannot, as academic discourse or our culture at large would have us believe, be attributed entirely to personal quirks or psychological idiosyncrasies. Rather, and as Ruth Benedict (1934) observed of the Greeks, we can be said to inhabit and reproduce a "shame-culture" wherein inclusion and exclusion, power relations, and pecking order are often overdetermined by shame-based rites and rituals (e.g., grading, writing dissertations, all manner of surveillance—including classroom observations and annual activity reports—and publishing or perishing). Of course, not everyone is equally susceptible to shame, and in a shame-culture, the less one feels (shame), or the better one is able to manage one's feelings independently, or the less likely one's feelings are to be misrecognized or dismissed by those in power—and here gender, ethnicity, and class loom large—the better one is likely to fare.

Refiguring the Emotions

Neither Damasio's theory, which details the neurological processes of the emotions in much greater specificity than purpose or space allow me to represent here, nor my own partial explication of it is intended to render emotion transparent or predictable, or to reduce individuals or their creative endeavors to simplistic biological formulas. Biological it may be; simplistic it is not. Rather, this biologically based theory of emotion, feeling, and consciousness, and the processes by which we make sense of experience and interpret text, whether oral, written, or behavioral, offers a way for us to understand what exactly is happening to our own and our students' bodies—to our organisms—as we engage in the constitutive activities of our culture: reading, writing, and talking about texts. We are surrounded by and encounter others' bodies and a myriad of attendant emotions and feelings everyday, but our direct vocabulary for naming and interacting with them is impoverished—blunt and diversionary. We talk constantly about emotion and feeling *formally* via tone, style, and structure, but bracket it *informally* as beyond the pale, the proper object of psychology, and/or as the accidents of working in close quarters with, as a former colleague once put it, "a bunch of nuts." Cognitive neuroscience offers one vital, extrapsychological language with which to reflect on our own nuttiness in a way that might well enhance empathy and strengthen the bonds of community.

Note

1. Many thanks to Eileen Schell for her insightful critiques of this essay in early drafts.

Chapter Three

The Pathos of *Pathos*

The Treatment of Emotion in Contemporary Composition Textbooks

Gretchen Flesher Moon

The *pathos* of *pathos* in current composition textbooks is twofold. *Pathos* as a rhetorical appeal gets very short shrift in textbooks and, even then, often suffers the ignominy of identification as or association with the fallacies. At best, textbooks discuss the traditional division of appeals—the *pisteis*—by Aristotle and note their interconnectedness in persuasion. Some textbooks say nothing at all about *pathos*—or about emotions, feelings, prejudices and the like even in sections on argument and persuasion. At worst, textbooks denigrate appeals to emotion and implicitly dismiss emotion in judgment. More problematic, *pathos* as a rhetorical appeal to the reader's emotions, values, and beliefs also generally constitutes the entire treatment of emotion in textbooks; it is a treatment inadequate for Composition.

When Aristotle delineates three appeals in the *Rhetoric*—*logos, pathos, ethos*—he establishes not only a system of classification, but a principle of valuation for study by the generations of rhetoricians to follow him. From the first sentences of the *Rhetoric*, he sets his course characteristically in the middle way, seeking to correct both the abuses of histrionic emotional appeals by contemporary rhetors and the rejection of emotion by those who feared such rhetors. Our textbooks reveal the skeleton of his classification system, faint and attenuated. They, too, propose a middle way, though offering minimal analysis and argument for their recommendations.

Aristotle understands, accepts, and promotes emotional appeals and devotes a major portion of his treatise to them. While we can discuss the three *pisteis* separately, we cannot effectively persuade an audience unless we learn to use all three in concert. He claims at the outset that "the man who is to be in command of [the *pisteis*] must, it is clear, be able to reason logically, to understand human characters and excellences, and to understand the emotions—that is, to know what they are, their nature, their causes and the way in which they are excited" (1156a 22). The rhetorician must cultivate in the audience a "right frame of mind"—a mind receptive to weighing arguments and then to ethical action. Christopher Johnstone (1980) argues that translators have sometimes misled us on the implication of "right frame of mind" by ignoring the use of the same word that in *The Nichomachean Ethics* clearly refers to the "morally right condition" in which one's emotional state is ready for rational guidance. Thus, when Aristotle argues that the domain of rhetoric extends across matters of public life for which no "exact knowledge" exists and in which judgment about what is true and just must prevail, he argues for the complete interdependence of reason and emotion in moving action.

But Jeffrey Walker finds that while Aristotle may not have intended it, his analysis of the *pathe* forces the conclusion that all "practical reasoning is pathetic reasoning" and, more surprising, therefore emotionally cathartic (2000, 91). Moreover, as our familiar identification of catharsis with drama would suggest, the rhetor's art in moving the audience may be understood as principally an art of style and delivery. Aristotle's classical successors clearly understood this implication: Cicero and Quintilian elaborate techniques for inducing emotion by *energia* (the rhetor feeling the emotion he wishes to provoke in the audience) and *enargeia* (creation of a scene vivid enough to create a desired emotional effect). That Aristotle, Cicero, and Quintilian make language the medium in which reason, will, and emotion work together is a central theme for Renaissance rhetoricians: the traditional Ciceronians understood the *pathe* under topics of invention, while the Ramists aligned *pathos* with style. We see the Renaissance enthusiasm for pathetic appeals in an elaboration of elocution and style manuals in which *pathos* is identified with performance.

Attention to *pathos* in English and Scots rhetoricians of the late eighteenth century figures prominently in their study and emulation of classical rhetoric. But in the eighteenth century, Campbell meets the new understandings of psychology with a new theory of association in rhetoric, and Blair posits a more romantic notion of individual inspiration. In the nineteenth century, Bain argues that volition is moved by the expectation that one's action will either sustain pleasure or alleviate pain, and that the rhetor's work lies in finding language adequate to recalling pleasure or pain. In the twentieth century, the New Rhetoric of Perelman and Olbrechts-Tyteca and the introduction of Rogerian argument by Young, Becker, and Pike return the rhetor's attention to invention, and at least implicitly, to the ethical dimension: the problem for rhetors in questions of value and judgment—that is, in the province of rhetoric as Aristotle defined it—is to find the common ground between rhetor and audience in attitudes and states of mind.

As we begin the twenty-first century, this long, if discontinuous and varied, theory of the emotions in rhetoric has faded and blurred beyond recognition, remaining only a shadow, a whisper of its former self in the textbooks that construct the rhetorical tradition for college students. This essay documents its abandonment in contemporary rhetorics. I analyze them by close reading and ask how their language about emotion might work on readers. I ask why they might say what they say and speculate about the meaning for writers of their scant attention to emotions. The data for the analysis I present is based on twenty-five rhetorics published after 1998. The sample is not exhaustive, of course, and it does not include older books that may still be in use. But I believe it will fairly represent conceptions of emotion that circulate in a range of currently available textbooks.

Rhetorics

Rhetorics serve not only as references to the conventions, but as guides, invitations to college writers to engage intellectually, experientially, in the practice of writing and sometimes in the study of discourse more generally. We might expect, then, that rhetorics would lavish a good deal of attention on *pathos* as rhetorical appeal and on rhetorical problems involving the emotions. In fact, in the twenty-five texts I sampled, this is seldom the case (Sources 23, 25 are exceptions). Five books make no reference to emotions, feelings, or *pathos* (Sources 11,12, 15, 20, 21). Several attend explicitly to emotional appeals or *pathos* as handbooks do, by defining the term and providing an example or two within a single paragraph (Sources 2, 4, 6, 8, 10, 17, 18, 22, 23, 24), or more briefly still (Sources 5, 19), or as fallacies (Sources 1, 16). Rhetorics sometimes direct writers to consider emotion at various stages of writing: as readers, during audience analysis, in drafting, and again in revising (Sources 3, 7, 9, 13, 14). The twenty-five textbooks consider emotions only in terms of *pathos*, the argumentative appeal to emotions.

Rather than the imperative voice heard in handbooks ("Appeal to principles, reason, and common sense, not to emotions, ignorance, and prejudices"), rhetorics, even when brief, generally address their readers in the conversational voice peculiar to textbooks, a voice whose *we* or *you* expects agreement:

> Whereas reason may help us formulate and solidify our beliefs, emotion acts as the catalyst that brings our actions and our beliefs together. . . . We are sometimes moved to do things even though we can give no good reasons for doing them. When an advertiser persuades us to buy a product that costs more money than we can really afford to spend or one that harms our health, we have been moved to take an action without having been convinced logically that the action is good for us. In such a situation, the advertiser's ability to separate reason and emotion makes his writing effective, even though what he is doing is not ethical. (Source 14, 364)

The writers this textbook imagines, and their audiences, are apparently apt to agree that emotions play a useful role, but a potentially unsavory one. In this drama, reason is a strong protagonist who needs a sidekick, a supporting actor, in emotion. Barely is this admitted, though, before the explanation turns to a warning against this powerful, unethical duo. Both in number of words and placement into the rhetorically stronger end of the paragraph, the case *against* outweighs the case *for* emotion.

In the next example, a less negatively slanted approach nevertheless downplays the role of emotions in persuasion. Following a paragraph that has cited the irrelevant references by Henry Hyde to Americans who gave their life for the country and by Clinton's lawyers to the Civil Rights movement during Congress' impeachment trial, the author warns readers that emotional appeals "wear off":

> The problem with appealing to people strictly through their emotions, however, is that it generally works for only a short time. An emotional appeal will get your readers' attention, but it is unlikely to convince them of the rightness of your position. Once the immediate effect wears off, your audience will no longer be persuaded unless your appeal is made—and holds up—on other levels as well. (Source 8, 32)

The section on using the three appeals has begun, as many do, with the assertion that effective persuasion depends on employing *ethos*, *pathos*, and *logos*. But no examples explicitly illustrate the effective combination of all three appeals.

These examples support propositions ostensibly arguing for the legitimacy of emotional appeals in argumentation, although each significantly undercuts that legitimacy on practical or ethical grounds. Others simply deny the validity of emotions in reasoning altogether. When argument is distinguished from persuasion, argument frequently attracts the desirable attributes of clarity, dispassionate evaluation of evidence, and contemplation, while persuasion involves obfuscation, loading of inappropriate evidence, and action (Source 16, 47).

The proscription, or at least qualification, of emotions in writing often emerges in discussions of word choice. Textbooks routinely advise against diction that is too emotionally powerful, or that falls too far from affective neutrality. One text warns students to avoid the emotionalism *invoked by such language as* "'swell the wallets of those fat cat rich who already hoard most of our nation's wealth'" and suggests instead "'augment the personal wealth of those who already control most of the nation's resources.' That kind of language reflects values but does not seem crudely emotional" (Source 25, 326). Indeed, the example is so gross as to be gratuitous. While the chapter goes on to assert the validity of both values and emotions, it exemplifies, illustrates, and analyzes only offenses of crude emotionalism.

It is possible to present *pathos* as important to argumentation without hastening to recommend suppressing it. The following textbook truly gives emotional appeals their third of the discussion; having begun with simple definitions of each of the Aristotelian appeals, it then discusses their integration:

> In some instances you may rely predominantly on one of these appeals. A student writing a technical report, for instance, will typically emphasize scientific or technical evidence (*logos*), not emotional or personal appeals. More often, however, you will draw on all three appeals in your effort to create a persuasive document. A journalist writing an essay on child abuse might begin her discussion with several examples designed to gain the attention of her readers and to convince them of the importance of this issue (*pathos*). Although she may rely primarily on information about the negative consequences of child abuse (*logos*), she will undoubtedly also endeavor to create an image of herself as a caring, serious person (*ethos*), one whose analysis of a subject like child abuse could be trusted. (Source 9, 157)

This discussion makes none of the assumptions common in most of the handbooks and rhetorics under review here—that students write only argumentative essays, that *pathos* is an appeal engaged only in persuasion, and that persuasion operates in the realms of advertising and politics.

In the fullest treatment in this sample, the introductory definition of *pathos* establishes the grounds for a serious study of the role of emotion in rhetoric:

> Our third term, *pathos* (Greek for "suffering" or "experience"), is often associated with emotional appeal. But *pathos* appeals more specifically to an audience's imaginative sympathies—their capacity to feel and see what the writer feels and sees. Thus, when we turn the abstractions of logical discourse into a palpable and immediate story, we are making a pathetic appeal. While appeals to *logos* and *ethos* can further an audience's intellectual assent to our claim, appeals to *pathos* engage the imagination and feelings, moving the audience to deeper appreciation of the argument's significance. (Source 19, 75–76)

After explicitly rejecting the temptation to "think of these three kinds of appeals as 'ingredients' in an essay, like spices you add to a casserole"—a temptation too many textbooks succumb to—the authors propose that the appeals are "ways of seeing rather than objects of sight" (Source 19, 139). They work through four verbal strategies for creating appeals to beliefs and emotions—concrete language, specific examples and illustrations, narratives, and a range of topics on diction—and then treat separately the use of visual images that figure so prominently in contemporary rhetorical practice. Their chapter includes the customary precautions about exploiting emotional appeals to distract the audience. But it does so in a context that provides grounds for understanding and appreciating the nature of emotional appeals. The cautions do not, that is, outweigh or completely undercut the justifications.

Implications

The dominant impression after such a survey is that appeals to emotion are understood to be a kind of compromise for the postlapsarian world, infinitely dangerous and detached from rational processes. If this impression is even partly correct, it's no surprise that many textbooks fail to address emotion at all. It's the rhetorical analogue of writing "G" textbooks by the motion picture industry's rating system, with emotion the rhetorical equivalent of sex and violence. But this dualism is not reinforced by contemporary theoretical or pedagogical writing by compositionists.

A secondary impression based on this survey is that while emotions may be defined to include a fairly broad affective dimension—feelings, values, beliefs—they are of no importance to students' writing outside the argument. They are not discussed explicitly as part of the scene of writing—as forces motivating the writer to write or inhibiting the writer from writing, nor even as legitimate players in the response writers have to their own reasoning as they use writing for discovery, clarification, learning, communication, expression, aesthetic creation, or recreation. Scholarship in both Rhetoric-Composition and in emotion studies provides for a much richer treatment of the role of emotions in writing. What can explain its slighting in textbooks? We might look to three interrelated phenomena.

First, the phenomenon of the textbook as cultural entity. The critics of textbooks beginning with Richard Lanham (1975) and continuing through Xin Liu Gale and Fredric G. Gale (1999) and, most recently, Libby Miles (2001) repeatedly lament the stifling lack of difference among composition textbooks. The textbooks condescend to students by settling conflicts behind the scene; they pronounce, gravely, the *way it is*; they reduce the complexity of composing to a linear sequence of steps. This is, at least in part, a graveness thrust upon them by cultural positioning. Mike Rose (1983) and David Bleich (1999) both refer to Thomas Kuhn's description of textbooks as digests of (scientific) theory, experimental confirmation, and application; composition textbooks, they suggest, cannot resist their readers' habits to read them as "knowledge of a certain kind: facts, data, information, theories" (Rose 1983, 211). That rhetoric traffics in a very different kind of knowledge—procedural, evaluative, context-specific—radically compromises the textbook enterprise, condemns it, as Rose says, optimistically I think, to "the realm of Moderately Useful" (1981, 65). We may hope to see greater textbook attention to the affective dimension of writing, as envisioned in the 1980s by pioneers Alice Brand and Susan McLeod and now carried on by many others. But the profession's critique of textbooks more generally suggests that we will need to sustain that hope over a very long time.

Second, disciplinary and interdisciplinary discomfort with what Lutz and Abu-Lughod (1990) distinguish as the discourses on emotion (theories about emotion) and emotional discourses (situated deployments of emotional linguistic forms). We don't know how to talk about emotion. Contemporary rhetoric does not have a unified rhetoric of the emotions, nor a psychology of the emotions. Psychology doesn't even have a psychology of the emotions, but several: evolutionary, psychophysiological, cognitive, and social constructionist or sociocultural theories of emotion all thrive and each entails a different relationship to language (see Cornelius 1996; Plutchik and Kellerman 1980; McLeod 1997). Scholars now find that the variety of states, attitudes, beliefs, and feelings we customarily lump together as *emotions* resist sharing a single category (see Rorty 1980; Brand 1987; McLeod 1997). Faced with the challenge of making sense of such complexity, textbook writers may have wisely decided that the better part of valor is discretion.

But it seems more likely that they have uncritically followed western culture's binary habits, which run deep and largely unchallenged. We have for centuries pitted reason against emotion, *logos* against *pathos*, *nomos* (law and culture) against *physis* (nature), masculine against feminine—and we have left for the most part unquestioned the assumptions that not only opposed these pairs but ranked them. Thus, despite Aristotle's admonitions, we have scant experience even in naming the emotions, much less in understanding them, in knowing "what they are, their nature, their causes and the way in which they are excited." Rather than potentially complementary, the binary oppositions may even be figured as implicitly hostile. Social epistemic and cultural studies approaches, for example, emphasize the experience and activity of groups rather than of the individual. Because emotions have, at least since Romanticism, been located in the individual—even identified *as* individual—they may seem trivial and bourgeois (see Brand 1991). Similarly, cognitivist approaches to composition schematize the highly conscious, linear processes of rationality and largely ignore the unconscious and chaotic affective ones (see Brand 1985–86). McLeod recognizes the interruptions in a writer's plans as emotional events (1987, 431). Quite early in the history of refiguring the affective dimension of writing, she also makes two moves not uncommon in Composition theory and pedagogy: she ponders the emotions she observes in her students as they write and speculates upon her own emotions as a writer. In the textbooks of any field, an objective stance is not likely to be remarked. But the teacherly remove of textbook authors from their readers is a bit puzzling in Composition because our professional discourse so frequently is not so.

Textbooks, reproducing one another and the discourse of academic argumentation, invoke the Aristotelian *pisteis*. But, while Aristotle may provide for Composition a respectable classical antecedent, a row of columns across the front of the classroom building where students are required to learn how to communicate information, the textbooks' rhetoric is not an Aristotelian rhetoric. In fact, the pedagogical practices implied by composition textbooks are only slenderly connected to their authorizing rhetorical theory. Despite the books' frequent reference to Aristotle and classical rhetoric, one might conclude that, at least as treatments of emotion, contemporary textbooks are rhetorically puny. Nor are their rhetorics explicitly aligned with any other theoretical perspective, although one or two books explicitly employ the rhetoric of Toulmin. They seldom sustain an attempt to understand the emotions—to know "what they are, their nature, their causes and the way in which they are excited"—for more than two or three paragraphs. They do not explicitly engage any theory of the emotions, or of the relationship between the emotions and other intellectual processes, or between emotions and ethics, or the implication of emotions in history, language, culture; in short they ground their admonitions to students in none of the long tradition of theory rehearsed and reread in Ellen Quandahl's essay at the beginning of this book. When they do discuss emotional appeals, they take the emotions for granted—as essential—and offer suggestions about *how* to excite them or, more frequently, simply allow that writers will find it useful *to* excite them. None of the textbooks I reviewed for this study engaged an analysis of the *pathe*—and certainly not of any particular emotion—as central to writing, to rhetoric, to a way to move.

What would a textbook that took emotions seriously look like? It would not make composing look simple. It would recognize and provoke analysis of both the discourse of emotions and emotional discourse. It would not trivialize emotions by taking them for granted, but would study them, interrogate their political and historical significance, inquire into their inflection by race, class, gender, geography. It would not restrict emotional appeals to the introductory and concluding paragraphs of an essay. It would not figure the writer as so clearly distinct from her readers—not pose her as the cool owner of information and argument and her readers as the victims, or at least stooges, of her feats of emotional manipulation. The ethical location of Aristotle's rhetoric of emotion, as Quandahl's essay reads it, arises in political action, especially action in language. It draws on the habitual dispositions of the rhetor as well as of the audience. But the long history of invoking Aristotle in textbooks has separated rhetor from audience, taken both as essential givens, and instructed the rhetor to act on (or refrain from acting on) the given emotions of the audience. A composition textbook that took emotions seriously would complicate this binary opposition as well. I'm tempted to say it would not look much like a textbook.

Third, the institutional context in which textbooks exist. That context figures composition as a service course with the mission of teaching students to produce clear expository prose in one year or less. In scientifically controlled assessments, success is defined as conformity to conventions, not only of standard edited English, but also of argumentation. Critical thinking is understood to be not only dispassionate but unpassionate, not only balanced and objective, but detached and neutral. Few writing teachers, I suspect, idealize these conventions or adhere to them in their individual practice. But programmatically, institutionally, composition and composition textbooks reproduce institutional culture.

American culture perpetuates its enlightenment roots in the binary structures that pit reason against passion, rational against emotional. Feminism, multiculturalism, poststructuralism notwithstanding, these binary discourses persist as powerful forces and discourage serious inquiry into the role of the emotions not only in Composition but also in the arena of rhetoric, that is, in public life. We dismiss emotional arguments as irrelevant or dangerous to decisions in public life. We look to science and the pseudoscience of expertise to guide objective, rational decisions. At the same time, we tolerate an uncritical cultivation of emotional display in the media. Television journalism daily engulfs viewers in hours of public outburst; in a parody of *enargeia*, networks strive to produce more anger, outrage, fear, pity, grief, and occasionally maybe even compassion in viewers than the competition. Is it any wonder, then, that textbooks warn writers against aligning themselves with advertisers and politicians? Or even that textbooks obscure the emotional dimensions of writing altogether?

Nevertheless, composition textbook writers must find a way to move. Not to do so misrepresents the nature of rhetoric and of emotion. Not to do so participates in the diminution of composition to service courses whose expressed purposes are not always the purposes of the profession. More important, not to do so encourages our students to continue in a thoughtless rejection of emotion as part of the good life, the reasoned life, the self-examined life. Not to do so feeds the sense that formal writing is a detached, personally meaningless academic exercise. Ultimately, not to do so denies emotion a place in public life and thereby separates the individual from the citizen.

Appendix: Textbooks Under Review

1. R. B. Axelrod and C. R. Cooper. 2001. *The St. Martin's Guide to Writing,* 6th ed.

2. S. V. Buscemi, A. H. Nicolai, and R. Strugala. 2000. *The Basics,* 3rd ed.

3. I. L. Clark. 1998. *The Genre of Argument.*

4. E. P. J. Corbett and R. A. Eberly. 2000. *The Elements of Reasoning,* 2nd ed.

5. R. Cullen. 2000. *Rhetoric for a Multicultural America.*

6. D. Daniel, C. Fauske, P. Galeno, and D. Mael. 2001. *Take Charge of Your Writing.*

7. E. A. Dornan and R. Dees. 1999. *Four in One: Thinking, Reading, Writing, Researching.*

8. D. Dunbar-Odom. 2001. *Working with Ideas.*

9. L. Ede. 2001. *Work in Progress,* 5th ed.

10. L. Faigley and J. Selzer. 2000. *Good Reasons.*

11. S. Fawcett and A. Sandberg. 2000. *Evergreen: A Guide to Writing with Readings,* 6th ed.

12. S. I. Fontaine and C. Smith. 1999. *Shoptalk for College Writers.*

13. A. Lunsford, J.J. Ruszkiewicz, and K. Walters. 2001. *Everything's An Argument,* 2nd ed, with readings.

14. R. F. Lunsford and B. Bridges. 2000. *The Longwood Guide to Writing.*
15. L. McMeniman. 1999. *From Inquiry to Argument.*
16. R. K. Miller. 1999. *The Informed Argument,* brief ed.
17. J. Nadell, L. McMeniman, and J. Langan. 2000. *The Macmillan Writer,* 4th ed.
18. J. D. Ramage and J. C. Bean. 2000. *The Allyn and Bacon Guide to Writing,* 2nd ed.
19. J. D. Ramage, J. C. Bean, and J. Johnson. 2001. *Writing Arguments,* 5th ed.
20. J. Rawlins. 1999. *The Writer's Way,* 4th ed.
21. D. Rosenwasser and J. Stephens. 2000. *Writing Analytically,* 2nd ed.
22. J. Siler. 2000. *The Essential Rhetoric.*
23. J. F. Trimmer. 2001. *Writing With a Purpose,* 13th ed.
24. J. D. Williams. 2001. *The LEA Guide to Composition.*
25. J. M. Williams and G. G. Colomb. 2001. *The Craft of Argument.*

Chapter Four

Moved by "Their" Words*s*

Emotion and the Participant Observer

Mary Ann Cain

> *[W]e have learned to code the political in specific, socially authorized ways, so that we might contain and control it. . . .[P]olitics was something I chose (or not) to bring in, through outside readings, assigned topics, or directed discussions, rather than an always present operative condition.*
>
> —Amy Lee, *Composing Critical Pedagogies*

When I consider Amy Lee's assertions above, I find it easy to exchange "the political" and "politics" with "emotional" and "emotions" and come to similar conclusions. Emotions, like politics, are encoded for social containment and control. However, unlike the political, which advocates of critical literacy have, as Lee notes, argued for as "an always present operative condition" (2000, 76), the emotional is more often cast in professional discussions as something that, like personal experience, can be readily included or excluded from writing, research, and teaching in Composition. The gulf between what is regarded as personal, and thus linked to one's emotion, and what is political, and thus somehow beyond individual lives and the emotions that shape them, is still wide in Composition Studies. Even after a decade of social constructivist arguments about the politics of institutional power and expressivist positions that locate personal experience and reflection as necessary for individual empowerment, discussions about the emotional as encoded in "specific, socially encoded ways" are rare. Such discussions tend to enfold the emotional within the question of "the personal" as something to either embrace or ignore but not to critically engage.

Emotion, as part of personal experience, is rarely engaged as a subject of critical inquiry, even as we as teachers, scholars, and writers routinely recognize it as a significant part of professional life. As Lee points out, we want to write and speak powerfully for a variety of purposes, including social justice, equality, and a democratic ideal. We want our students to be able to do the same. Power matters, and to the extent that it necessarily engages one's emotions, it would seem obvious that we would care as much about how emotions shape our sense of what makes writing powerful. And yet this is a question that is rarely asked. Scholarly journals such as *College English* and *College Composition and Communication* sometimes include first-person narratives (see Brodkey 1994; Sommers 1992) as a gesture towards embracing "the personal" (and presumably the emotional) as a form of knowledge. Yet most professional discourse remains decidedly conventional; writers make claims, provide evidence, and draw conclusions that do not appear to engage the writer's own experience. What is curious about this recent trend towards the personal, however, is not that it is, finally, being *included* but the perception that it has been previously *excluded*, and is now only allowable under heavy disciplining and with virtually no critical engagement.

During a 1999 CCCC panel on "Making Rhetoric Visible: The Critical Turn in Creative Writing," Lil Brannon raised this question of critical engagement when she called upon compositionists to critique the arguments embedded within personal narratives. She demonstrated this critical move by responding to a memoir by Lynn Z. Bloom in which Bloom, as the story's protagonist, is celebrated for fleeing naked from a college dormitory to escape a rapist's attack. Reading this narrative as a questionable metaphor for the choices that women make in their professional lives, Brannon illustrated the possibilities for re-visioning this story in less binary terms of either passively succumbing to an attacker or fleeing naked and vulnerable into the night. Brannon's reading demonstrates that however much we, like Bloom, may embrace our emotions to determine what we know and how we value that knowledge, we are nonetheless reluctant to get "too personal" in the process of engaging the social controls that shape them. Conventional readings of stories like Bloom's offer little critical engagement and as a result, do not address the story's tacit argument that women have little control over their lives. Instead of recognizing the emotional as similarly formed and encoded as other forms of knowledge, we more often than not construct such discourses as the privilege of those already authorized by the profession to speak, or quarantine them in "special issues" of a particular journal.

This intersection between the social and individual, the political and personal, is where the scholarship of Composition may take a turn from the rhetorical towards the poetic aspects of discourse, to make visible previously "unthinkable" forms of emotion that inform discursive practice. Contemporary fiction writers, for whom the problem of Modernism's legacy of the individualized, even self-contained, psyche is hardly new, have already launched such inquiries into narrative form. Avant-garde writers such as Carole Maso, Rachel Blau Du Plessis, and Ursula LeGuin, to name a few, reject a narrow psychologizing of characters even as they employ a radical first-person narration to disclose both the possibilities and limitations, the political gains and hardships, of speaking as an "I." Such authors rewrite the singular "I" into multiple, competing voices speaking through a variety of discursive forms that intersect within the "I." As LeGuin writes,

> The writer at her work
> is odd, is peculiar, is particular,
> certainly, but not, I think,
> singular.
> She tends to the plural. (1991, 216–17)

Instead of capitulating to objectivist assumptions about discourses and texts as speaking in a singular voice without contradictions, struggle, or contestation, I think we should strive to engage rather than defer to readers' assumptions about not only what they read but how. In short, we need narratives that will, on one hand, make readers aware of how certain discursive practices invite one to "overtake" a text and, on the other hand, offer possibilities for resisting such "overtakings" in our reading practices so that alternative viewpoints may be articulated.

Imaginary Spaces: Research as Discursive Exchange

In a recent article entitled "The Materiality of Language and the Pedagogy of Exchange," David Bleich notes how language learning takes place through a "mutual, collective, and reciprocal, as well as individual" exchange (2001, 117). Part of how such an exchange transpires would seem to include an exchange of the forms that emotions take. Unfortunately, according to Bleich, academic traditions and values "have separated 'knowledge' of anything from the pedagogical practices that pass it on," which would seem to include not only the uses of language but the forms of exchange (2001, 117). If, as Bleich argues, all uses of language constitute a "pedagogical scene" where language is exchanged in a reciprocal way, then the figure of the "neutral" researcher is a trope that conceals the pedagogical aspects of research. Repositioning researchers as those who exchange language (and knowledge) with their subjects opens into questions of how such relationships are already a site of overtaking and/or resisting another's language uses. In this view, research is also pedagogy, as language is exchanged between researcher and subjects. Current assumptions about neutrality, however, conceal the pedagogical aspects of research. As a result, our knowledge of what forms emotions actually do take in such inquiry, how they are used in social control, and their potential for re-formation through mutual exchange, is unavailable; it is simply "unthinkable."

According to Nancy Welch in her book, *Getting Restless: Rethinking Revision in Writing Instruction* (1997), introducing a "third factor" in our readings/revisionings of discourse can provide a strategy for such inquiry. She cites feminist philosopher Michelle Le Doeuff's construct as follows:

> In Le Doeuff's narrative, it's straying from a strict focus, venturing into a discourse viewed as outside (and beneath) her work as a philosopher, that enabled her to return to philosophy with a new critical and creative focus. Her involvement in feminist activism worked as what she called a 'third factor,' disrupting her relationship to philosophy and showing how as a *feminist* philosopher she could start to intervene in what her discipline took to be evident, natural common sense. (1997, 28)

Thus, to disrupt the binary opposition between "subjective experience" and "objective resource" requires this "third factor." Feminist geographer Gillian Rose makes a similar argument in her discussion of "imaginary space." Rose invites us to consider Luce Irigaray's concept of the imaginary in which "the distinction between the individual and the broader social structures in which they are embedded" is displaced (1996, 65). The "imaginary" is an "in-between" space, one different from the "real" ones of the practical world and the "imagined" ones of metaphor, a space where the categories by which "real" and "imagined" are called into question, and where "the imaginary relation between self and other is performed" (1996, 62). Using the imaginary as a framework for discursive relations allows us to revisit the distinctions between the "social and symbolic, or the real and the textual, or between the bodily and the cultural, or between agency and structure" (1996, 66). Nonhierarchical, reciprocal meanings *between* binary oppositions—between the "real" and "symbolic" as well as between seemingly contradictory or conflicting language uses—are possible.

The rest of my article will show how I use ethnographic narratives to articulate cultural assumptions about the emotions that "overtook" me as a participant-observer. I will also discuss how I used these narratives about emotion to reposition myself in relation to my research subjects towards a more "mutual, collective, and reciprocal, as well as individual" exchange of language, to quote David Bleich. I will employ the radical *I* described above by including two first-person narratives (one written as a collective *We*, the other as a singular *I*) that a third, analytical I/eye will engage to help readers reposition themselves in a similar manner. In the "imaginary spaces" between these multiple *I*'s, readers are invited to construct more of a reciprocal exchange between their own discourses and those of this research, as well as between their own and others' subjectivities by becoming more aware of the cultural narratives regarding emotion that always/already overtake them.

Moving Through Opposites: Improvisation and Discursive Exchange

> [A] story not told is told over and over again in mimed gestures of shyness and fear and conscribes a place in the body which holds this old suffering almost with tenderness.
>
> —Susan Griffin, *A Chorus of Stones*

Lisa grabs the rope with both hands from its pile in a corner of the studio. Muscles in her arms tighten as she drags the heavy, twisted fibers across the floor. The rope thumps as it uncoils, but Lisa is quiet and focused. Her head is bent slightly, as if listening to something very near or distant. She circles the studio, the rope bending and twisting obediently against the smooth wood floor until a kink or knot surfaces, and she pauses to shake it out. The rope settles into one large circle whose perimeter Lisa now walks with slow, steady steps, as if soliciting the answer to a question. Then she returns to the pile for a smaller length of rope, which she carries in her arms into the middle of the newly formed circle. Heavy fibers stream to the floor between her palms. Once the second circle is formed inside the first, she stands back to regard her work.

The teen boys and girls are still talking and laughing when Lisa interrupts to introduce us to the ropes. She invites us to reach down and touch them. They are rough, weightier than expected, and darkened with age and use. They smell like hay and mildew.

"This rope comes from the barn of a farmer friend of mine," she tells us. "A man of the earth. He used it with these huge horses he owned."

Some of us start walking the edges of the circles. We want to follow those shapes but also trespass the boundaries they set. Yet no one kicks the ropes or pulls them out of shape. The circles remain unbroken even as we start to move around, over, and under them.

For six months in 1999, I followed dance and movement artist Lisa Tsetse in her work with youths from northeastern Indiana. I wanted to understand how movement, as a "third factor" that gave form to otherwise invisible emotions, might help youths find ways to re-vision the choices in their lives and move them towards greater awareness of body, mind, and spirit. Lisa worked with a team of local artists in the CAP on Violence project, a court-ordered program designed to teach youths alternatives to violence through the use of artistic expression.[1] Lisa and her fellow artists met with groups of boys and girls once a week for twelve weeks.[2] The project culminated in a public performance by teen volunteers from the CAP project, as well as from area schools. Lisa and the other artists helped the teens develop a theme, learn to play percussion instruments, choreograph movement, write a script, and create stage decorations for this performance. Rehearsals started in late April at the Fort Wayne Dance Collective studios, with a mid-June date for the performance.[3]

On the first night of rehearsals, Lisa introduced the teens to an improvisational exercise using two ropes laid out in concentric circles on the studio floor. She and the other artists sought to engage the youths in various activities such as this to generate possible performance themes and develop a sense of connection. This improvisation proved later to provide me with an important key to making visible the forms of emotions that controlled and/or overtook participants. The resulting movements offered a third factor in which to critically engage in rereadings of those forms as social controls that shaped emotion and ultimately re-formed them for more liberatory purposes.

Body Talk/Body Text

I was taking Modern I for the third time in 1998, doggedly clinging to the hope that 20+ years as a runner and an occasional venture onto the dance floor at parties would somehow translate into coordination as a dancer. Yet up until that point, every class was a painful reminder of how little "body memory" I had. Lisa (who was not my instructor) suggested that I try other forms of movement. After working with a variety of modalities, including Feldenkrais Awareness Through Movement, Body-Mind Centering, Pilates, and Authentic Movement, my perception started to change. The pain became meaningful; my body started to "tell" me its story as I moved around the studio. I wasn't simply untalented or too old to move well. Instead my "failures" helped me identify chronic physical conditions that had gone unnoticed for years. It took another two years as I learned to ask the right questions of my body and find the necessary help to heal. Until I was able to "read" the emotions that shaped my body's movements, I was unable to re-form them towards greater ease, coordination and expression.

> *Lisa tells us that these ropes are powerful to her because of their connection to this friend, his horses, and the earth he farmed. She asks us to improvise movements using the rope's circles as a form. The larger circle, she says, is A. We need to find a way inside that first circle. She demonstrates different possible moves: stepping over, one foot at a time; jumping in with both feet; touching inside with one foot then another; going under the rope. Once we are inside A, we are to strike a pose that shows how others see us. After we move in A, we are to find a way into B. She tells us even somersaulting backwards is a way in. Once inside B, we are to strike a pose that shows how we see ourselves.*

The rope circles provided by Lisa introduced an "imaginary" space through which to inquire into the complicated social, intellectual, emotional, and psychological relations by which we as participants in this project were bound—in other words, the cultural narratives that currently "overtook" us, shaping our pedagogical "exchanges." Specifically, the ropes embodied various discourses on identity, discourses that are structured around binary oppositions between Self and Other. The "inside" space constituted the Self, or, in other words, the totality of an individual's identity. The Self occupied a space that was defined by the ropes, yet was still contained within the larger space of the studio. Within this Self there was an outer and inner self. The outer self is that space where we perform the Self (or Selves) that others see. We may or may not embrace this Self, but it is, nonetheless, part of the larger Self. The inner self is one we do embrace. But because it is encompassed by this larger, external Self, others do not see it.

Lisa's invitation to move in and out of the circles was, in essence, an invitation to inquire into the binary oppositions that shaped the participants' sense of self, as reflected in our physical movements. These binary oppositions were evident in the structure of the circles. The first opposition, as mentioned above, is the boundary between Self and Other represented by the outer circle. The space within the outer circle is constructed as public, a physically larger space, and ultimately what is seen by many. The smaller circle is constructed as private, a smaller space, what is seen by few, if any. Thus, a clear hierarchy exists between the "outer" and "inner" selves contained within the larger Self. The "inner" self is not visible to others; it is out of sight of public view. On the other hand, the "outer" self is wholly visible, yet can perform only what others outside already know and expect. Such a hierarchy, then, precludes any possibility for new constructions of the Self by maintaining this opposition between the inner and outer selves contained within. It is also a gendered

Double Moves

At first it seems simple: step inside A, strike a pose, step inside B, strike another pose. Lisa mentions a few possibilities to get us started, but that's all. I start moving. Something about the braided coils of the rope draws me to trace its perimeter, stepping inside with my right foot and outside with my left, criss-crossing my steps. My ankles ache with all the twists and turns, and I spread my arms for balance. I manage to do this for a while without losing my rhythm. Others around me make their way inside A. I'm not sure how to go inside, so I wait to see what others will do. Eventually I hop, both feet pressed side by side together, over the rope, then immediately hop backwards, again challenging my balance, not to mention anyone behind me. Hopping isn't quite right. I try again, take one big stride inside the circle, then bring the other leg in. I stand there, waiting. Everyone else's movements in and out are much more interesting. I step outside again, start braiding my steps along the rope again. In and out, in and out. Restless. As if I just can't commit one way or another. In and out. To my left, Angel dives gracefully to the floor, arms flung forward, fingers scooping beneath the heavy rope. She ducks her head as the rope glides over her. I bend over and grab her feet—this is the way in! She pulls us both under and through.

Once inside A, I somehow have to convey what others see as "me," all within a single pose. My arms move heavily; I feel daunted. How can one pose say everything? As my arms and head bend and twist, I realize that I can't settle on a single pose. And yet as I move, and others around me settle into their poses, I stop trying to figure it out. Some keep moving in and out of both circles, striking one pose after another, as if trying them out and rejecting them until they find the "right" one.

But perhaps they are also exploring how many different poses can answer the question of how others see them. My hands cup my face, my wrists join together like a seedling plant, and my back hunches over protectively. As if some invisible puppeteer were pulling strings, a movement in one body is echoed in another. I hunch over as someone else straightens and puffs out his chest. But I don't think about it. Movements happen without thought, whether "I" notice them or not.

Finding my way inside "B" seems trickier. Not as many will fit within this smaller circle, so timing is important, unlike A, where I can come and go with little thought of others. Again, I feel daunted by the prospect of striking a single pose to convey all of who I truly am, of knowing the differences between the "outside" and "inside" "me," if there even are any real differences. Those around me appear not to share my dilemma. They keep moving and posing. So I keep moving. Perhaps inspired by Amy's dive, I somersault backwards inside of B, then stand, arms outstretched over my head, hands splayed in triumph. A moment of celebration—that felt like the "right" way in! Over my shoulder I catch sight of James, standing still against the brick wall. His arms are crossed, and his eyes are trained on some distant spot across the studio. His stillness almost makes me stop myself.

Until now, I have enjoyed this invitation to move, to be overtaken by the movements of others, and have others be overtaken by mine. Yet here

hierarchy, in which smaller, private, and "personal" spaces are feminized, invisible outside the Self.

However, moving through these apparent oppositions made it possible to *feel* them as forms, and thus to feel how these discourses, as social constructions, shaped our bodily movements and, by implication, our emotions. Movement, then, gave form to emotion, embodying the social controls that regulated our bodies. The limits of how we could feel were materially manifested in the limits on how we could move. For instance, as the group moved, I not only felt my own, individual movements *as* movements but felt them in relation to the movements of others. I saw in their movements possibilities I had not previously imagined. I also saw how the movements I made were reflected in others. This awareness of others actually fostered an *exchange* of movements between one mover and another. New movements were improvised from the existing social constructions. The "either/or" constructions of the binary oppositions were transformed into a more reciprocal "with/and" through this exchange. Our improvisations, then, re-visioned the oppositional social constructions that had regulated our bodies and our emotions. The binary oppositions could not, in any absolute sense, contain all of what our bodies actually enacted or, in turn, what we felt.

One of us does not come inside the circle, does not move. One of us stands straight, arms crossed, back to the wall, to the windows, which let in that last light, making shadows on the floor. One of us says No! to inside/outside. No! to true and false. No! to individual vs. col-

lective. One of us stares across the ropes while the rest of us keep moving, in and out, in and out. One of us stays totally still, only breathing, blinking, swallowing. One of us has eyes that do not wander. One of us refuses the invitation to inquire. One of us is not "us."

Lisa traces the outer rope with quiet steps, weaving in and out as her hands draw pictures in the air around her. She walks slowly, without hesitation, past the one who stays outside. She looks down, watching her feet take their steps. Her hands and arms lift outward, not enough to touch the wall, but enough to touch that space just outside the circle and bring it inside, making what is inside stretch outside as well. She moves on as we collapse on the floor. We need that one standing outside so much it hurts. So we get up once more and start moving past him, acknowledging him with our movements even as we keep our eyes trained to our own bodies. What could be so difficult, except to stop?

is someone who refuses this "freedom." His refusal casts doubt on my triumph of getting it "right" inside B. He does not want to be overtaken. He does not want to exchange. He will not enter the circles. He stands, bearing witness to the rest of us who do. His refusal arouses my curiosity as well as my dis-ease. Why doesn't he join us? Is there a way to make him feel more invited? Seduction? Appeals? Is it because he is large and feels awkward? Or maybe it's the ropes themselves, their inside/outside oppositions that we all depend upon? Maybe he finds that in stillness he is not reducible to A and B, can resist the contradictions, refuse to play the discursive game, reject the master's model. He's too smart for that. This disturbs even as it fascinates me. He's chosen not to be "one of us."

We keep moving. What is bound is soon unbound. As we keep moving, nothing stays the same. Nothing stays the same, so we keep moving. When we finally stop, James leaves the wall. I think how much we needed his stillness to know how else we might move.

Within the imaginary spaces of these circles, the cultural narratives of emotion and how they "overtake" the forms that one's feelings, and, in turn, one's body take, became apparent to me as a participant *and* observer of this particular "pedagogical scene." One narrative was that of emotional control. Within this narrative, I assume that I am in control of my own movements as well as my emotions. Control of one's movement and body is assumed to come from within the individual. Thus within this narrative, "I" am cast as the one who not only chooses the forms that my body and emotions take but also controls them by choosing when and how to move.

The narrative that stands in opposition to emotional control is that of emotional freedom. In this narrative, movement forms are assumed to offer a space through which my emotions can be freely expressed, even "unleashed" without any negative consequence, either to myself or to others. The ropes provide a "safe space" to express a full range of possible emotions, including anger, rage, and fear, as well as joy, hope, and love. The freedom to express one's emotions coincides with the freedom to move and be moved by others' emotional expressions. One is not in control of such emotions, per se; instead, one is free to express them as they arise. The source of such emotions is assumed to be outside the individual. One does not choose one's movements or emotions; instead, one is overtaken by them, and within this context, can freely express them.

One moment in each of the first-person stories I've included inquires into these oppositional narratives and brings them into a more reciprocal exchange, thus articulating alternative ways of understanding how emotions work, as well as offering other possibilities for what is actually being exchanged and how. This moment came when I noticed that James, one of the boys from the CAP project, was standing still against the studio wall instead of entering either of the circles, arms crossed, eyes focused beyond the scene. On one hand, one might read James' posture as a refusal to participate: he is standing still while everyone else is moving; he remains outside the circles instead of going inside; he implies dissent, even disbelief in the social construction of Self that shapes everyone else's movements and emotions. He remains impassive, unmoved, literally and figuratively. Such a reading, of course, depends upon the cultural narrative of emotional control in which it is possible for the individual to control his movements and emotions in the face of social oppression.

Another reading of James' actions, on the other hand, would focus on James' expression of his emotions, in this case his possible discomfort with movement and thus with such self-expression. His "freedom" is to be able to express his discomfort by standing still. As I looked at James, considered his rather large and bulky frame in relation to the thinner, more lithe bodies of most of the other youths, of Lisa, who is herself a dancer, small and fluid in her movements, or myself, somewhat tall but not quite as broad, I did, indeed, wonder if he wasn't genuinely uncomfortable with moving his body, embarrassed by his size and stature and his inexperience with moving in a nonfunctional way. He might have been expressing a discomfort that many of us may have felt, but for various reasons, did not express ourselves, or at least in quite so obvious a way. James' possible discomfort made me consider what discomfort I was contending with in order to perform this improvisation.

This second reading of James depends upon the narrative of "free" emotional expression. It stands in direct opposition to the first reading of emotional control, in which James is in control of how he feels and actively resists the social controls that seek to overtake him. The second reading shows James as being overtaken by his discomfort and self-consciousness and freely expressing these emotions. He doesn't resist social controls overtaking his emotions as much as he is a vehicle for expressing how those controls affect him. Thus, both readings support the oppositional, contradictory views upon which the social construction of Self relies.

This opposition creates a seemingly unavoidable impasse for the researcher as an observing "I/eye" seeking to assign a conclusive meaning to James' behavior, except that he may, in fact, be refusing to participate. But why and how he refuses remain questions for "mere" speculation; the binary opposition, finally, places such answers as "outside" evidence and thus unknowable. Such questions are not, within this framework, "real" questions. However, when a "third factor" is introduced into this opposition, what is "real" and "unreal" shift ground. This "third factor" came in the form of Lisa as she moved past James and around the circle.

Soon after I noticed James against the wall, I also noticed Lisa moving in front of James, with a certain quiet deliberateness that made me think she was aware of James' presence and through her movements was acknowledging it. She twisted her torso and raised and lowered bent arms, softly and slowly, yet with what I considered great concentration. I thought about how I, as a teacher, would deal with a similar "refusal," and it seemed that my choices would ordinarily be to either insist on participation, ignore it, or make allowances for a "personal choice" to opt out. But Lisa's movement struck me as a re-visioning of the scene. Instead of thinking of James as being *either* a participant *or* an observer, as either "one of us" or an "outsider," Lisa's movements prompted me to reconsider James as fully participating in the exercise even as he refused to move in the ways that Lisa had initially suggested. Lisa's movements seemed, at once, to weave a web of connection with James even as they acknowledged his separateness from the rest of the group. I felt a certain tender questioning, "Are you alright?" even as I felt an affirmation, "You are exactly where you should be," as well as an acknowledgement, "I see your separateness." In short, Lisa's movements embodied for me those oppositions but enacted them as opposites in a dialectical tension, creating dialogue between categories of thought. When I saw how these oppositions could actually move together as "both/and" and not simply "either/or," I could also re-vision James as in a dialogue with the rest of us about the construction of Self that had overtaken us. James was, in this sense, an important counterpoint to raise our collective awareness that we were, in fact, all overtaken by movements and emotions that have been socially constructed and even imposed. He made me aware of how my movements weren't, in any final sense, my "own," and yet by feeling their forms, I could recast my choices, imagine other possible moves to make, including "not moving."

Conclusion: Towards a Critical Engagement of Emotion in Composition Studies

Emotion is typically difficult, if not impossible, to engage critically because of the oppositional narratives that shape how we live by and through emotions, narratives that we often experience not as socially constructed forms but as uncontested "reality." As a result, we tend to regard feelings as "personal" and not subject to critical engagement. At the same time, we routinely interpret and even judge emotions through various critical perspectives. For instance, we read emotions psychologically as "repressed," or "dysfunctional," philosophically or morally as "wrong" or "dangerous." We might aesthetically evaluate the artistic expression of "deeply felt" emotions or "free expression," and at the same time chide ourselves for taking our emotions "too seriously" or for feeling "out of control." Yet we rarely consider how the cultural narratives that shape our experience of emotion—namely that we either control or are controlled by them—can and should be critically engaged, in order to see beyond such dichotomies towards other possibilities.

Similarly, in Composition scholarship, we either embrace emotions acritically (as in classroom narratives and professional memoirs) as "powerful" or ignore them (as in conventional research) since no "evidence" exists to "prove" an interpretation of a subject's emotions (as in the above example of James' refusal to move in the rope improvisation). When we frame the "personal" (and, in turn, emotion) as a problem, as a matter of whether, when and how to include it in scholarly practice, emotions are not only understood as irrelevant to critical engagement, but also make critical engagement with a subject impossible. Yet when scholarly practices preclude critical engagement with the emotional, they also deny the pedagogical aspects of all discursive exchanges, including those between researchers and subjects. In Composition Studies, such a denial seriously limits our profession's ability to more fully realize the interrelationships between theory and practice, and between scholarship, writing, and teaching. For instance, when research is constructed as a singular, neutral perspective through which the research subject is made visible, it perpetuates an opposition to the subject's presumed partiality. Since much of Composition's research involves teachers and students of writing, such oppositional dichotomies reinforce professional hierarchies in which research is regarded, in and of itself, as "sufficient" while teaching "depends" upon theory and research to be successful.

However, by reframing the personal (and, in turn, the emotional) as always/already present within social formations of control and regulation, emotion as a "third factor" in both scholarship and teaching in Composition Studies can serve to make the cultural forms it takes more visible. We can theorize about conventional discursive practices in teaching and scholarship in Composition by rereading them through less conventional forms. For example, multiplying the "I" of one's discursive self, as I have done here, is one way to facilitate such a rereading, illustrating the ways emotions are socially constructed and regulated, but also offering the possibility of re-formation. Also, inquiring into other "emotional" forms such as movement can similarly provide a means of engaging the cultural narratives that underwrite presumably "unemotional" research discourse. Thus, we can prompt rereadings of presumably "impersonal" (and unemotional) discourses in light of the "personal" (and emotional) disclosures they in fact make, how they make them, and what ends they serve. By reading these narratives with a critical eye towards re-visioning the choices and possibilities they forecast for us as individuals, we might more productively question the emotional forms through which we currently move. As a result, research and scholarship may contribute more fully to a "mutual, collective, and reciprocal, as well as individual" discursive exchange between scholars and teachers, as well as between researchers and subjects, and teachers and students. And in that questioning, we might also improvise other forms of emotion as part of a discursive exchange to move our thoughts and actions into the unknown and unthinkable spaces of the imaginary.

Notes

1. Lisa coordinated the CAP program as the Outreach Director for the Fort Wayne Dance Collective. This outreach was in conjunction with the Fort Wayne Center for Nonviolence, which provided a structured curricula of nonviolence education that the CAP project complemented.

2. The CAP on Violence Program had already been in operation some years before I joined the artists and continues today.

3. Unlike other rehearsals that followed, I did not video- or audiotape this first one. Up until that point, I had limited my data collection to writing reflections the day after a meeting. This was primarily to ensure that teens from the court-ordered program felt "safe" to speak and move freely. Even taking notes on site interfered with my ability to participate in the groups' activities fully, something that Lisa had stipulated I do. But on this first night of rehearsal, in the dance studio for the first time with a mixed group of boys and girls, I could have recorded the night's activities. However, I felt that I did not want to be "outside" the group, operating a video camera. Nor did I feel comfortable thrusting a tape recorder into our midst while we sat and "checked in" for the evening. To grasp more fully what was developing between us as a group, I felt that I needed to participate in the conversation without any equipment mediating my experience of the discussion.

Chapter Five

What's Love Got to Do with It?
Eros in the Writing Classroom

Susan Kirtley

My eroticism is my participation in the universe.
—Carter Heyward, *Touching Our Strength*

I was an awkward eighteen-year-old freshman and I was giddy in love. Not so uncommon, I suppose, even if it was with my English professor. He was sixty-two years old with children my age, but he was still dapper, dressing in Timberland hiking boots and snappy khaki and flannel combinations. With his silvery hair and dark tortoiseshell glasses he had a way of smoking that oozed sophistication. Although stricken with asthma I wheezed happily at his side during the regular smoke breaks we took from class, just to hear his thoughts on literature and sometimes, on life itself. Although I loved my jaunty professor, I did not lust after him. When I waited outside his office for the chance to speak with him I did not hope for a torrid affair. I was in love with something he represented—a way of being in the world that embraced learning and literature. And though I can honestly say I did not desire a sexual relationship with him, my reaction to him was quite physical. In his presence, when discussing Foucault or Lyotard my pulse would beat frantically, an erratic, inebriated rhythm. Years later I still love him with a grateful, sweet longing. He taught me what it was to learn and work passionately.

Now I am an instructor of writing and literature at a large university, and even though I remember my own affections as a student I have become somehow ashamed of them. Juvenile emotions, I thought several years ago as I began my teaching career, and not fit for the classroom. As a young, female graduate Teaching Associate I knew I needed to prove my intellect, not my passion.

And yet, despite my attempts to remain a brain alone, my heart has betrayed me and I have fallen in love again, this time with a student—a whole class of them in fact. I know it is taboo to feel such affection for students (or at least it feels that way), but somehow I couldn't help it. When class first met I was nervous as I always am with new people, but as time progressed all the signs of a romance in bloom emerged. Once again I felt the fast, familiar rhythm of my silly schoolgirl heart, and I found myself wandering into daydreams of imaginary class meetings. I was elated during class sessions and when the semester ended I grew depressed, knowing how desperately I would miss them. It has been several months since class ended, and I still feel a bittersweet longing when I think of them.

This emotion, this love I speak of is something I have found embarrassing and exhilarating. In my own thinking I defined this love I experienced in both my roles as teacher and student as eros. My quest in writing this essay is to investigate eros, by borrowing from past and present theories, and to create my own constructions of eros. In the process I hope to explore how these many theories of eros might assist in my goals as a Composition instructor.

A caveat—I do not claim to be an expert on eros or Plato, or for that matter on love or any other emotion. However, I take comfort in the words of Theodore Reik, who offers his own confession in the preface to his work *Of Love and Lust*. "This is not the book of a learned man," he writes, "but of a seeker after truth. I do not pretend to know all the answers, I do not even know all the questions" (1957, 6). This is not the essay of a learned woman, but rather a "seeker after truth" who hopes to explore how eros might be reimagined as a site where teachers and students connect emotion with intellect in the writing process.

The Problem: The Absence of Bodies and Emotion in the Academy

> What did one do with the body in the classroom?
>
> —bell hooks, *Teaching to Transgress*

> The thing I want to say is that I've been hiding a part of myself for a long time.
>
> —Jane Tompkins, "Me and My Shadow"

I am a woman who weeps during Hallmark commercials. It is as difficult for me to hide my feelings as it is for me to hide my body. My emotions register with smiles and frowns, and since I have entered the academy I have often felt that my body and its attendant sentiments do not belong. Perhaps it is not surprising that I sense a distinct divide between body and mind in the academy given its history. In his essay "The Politics of Middle English Writing," Nicholas Watson explains that within the medieval church and its offspring the academy, "heart knowledge" or *sapientia* was quite different from "head knowledge" or *scientia.* He writes, "*Sapientia*, which did not require formal theological training . . . was available to all. Associated with the body, the emotions, women, and Christ's human nature . . . *sapientia* was also figured by the mother tongue and its audience" (1999, 339). It was thus early on that "heart knowledge" was linked with "the body, emotions, women" as well as the vernacular or common language, and therefore devalued, hidden, and concealed. It was *scientia,* the knowledge of the head that was lauded by the academy, but how is it possible to have a head without a heart? It is this dichotomy that has haunted me as a teacher, scholar, and writer.

As a teacher I have often felt the need to relinquish my feelings in order to be a "real" instructor. I feel literature, I feel my connection to my students, and I feel my writing in my body. However, I also feel compelled to hide what I have been taught is a weakness: my emotions. As Deborah Chappell explains, "even though I saw my students as whole human beings, possessing bodies, minds, and spirits, I was coming into the class pretty much as a disembodied brain" (1992, 3). I, too, feel the pressure to present myself only as an academic "brain."

It was thus with great delight that I read the work of feminist scholars who posit eros as a way back to our bodies and feelings as scholars and instructors. In her dissertation, "Uses of the Erotic: Contemporary Feminists and Plato on Eros, Power, and Reason," Cheryl Ann Hall points out that many prominent feminist theorists such as Audre Lorde, Haunani-Kay Trask, and bell hooks focus on "the way in which the repression/denial of eros creates the split between mind and body. . . . Mind and body are not, according to this view, inherently opposed; they only become so through the refusal to accept eros as part of the self" (1993, 26). hooks argues that "when eros is present in the classroom setting, then love is bound to flourish" (1994, 199), and Lorde suggests that "the erotic is not a question only of what we do; it is a question of how acutely and fully we can feel in the doing" (1997, 54). Hurrah for eros, I thought as I read the words of these great scholars. But as I reflected on these works, I became concerned about the recurring association of eros as a concept not clearly defined, but lauded instead as an almost entirely positive force.

Shulamith Firestone posits that eros is not a source of power for most women but rather a source of subjugation. She reveals, "eroticism is only the topmost layer of the romanticism that reinforces female inferiority" (1989, 38). What has happened to my joyful reunion with eros? Hall asserts that the deepest problem underlying the position of these feminists is "the idealization of eros" (1993, 63), in which eros "comes to stand for 'the good,'" and consequently leaves "the realm of ordinary, complex human desire behind" (1993, 76). Hall turns to Plato to help her find a way out of this dilemma and discovers that his vision of eros is not an "ideal state" (1993, 140) as some scholars suggest, but rather a "source of movement" (1993, 141). For Plato eros is a process of movement inspired by desire. And though I am critical of eros, I choose not to abandon it; I turn, instead, to Plato's *Symposium.*

The Clarification: Diotima Explicates Eros

> A loves B because Eros has caused A to love B, regardless of whether B looks attractive on any objective criteria.
>
> —Catherine Osborne, *Eros Unveiled*

> If I love A because of ∅, is what I love in A the object of my love and different from A in such a way that what I really love is ∅ and not A?
>
> —L. A. Kosman, "Platonic Love"

> 1. A knows B (or at least knows something of B)
> 2. A cares (is concerned) about B
>   A likes B
> 3. A respects B
>   A is attracted to B
>   A feels affection for B
> 4. A is committed to B
>   A wishes to see B's welfare promoted
>
> —W. Newton-Smith, "A Conceptual Investigation of Love"

As we've seen previously amongst scholars such as hooks and Lorde, defining eros is a difficult task. Kerry Burch points out, "Eros itself is a contested concept and we need to acknowledge the politics of its representation, as a first step. We should do this not only in the interest of sound scholarship but also to underscore the richer textures of the concept" (2000, 130). He further posits that "the exact meaning of a complex symbol like 'eros' is not pre-given, but fluid, dynamic, and contested" (78). Scholars of Plato indicate various equations of eros in their own attempts at definition and clarification. Though I find them intriguing, ultimately they provide me with little guidance.

The online *Oxford English Dictionary* defines eros as "Love, the god of love" or "earthy or sexual love, contrasted with AGAPE." As indicated by the OED, over time eros came to be associated with sex and sexuality, as opposed to *agape*, the spiritual Christian love. Burch argues against a devaluation of eros as *only* sexual love, maintaining, "I do not agree that eros should be reduced to sexuality at the expense of other valid associations. We need to exercise a finer sense of discernment about the boundaries of eros" (2000, 130). Rollo May agrees, claiming in his book *Love and Will*:

> Eros is the drive which impels man not only toward union with another person in sexual or other forms of love, but incites in man the yearning for knowledge

> and drives him passionately to seek union with the truth . . . The Greeks also knew that there always is a tendency for eros to be reduced simply to sexual desire—*epithymia* or lust in their terms. But they insisted that the biological is not denied but *incorporated* and *transcended* in eros. (1969, 79)

While I agree with May that eros is much more than sexual desire, I do feel it is important to acknowledge the abusive actions that some teachers have taken in the name of eros. We have all heard the stories of professors seducing students, of sexually abusing and/or harassing the pupils they are charged with instructing.[1] Much has been written about such abuses; such exploitation is known and should be addressed and combated within our profession. Sadly, some teachers believe that their actions were guided by eros; I would disagree. Eros, as May explains, is more than lust for sexual activity—it is also the desire for knowledge. It is this eros, the eros that does not exploit but educates, that I wish to explore.

Although my thinking is informed by the multiple meanings ascribed to eros by hooks and Lorde as well as other scholars, it is in Socrates' dialogues with Diotima in Plato's *Symposium* that I find the explanation of eros that most assists me in my work as a teacher of writing. I readily admit to utilizing some of Plato's teachings while resisting others, and ultimately I choose to focus on Diotima's lessons, rather than on the entire oeuvre of Plato's texts, or even the entirety of *The Symposium*.

In *The Symposium* Plato depicts a jovial dinner party in which guests offer speeches on eros, one by the great Socrates himself. Given the many speeches and their various contexts, it is impossible to discern one precise, unassailable definition of eros. Yet it is to one speech in particular that I turn my attention—that of Socrates. In his address Socrates claims that his teacher on matters of eros was the great and wise woman Diotima.

Though his time with her has passed, Socrates recreates his discussions with Diotima for the edification of his listeners and explains how Diotima understands eros. Jim Garrison states, "Diotima begins by teaching Socrates that eros is one of the daimons. In ancient Greek religion daimons were a kind of personality midway between humankind and the gods" (1997, 3). As described by Diotima, eros occupies a special position *between* humanity and the heavens. When Socrates asks about the function of a *daimon*, Diotima explains that a *daimon* will "interpret and convey messages and sacrifices from gods to men and to men from the gods, prayers and sacrifices from the one, and commands and rewards from the other. Being of an intermediate nature, a spirit bridges the gap between them, and prevents the universe from falling into two separate halves" (1951, 81). As a *daimon,* eros is dialogue, which includes human requests and heavenly responses. Eros is movement, a speaker's wish to communicate with an audience. Through this action, the *daimon* holds the world together, uniting the mortal and the immortal through language. Eros then as a *daimon* works to connect ideas that may seem incompatible. While heaven and earth are certainly divided, eros the messenger helps bridge the gap. Writing functions similarly to eros, bringing together author and audience and making connections between separated parties.

How is it that eros came to be always in motion, always searching? Diotima explains to Socrates the origins of the personified Eros in mythology, illuminating how the concept of eros came to be defined. Diotima explains:

> On the day that Aphrodite was born the gods were feasting, among them Contrivance the son of Invention; and after dinner, seeing that a party was in progress, Poverty came to beg and stood at the door. Now Contrivance was drunk with nectar . . . and went out into the garden of Zeus, and was overcome by sleep. So Poverty, thinking to alleviate her wretched condition by bearing a child to Contrivance, lay with him . . . (1951, 82)

The conception of Eros, the mythological figure, further emphasizes the idea of "a space between," and a coming together of opposites. Eros was conceived at a feast for beauty in the garden that marked the boundary between excess and lack. Eros then, according to Kay Alston, is "halfway between the mortal and the divine, the child of Need and Resource" (1991, 388). Garrison resolves that "if Diotima is correct, eros is the principle that unified opposites, such as need and fulfillment, throughout the cosmos" (1997, 8). Diotima carefully crafts eros as occupying a space between ideas, but never quite reaching a final destination. Much like writing, this eros originates both in abundance and lack. As writers we want to share our language and spread our message beyond ourselves.

In *The Symposium* Socrates makes the mistake of suggesting that eros is beautiful, a common idea in contemporary as well as classical thinking. Diotima, however, corrects this prevalent misunderstanding, arguing that many confuse the object of affection for eros itself. While the object of our affection might well be beautiful, gorgeous even, *the feeling of longing itself* is much more complicated. Diotima uses the mythological figure Eros to emphasize the unsettled nature of the concept, suggesting that he takes after both of his parents: "He is always poor, and, far from being sensitive and beautiful, as most people imagine, he is hard and weather-beaten, shoeless and homeless" (1951, 82).

The Eros depicted by Diotima is a wanderer who bears little resemblance to the pudgy, rosy-cheeked cupids of Renaissance paintings, but this personification has its own appeal. Diotima's eros offers something we humans might more readily understand, for this *daimon* experiences deficiency and desire. Furthermore, the image of disorder appeals to me. Writing and teaching and learning are often messy enterprises; we struggle and make mistakes and occasionally lose our way. As a teacher I am sometimes tempted only to "clean up" students' writing, becoming a diagnostician who corrects prose and tames students' wandering thoughts. I believe it is important not to forget to encourage students to enjoy the origins and the journey of writing as well as the final crafting.

What then does eros create through this continual wandering? Diotima suggests that in the quest for knowledge, eros finds immortality. Diotima maintains that the function of eros "is to procreate and bring forth beauty" (1951, 87). Socrates is confused, but Diotima continues, "procreation is the nearest thing to perpetuity and immortality that a mortal being can attain" (1951, 87). And while some beget children as their glimpse of immortality, others beget knowledge. Diotima clarifies, "there are some whose creative desire is of the soul, and who long to beget spiritually, not physically, the progeny which it is the nature of the soul to create and bring to birth. If you ask what that progeny is, it is wisdom and virtue in general" (1951, 90). Diotima here makes an important clarification—while she doesn't deny feelings of physical desire with the potential of begetting children, she indicates another idea of eros, a spiritual longing to bring forth wisdom. Reading this I am reminded of the teacher and the writer, whose desire for connection results, we hope, in wisdom. May describes eros in such a way that it becomes an opportunity to "open ourselves" to new ideas and knowledge. Furthermore, he suggests that participating in the larger community around us requires "imagination" as well as "emotional and spiritual sensitivity" (1969, 79). To become great participants in the "forms and meanings beyond us," we must enlist our passions. As a writing teacher I ask my students to explore, to investigate, to question their understanding of the world, and to resist easy endings or conclusions. To cultivate this type of eros in students and teachers might allow us to "bind" our own wonderings with new knowledge. Eros helps us move from simply existing as objects in the world to becoming thinking, questioning subjects.

Eros is represented as a journey, progress towards understanding. Diotima seems hesitant to explain her final lesson to Socrates, wondering whether he is capable of grasping "the perfect revelation" she is to impart. Diotima then relates her controversial theory of the ascent of eros, positing,

> This is the right way of approaching or being initiated into the mysteries of love, to begin with examples of beauty in this world, and using them as steps to ascend continually with that absolute beauty as one's aim, from one instance of physical beauty to two and from two to all, then from physical beauty to moral beauty, and from moral beauty to the beauty of knowledge, until from knowledge of various kinds one arrives at the supreme knowledge whose sole object is that absolute beauty, and knows at last what absolute beauty is. (1951, 94)

I realize that my interpretation of this key passage differs from others, yet I believe that this ascent, this journey towards "absolute beauty" does not necessarily have to leave behind the body, but might instead incorporate the lessons and feelings of the physical form in the expedition of eros. In Diotima's idea of ascension, eros begins in our feelings for other bodies and in the feelings and emotions present in our own bodies. It is these emotions that lead us from the desire we feel in our bodies to the desire for beauty in people—their minds and thoughts—to the desire for wisdom or "supreme knowledge." Now this is perhaps a scary moment; I am not advocating that we as instructors focus only on student bodies as the starting point for an ascent to wisdom. I am, instead, suggesting that we begin by acknowledging our feelings and desires and encouraging our students to do the same, as we progress towards deeper understanding and knowledge—what Diotima calls "absolute beauty." I realize that I am in some sense reinventing Plato here, for he is not known for celebrating the body. My intention is not to disrespect Plato; rather I hope to reclaim what I believe to be a particularly useful concept for contemporary instructors.

I believe that the journey towards eros is never complete, for those who undertake it always desire more. However, I like to believe that those who undertake such a voyage carry with them physical love and love of knowledge itself. Eros can then be seen as a continual movement forward, a perpetual striving that emerges in emotion and leads to wisdom. Perhaps it is in this reflective, inclusive understanding of eros as outlined by Diotima that I might find a way to connect passion with reason, as well as teacher with student.

Eros in Education: Pedagogy and Desire

> On whose authority is it accepted that the theme of love cannot be educationally considered?
>
> —Kerry Burch, *Eros as the Educational Principle of Democracy*

> We become what we love. Our destiny is in our desires, yet what we seek to possess soon comes to possess us in thought, feeling, and action. That is why the ancient Greeks made the education of eros, or passionate desire, the supreme aim of education.
>
> —Jim Garrison, *Dewey and Eros*

Although scholars within Composition are for the most part silent on eros, several scholars within education have found something lacking in contemporary pedagogy and have turned to the idea of eros as a way to bring passion into teaching. Though at times I question bell hooks' notion of eros, I believe she is quite right when she argues, "To restore passion to the classroom or excite it in the classrooms where it has never been, professors must find again the place of eros within ourselves and together allow the mind and body to feel and know desire" (1994, 199). In his book *Dewey and Eros: Wisdom and Desire in the Art of Teaching,* Garrison wonders, "What is this thing that every teacher intuitively understands lies in the middle of everyday practice yet is missing from almost all theory and research on teaching? It is loving, life-affirming, passionate "desire," or eros. Eros is the most basic type of desire. All practical reasoning is about obtaining values we desire" (1997, xix). In Garrison's thinking, "teachers may act like daimons mediating between students' present needs and their future good" (1997, 5). Thus, teachers may act as "mediators" assisting students in following their desires for wisdom, and educating these desires towards the good that Socrates longs for. Of course, as a teacher I also find myself following my desire for wisdom. In fact, engaging in the journey of eros may serve to diminish strict boundaries between teacher and student. In the classroom we become fellow travelers, though some are more experienced and thus more able to act as *daimons* for others.

Burch traces the evolution of eros throughout history in his book *Eros as the Educational Principle of Democracy*. Burch argues, "as an educational principle, eros can provide the vocabulary and symbolic value system that critical pedagogy needs to rejuvenate both the vocational identity of teachers and the hope of democratic renewal in America" (2000, 2). After his comprehensive analysis of the etymology of eros, Burch concludes, "the most powerful and transformative forms of education are those that provoke students to reflect upon the social orchestration of their desire" (2000, 160). Eros thus encourages teacher and student to discover their own desires, and reflect on the construction of those desires. In doing so, students gain perspective and are able to evaluate their yearnings and what might have inspired such desires.

Alston argues for the incorporation of eros into classrooms in the article "Teaching, Philosophy, and Eros: Love as a Relation to Truth." Alston states, "eros is suggested as a candidate for a relationship between teachers and students that is mutually participatory, dynamic and developmental" (1991, 386). Despite the value these scholars of education find in eros, they also advise caution. Burch argues, "eros as an educational principle should not, therefore, be imagined as completely unmoored eros, unmediated by critical reflection" (1991, 189). As instructors we must continually question our own motives. Similarly we must invite our students to reflect on their own wishes. What is it we desire? As a student I felt desire for what my English professor represented. I wanted to be like him, to think like him, to be a part of that life of learning. I still desire knowledge and understanding and probably always will. Through this eros I have become a teacher myself and now feel a similar connection with my students. I want them to *feel* literature and to experience the joy and connection and even struggle of writing. I desire for them to think and feel fully in the academy and in their lives.

Garrison, Burch, and Alston all exhort the possibilities of eros to transform education into a space where passion and desire guide *whole* students and teachers towards wisdom. They position eros as action, a desire that inspires questioning, thinking, and movement. I believe their scholarship makes a strong case for encouraging eros in all classrooms, yet as I contemplate desire, as well as connection and procreation, it seems to me that eros might be suited particularly well to the writing class.

Writing and Eros in the Everyday Classroom

Desire moves. Eros is a verb.

—Ann Carson, *Eros the Bittersweet*

For me writing has always been about longing. As a shy girl I wrote endlessly in my diary, secretly hoping that someday my writing would be discovered. Writing feels to me like an attempt to make an association. The power of composition resides in this "space between." Though the author may be long gone, once a link is fashioned with a reader, immortality is indeed achieved.

Writing is erotic. Words allow for an exchange, for a bridge between people. Ann Carson describes the erotic elements of composition eloquently in her book, *Eros the Bittersweet.* She clarifies, "As the vowels and consonants of an alphabet interact symbolically to make a certain word, so writer and reader bring together two halves of one meaning, so lover and beloved are matched together like two sides of one knucklebone. An intimate collusion occurs" (1986, 108).

There is an intimate, alluring element in the composing process—isn't writing an attempt to seduce readers, to entice them to see and feel the world as you wish them to? The writer issues an invitation and reaches out to the reader, much as the lover beckons to the beloved. Carson further suggests, "What is erotic about reading (and writing) is the play of imagination called forth in the space between you and your object of knowledge" (1986, 109). To write is to call forth the *daimon*, the messenger between one imagination and another.

And yet, neither writer nor reader fully achieves completion. As writers we rarely know our readers, and even when we do, our vision is never received absolutely. Rather, it is re-interpreted through the mind of the reader. Carson asserts, "neither reader nor writer nor lover achieves such consummation. The words we read and the words we write never say exactly what we mean. The people we love are never just as we desire them. The two *symbola* never perfectly match. Eros is in between" (1986, 109). Eros is thus my desire for the reader to understand me. My passion is in the attempt, not the conclusion. I teach my students that the joy of writing is not only in the product, but in the process as well, in the act of crafting language. Eros is the invitation we issue as writers, an attempt to find immortality with another.

Eros, like writing, is a verb. Eros and writing share other commonalities, such as lacunae or absences and the desire to reach across them to create a bond with another. For me the erotic writing class is about an embodied, intellectual passion that bridges gaps as a *daimon* might. Teacher—Student. Longing—Possession. Writer—Audience. For many of us the pleasure of writing is the journey it takes us on, and the mystery when it is sent off into the world to reach others.

Am I idealistic to think this concept will be palatable as well as practical to other writing instructors? I imagine that I am a bit of a romantic. However, though I am enthusiastic about the potential of eros, I do believe it is important to be aware of power imbalances in the classroom no matter what the pedagogy, with eros being no exception. When eros is incorporated as a point of connection between people (not necessarily opposites) I hope not to gloss over imbalances, but to create bridges that recognize these disparities.

I find eros everyday in the writing class, in even the smallest things. Eros is the essays students write and the letters I write in response. Eros is the palpable excitement in the writing class when we share our research projects, projects designed to draw on the students' desires as well as my own. As the students and I share what we are working on, other class members offer suggestions, sources, advice. When I receive these final papers, knowing the energy and passion that went into creating them, I am eager to read them.

As I indicated in the opening of the piece I do not claim to have all the answers about eros, and I realize that others might understand the concept quite differently. However, this is a discussion we need to have in Composition, despite any taboos. Unfortunately, fear has limited many scholars from discussing our passions in the writing classroom. We should not be afraid to address our desires and emotions, the feelings that inspire and limit us. Over time and through my investigations I have come to think that writing and teaching with eros allows us to join with others. It is a passionate offering marked by perpetual movement. And although I still have many questions and make no claims to final conclusions, I like to think that Diotima had it right all those years ago, and that if we are willing to mindfully embrace eros in our classrooms, it will guide us to traverse boundaries, coming to a place where desire leads to wisdom.

Notes

1. Although not addressing the term "eros" specifically, in her book *Feminist Accused of Sexual Harassment* Jane Gallop makes the argument that consensual sexual relations between students and teachers should not be prohibited, and that such restrictions might actually diminish pedagogy. It would appear that for Gallop engaging in a sexual relationship does not alter a teacher-student relationship; I would argue that for most students and teachers, such a relationship would significantly alter a teaching dynamic, most likely in damaging ways. I believe that it is possible to teach with passion without having sex with students and that in being mindful and careful of students' boundaries we are, in fact, "treating them as human beings."

Chapter Six

Error and Racialized Performances of Emotion in the Teaching of Writing

Donna Strickland and Ilene Crawford

In a recent McDonald's television commercial, a little boy asks his mother to clarify a bit of grammatical usage for him: should he ask "*may I* or *can I* have a Happy Meal"? Empowered by her response, he confidently faces the young worker across the McDonald's counter to ask, "May I have a Happy Meal please?" In the closing shot, the boy enjoys his fast food under the approving gaze of Ronald McDonald himself. "Ronald thinks you did good," his mother tells him. Flush with his grammatical success, the boy corrects her: "I think I did *well*."

This commercial is striking in its effort to align a multinational company with something as seemingly mundane as "proper" grammar.[1] But it is striking also in its effort to school its viewers' emotions— to elicit approval as we watch the small child wield hypercorrect usage, as if he might be denied his burger and fries were he to err with a sub-par "can I." We are invited to look on the boy through the eyes of Ronald, who watches the closing scene with his enigmatically mute smile, and to feel a warm connection to this interplay of consumerism, homogeneity, and correctness.

What is also noteworthy about the commercial is that the mother and child are Black, while the McDonald's worker and, indeed, Ronald himself, are white. This performance of correct(ing) language can be read as racialized and racializing in distinguishing, on the basis of skin color, between those who correct their language and those who approve and reward such corrections. Although the performance may seem insignificant in the scheme of things—a momentary blip on the screen—Pierre Bourdieu's critical work on language and schooling persuades us that "the factors which are most influential in the formation of the habitus are transmitted . . . through suggestions inscribed in the most apparently insignificant aspects of the things, situations, and practices of everyday life" (1991, 51). The "habitus," for Bourdieu, "is a set of *disposi-*

tions which incline agents to act and react in certain ways. The dispositions generate practices, perceptions and attitudes which are 'regular' without being consciously co-ordinated or governed by any 'rule'" (Thompson 1991, 12). Apparently insignificant, regularized practices, in other words, are both generated by and generative of normalized inclinations, inclinations that tend to support the status quo. Though they may appear insignificant, these regularized practices enact "invisible, silent violence," the effects of which are "never more manifest than in all the corrections, whether *ad hoc* or permanent, to which dominated speakers, as they strive desperately for correctness, consciously or unconsciously subject the stigmatized aspects of their pronunciation, their diction . . . and their syntax" (Bourdieu 1991, 52). For Bourdieu, himself a native speaker of a stigmatized dialect in France, the performance of correcting language is symptomatic of internalized, symbolic violence. The McDonald's commercial, according to this view, can be seen as a performance of self-correction, one that regularizes the desire for homogeneity and that articulates invisible, internalized violence with consumerism.

The symbolic violence that maintains the habitus, Lynn Worsham has argued, "educates emotions and inculcates an affective relation to the world" (Worsham 1998, 216). Further, the primary work of this dominant pedagogical violence "is to organize an emotional world, to inculcate patterns of feeling that support the dominant interests, patterns that are especially appropriate to gender, race, and class locations" (1998, 223). Advertisements like the McDonald's commercial help to establish and reinforce such patterns of feeling—in this case, the feeling of approval as a child recognizes himself as a dominated speaker in need of correction, approval as he literally trades on the cultural capital of corrected speech, thus establishing the "rightness" simultaneously of the dominant cultural and economic systems. The viewer is asked to share in the child's pride over his self-correction, a sharing that depends on a kind of conceit: the viewer recognizes the child's desire for correctness as a good thing, a proper thing, insofar as the viewer her- or himself believes in the value of the dominant culture.

Teachers of writing, we believe, have an obligation to think through the ways in which these dominant pedagogies, played outside of the classroom, shape classroom performances and pedagogies. Those of us who teach writing know that few issues seem to evoke more intense emotions from colleagues and people on the street than that of "correct" grammar. As anyone who has been involved in the administration of writing programs can attest, colleagues from across the university often indict writing programs for failing to "do their jobs"—that is, for failing to teach "correct" grammar. For at least three decades now, teachers of writing have answered such institutional and public denunciations with an appeal to authoritative knowledge: the research shows that direct instruction in grammar (for example, drills in grammar) have little or no transfer into students' writing. We all know the response to give to people who seem obsessed with grammar, and yet the tendency to dismiss our critics as "misinformed" has done little to change the overwhelmingly emotional response that the perception of error evokes. The McDonald's commercial, for example, depends upon an audience who will respond on an emotional level to the performance of correctness, respond with a kind of sadomasochistic sharing in the boy's pride as he submits to the symbolic violence of correcting his own language. To simply suggest that the boy would have been able to get a Happy Meal whether or not he used "may" is beside the point. The commercial obviously is not schooling its audience in the skills of "correct" English, nor is it making a direct claim that a person must use appropriate language to be able to purchase fast food. Rather, it is aligning consumerism with what the advertisers assume to be shared values toward correctness and thus reinforcing patterns of feeling that support the dominant culture.

The field of Composition Studies has been relatively silent on the emotional schooling of correctness. Elspeth Stuckey (1992), of course, has attuned us to the "violence of literacy," a violence that she sees primarily inflicted upon—and thus, at issue for—speakers of nonstandard languages and dialects. We would like to shift our attention away from those students who are generally represented as "other" to the ways in which this violence is perpetuated through racialized performances. In this case, we are thinking of the performances not of the child and his mother in the commercial, but of Ronald, and, by extension, the viewer who recognizes his or her own subjectivity in that white-faced, approving smile. In this essay, we want to consider how emotional investments in "correct" language are schooled and how they might be reschooled. However, as Worsham points out, "we cannot simply unlearn what dominant pedagogy teaches by mapping a new regime of meaning onto an old one" (1998, 222). To be sure, the more the two of us engage in the project to reschool emotional investments in correct language, the more we question our initial assumptions and approaches. In attempting to reschool students' emotional investments in nonstandard languages such as Ebonics, we found that this focus may paradoxically reinforce the negative emotional associations we hope to change. In this chapter, we would like to offer a different strategy, one in which we "turn the othering gaze on ourselves," as Wendy Hesford has advised, in order to begin to make visible the role emotion plays in the construction of white subjectivity (1999, xxx). Making visible the emotional investments and performances that constitute whiteness has the potential to better prepare teachers and students to question and change the unequal social relations that an uncritical investment in correctness supports.

To begin, we will demonstrate the racialized dimensions of emotional responses to what is perceived to be "error," a dimension that became particularly clear in the wake of the Oakland Ebonics resolution of 1996 and the ensuing public controversy over this resolution. By subsequently describing and reflecting on our own attempts to address this controversy in our classes, we hope to both trouble our own assumptions and to move toward more productive/disruptive pedagogies.

Correctness, Affect, and Race

We are by no means the first to notice that questions of grammar and correctness produce intense emotional reactions in many people. For example, in his classic 1981 article, "The Phenomenology of Error," Joseph M. Williams catalogues the raw emotional responses grammar and usage errors often produce in people. In pointing out that William Zinsser, for example, describes such "errors" as the use of "hopefully" and "ok" as "vulgarities" and "horrible atrocities," Williams wonders why certain errors regularly elicit a fury remarkably out of scale with the actual damage they inflict (1981, 152). After all, he says, shouldn't we reserve a term like "atrocity" for events in Cambodia and Afghanistan, or perhaps the actions of Idi Amin? Williams argues that in order to understand the source of this fury "we will have to understand better than we do the relationship between language, order, and those deep psychic forces that perceived linguistic violations seem to arouse in otherwise amiable people" (1981, 153).

Williams, however, primarily focuses on "the variety of responses that different 'errors' elicit," leaving the question of the relationship between language, order, and the psychic forces of emotion largely unexplored (1981, 153).[2] But in tracking responses to error, he does provide an important clue about what lies at the heart of that relationship. Williams discovered that people claim to be equally sensitive to all errors when, in fact, there are a number of errors people miss most of the time. Most likely to be noticed and responded to immediately are errors that violate "the rules that define bedrock standard English" (Williams 1981, 159). As examples of these he names "double negatives, incorrect verb forms, many incorrect pronoun forms, pleonastic subjects, double comparatives and superlatives, most subject-verb disagreements, certain faulty parallelisms, certain dangling modifiers, etc." (1981, 159). It is interesting to note that a significant number of these "errors" that elicited strong, immediate, and often emotional responses are characteristic of Black Language/Ebonics.[3] Ebonics, Geneva Smitherman reminds us, has complex negation patterns involving multiple negatives ("Wasn't no girls couldn't go with us") (1985, 30–31); uses *be* patterns to express habitual action ("The coffee bees cold") and future action ("I be going home tomorrow") (19); uses *been* patterns to express recently completed past action ("She been tardy twice this semester") (21–22); uses *done* to indicate past action ("I done my homework yesterday" or "I done finish my work today") (24); does not add -s or apostrophe -s to show plurality or possession ("Two boy just left" and "That was Mr. Johnson store got burn down") (28); does not use -ed verb forms "in either past tense or past participle" ("I look for him last night" and "This guy I know name Junior") (26); often repeats the subject "for emphasis" ("The boy who left, he my friend") (28); and does not mark most verbs for person ("She have us say it") (26). People troubled by these deviations from standard usage often read them as proof of the writer or speaker's laziness. Other types of usage errors, Williams found, were not noticed as often, such as count and non-count noun errors. Television news personalities and even an occasional colleague say things like "large amounts of books" more and more often. The stigma of laziness does not seem to apply to these errors in quite the same way, however.

While Williams ultimately focuses more on "the variety of responses that different 'errors' elicit" than on the question of the relationship among language, order, and the psychic forces of emotion, he does make an argument about why we respond emotionally to the *idea* of error as much as the reality of error (1981, 153). He argues that "it simply feels more authentic when we condemn error and enforce a rule" (1981, 165). Given that what many people perceive as "error" in fact conforms to the grammar of Ebonics, we argue that this sense of authenticity and order is often a *racialized* sense of authenticity and order. An emotional investment in "correctness" is one means by which racial identity is maintained in America.

Racial identity in American culture has been historically premised in part on the perceived character and morality of white people in contrast to racialized Others. For example, the construction of white people as moral and of good character depended on the construction of Black people as morally suspect. Tracing the emergence of "whiteness" as racial identity in the pre–Civil War era, historian George Rawick argues that Anglo-Americans created a new ethos for themselves by embracing capitalist principles and learning to value strict controls on time, sexuality, and gratification (Roediger 1991, 95). By collectively "adopting [this] ethos," Anglo-Americans were then able to "cast Blacks as their former [undisciplined] selves," with the result that "blackness came to symbolize what the accumulating capitalist had given up, but still longed for" (Roediger 1991, 95). Historian David Roediger calls the performance of capitalist values to create racial distinctions the new "industrial morality"(1991, 96).

In addition to controlled behavior, controlled speech was another important way in which whites could distinguish themselves as morally different from Blacks. Speaking standard English has been an historically important way to demonstrate one's character and morality. As Denis Baron argues, the "connection between good speech and good character" was made in seventeenth- and eighteenth-century school primers, a connection that "persists to this day in American schools and culture" (1982, 126). The versions of the English language codified and taught in the schools in the early centuries of American culture helped to "establish in the minds of Americans the inherent connection between language and morality" (Baron 1982, 167). Black people were historically denied subjecthood because their supposed immorality—"proven" not only by uncontrolled or disordered actions, but also by their language, characterized as uncontrolled or disordered speech. Smitherman, for example, cites nineteenth-century descriptions of Ebonics speakers as "slovenly," and "careless of speech," who "wrapped their tongues about [English] as well as they could," but with "characteristic laziness . . . took short cuts" by "using as few words as possible" (1985, 172). The evidence cited by Roediger, Rawick, Baron, and Smitherman suggests that in America, racism—a performance of hate that serves to maintain a racially ordered hierarchy—is historically grounded in beliefs about whose behavior and whose language is orderly. Taking on orderly (procapitalist) behavior and orderly (standard English) language helped Anglo-Americans create an authentic racial identity as "white" people.

These racialized associations among language, emotion, and order are not historic relics. In *Feeling Power: Emotions and Education* (1999), feminist theorist Megan Boler documents powerful contemporary connections among emotion, morality, race, and the capitalist subject in her study of emotion and education. Boler examines the EQ ("emotional quotient") movement, whose proponents maintain that the capacity to manage emotions is a measurable form of intelligence. Boler finds it is increasingly common in schools to conceptualize emotion as a "skill" to be taught, just as language—specifically the mastery of standard English—is considered a skill. More important to our line of inquiry here, teaching emotional "skills" and language "skills" are seen as dual means of instilling an appropriate sense of morality in students. Students who learn to control their behavioral impulses and their language are "skilled" and thus successful.

The similarities between emotional and linguistic schooling are telling. Both are a set of skills that "normal" children develop to succeed in life—in the schoolyard and later in the workplace. Children marked by race or class are frequently read as lacking the ability to monitor their emotion and speech and thus needing to be taught the skills and the virtues of emotional and linguistic management. Boler's contemporary example again begs the question of whose behavior and whose language is considered orderly. Schooling children of color in orderly behavior and orderly language reinforces capitalist ideology and the American racial hierarchy.

These historical and contemporary examples demonstrate that the schooling of language and the schooling of emotion are never far apart. The schooling of each proceeds in similar ways, becoming increasingly difficult to distinguish one from the other. Language and emotion are reduced to "skills," stripped of their social and historical contexts. This reduction obfuscates how their symbolic power "takes hold of and binds the individual, in complex and contradictory ways, to the social order and its structure of meaning" (Worsham 1998, 216). Worsham argues that "our most urgent political and pedagogical task remains the fundamental reeducation of emotion" (1998, 216). One way in which we might undertake this reeducation is to make visible the historical and social contexts that inform the practice of language and emotion. We have chosen to make the classroom an important site of this revisioning, asking students to think about how their performances of language and emotion locate them as raced, gendered, and classed subjects. At the same time, our experiences in the classroom have caused us to reflect on our own social locations and performances.

Language Panics and the Question of Pedagogy

When, in December 1996, the Oakland school board passed a resolution that, in part, recognized Ebonics as a language, a nationwide firestorm erupted, at the heart of which burned the question of the status of Ebonics as more than "slang" or "bad English." In a recent article that examines the public discourse on the Oakland controversy and the antibilingual legislation in California, Jane Hill demonstrates that "language panics are not really about language. Instead, they are about race. . . . They comprise one small part of a struggle over who will be 'racialized' and how the nature of racialized people is to be understood" (2001, 245). She argues that language scholars and educators need to change their strategies: "scholars must reshape their messages so as to directly engage racist culture and show how thinking about language within that system is inevitably as damaging and distorting as racism itself" (2001, 249). Our own efforts to directly engage racist culture have convinced us of the need to engage the emotional performances of whiteness.

The emotional reaction to the Oakland resolution, it seemed, was overshadowing the expressed intentions of the Oakland school board. Seeking to correct the "error" of what we saw as uninformed criticisms of the Oakland resolution, both of us dealt with the issue of Ebonics in our writing classes shortly after the controversy became news, and both of us experienced students simultaneously understanding the issues but being unable to separate themselves emotionally from their aversion toward what they labeled as "bad English." Donna, for example, made the Oakland Ebonics controversy a topic of inquiry in a sophomore-level academic writing class that enrolled primarily education majors in the spring semester immediately following the December 1996 controversy. She facilitated students' use of the classical questions of stasis (conjecture, definition, quality, and procedure) as a way to work through the various positions taken in the media coverage of the controversy. The students in the class quickly recognized that the various people taking positions in response to the Oakland resolution were not at stasis; that is, there was no common point of debate. Rather, for example, some people were caught up in a question of definition—"Is Ebonics a language or a dialect?"—while missing the fundamental question of conjecture on which the Oakland resolution was based: that students whose home language was Ebonics were failing to succeed academically at extraordinarily high rates. The students in the class became quite skilled at recognizing the conflicting stases within the Ebonics controversy, and working through the questions of stasis enabled many students to see the complexity of the issues. However, when they were asked to take a position in response to a question raised by the controversy, many deferred to the question that was most distinctly *not* at issue: should students learn standard English? The Oakland committee clearly wanted students to learn standard English; indeed, that was the whole point of the resolution. The resolution charged the Oakland superintendent to "immediately devise and implement the best possible academic program for imparting instruction to African-American students in their primary language for the combined purposes of maintaining the legitimacy and richness of such language . . . *and to facilitate their acquisition and mastery of English language skills*" (Oakland 1998, 145; emphasis ours).

It seemed odd that many students, who were primarily white, could simultaneously map out the various questions that *were* at issue (for example—should Ebonics be used as a teaching tool? What's the best way to teach standard English?) and yet defer to an uncontested argument about the need to learn standard English. Even more disconcerting were the white students who would come to Donna's office and confess—out of earshot of the two African American students in the class—that while they "understood" the motivations behind the Oakland resolution, they just "couldn't stand it" when people used "bad English." Some also expressed dismay at one African American class member's defense of Ebonics, since that student used and apparently understood the benefits of standard English. In these conferences, Donna found that white students often attempted to enact a kind of racialized solidarity as they would distinguish between how "we" (i.e., white people) speak and how "they" (i.e., Black people) speak. They seemed to expect Donna, a white teacher, to share their feelings of abhorrence over error and, in the private space of her office, to enact racialized performances of abhorrence with them. As the ideal viewer of the McDonald's commercial is expected to share the boy's feelings of pride in his corrected speech, so was Donna apparently expected to share in her students' feelings of disapproval of what they took to be uncorrected speech.

To her surprise and discomfort, then, Donna found that exposing students to the Ebonics controversy was, in some cases, having a racializing effect—exactly the opposite kind of effect that she was hoping for. While she had hoped that providing students with a more complex and systematic understanding of the controversy would enable all students—however they identified themselves—to recognize that Ebonics is not "bad" English and that the Oakland school board intended to help students acquire standard English, it seemed as if many white students, in particular, had a difficult time getting beyond a basic commonplace: standard English is good and, thus, necessary. Their emotional attachment to the goodness and necessity of standard English seemed to make any other question moot.

Ilene had similar experiences in several basic writing courses she taught. In one unit, students used stasis theory to read articles about the Ebonics controversy and then wrote exploratory essays. In their exploratory essays, students were asked to consider the multiple points of view represented in the readings and were asked to deepen their questions about the Ebonics controversy rather than arrive at a firm position on it. While many students developed a different understanding of the historical origins and grammatical logic of Black English by reading, writing, and thinking about essays by authors such as Geneva Smitherman and Lisa Delpit, they had difficulty questioning several positions that had become axiomatic for them: white people "naturally" spoke standard English; standard English was "proper" English; and people who did not write and speak "proper" English were less intelligent than those who did. Ilene saw a gap between the knowledge they had gained about Ebonics and their feelings about people who used Ebonics versus standard English. These feelings extended to themselves as writers. Many of these basic writers considered themselves Ebonics speakers; all of them were nonstandard language users in the eyes of the university. It was very difficult for them to move beyond these axioms and consider the possible value Ebonics might have outside of relationships with family and friends. While they enjoyed their new knowledge and corroborating the author's claims with their own knowledge of how Ebonics signified differently than standard English, it was difficult to imagine the place or value Ebonics might have in a school setting.

And who could blame them for their inability to imagine? Clearly, their education had been marked by incidents that schooled them to feel shame, embarrassment, even disgust about Ebonics. In a large-group discussion about a model paper, for example, several students in one class pointed to its Ebonics markers and concluded that the writer was "lazy." "I'm not even going to finish reading this," one student—herself an Ebonics speaker—said as she tossed the paper aside; "this writer is too lazy to be worth reading." Students have been schooled to read Ebonics as signifying highly racialized traits like laziness. They know that Ebonics "often marks students as different—or worse, deficient" in the eyes of their teachers (Mutnik 1996, 99). They know that their deficiency is constructed as a *cognitive* deficiency in the eyes of their teachers. Even basic writing scholarship, Bruce Horner argues, "tend(s) to place BW students at particular stages of cognitive development or language acquisition in ways that, unfortunately, continue what Susan Miller has observed as composition's tendency to treat students as 'emerging, or as failed, but never as actually responsible 'authors'" (Horner 1999a, 117). And even when basic writing scholarship recognizes that "errors" are historically and socially constructed and situated, Horner notes that "all this seems to be viewed as a fait acompli, 'history' in the sense of something in the past about which there is little to be done" (Horner 1999b, 139). There are in fact few precedents for imagining a valued space and function for Ebonics in school. Thus, it is difficult indeed for students to set aside their emotional schooling.

Given the racializing function of language panics, it may be that simply leading students to rationally understand the many layers of the panic does little to disrupt that function. Indeed, it could be that the exposure may do more to *reinforce* the racialized schooling of emotion. In a study designed to "neutralize" the force of political attack ads, researchers at the University of Pennsylvania found that while the participants in the study were able to recognize the "errors and misleading claims" in the attack ads, the impact of the attacks still remained (Cappella and Jamieson 1994, 342). In fact, they found that "once a television ad plants an image in the mind of the receiver, subsequent airing of the spot, even in the context of an adwatch [to critically analyze the ad], may have the effect of reinforcing that image" (Pfau and Louden 1994, 328). As Charles Paine has commented, "One might say it is a case of pathos overpowering logos" (Paine 1999, 15).

Moreover, Donna's very presence as a white teacher may have seemed to some students to be a racialized performance. To be a white teacher speaking and writing standard English while talking *about* Ebonics has the potential to be read as a racialized performance that articulates standard English with whiteness. Similarly, while Ilene asked her basic writing students to see the value in Ebonics and to imagine a place for nonstandard languages like Ebonics in school, she felt that in two ways she failed to see what David G. Holmes calls "the danger of conflating race and voice": she felt that her discussions with students about race and language failed not only to disarticulate *blackness* from *Ebonics*; they also failed to disarticulate *whiteness* from *standard English* (Holmes 1999, 62). Holmes criticizes "racially reductive" theorists who treat Ebonics as "something that belongs to [black people] in more than a sociolinguistic or cultural sense . . . but racially and, therefore, existentially theirs" (1999, 64). Instead, he argues, "if we are to rid ourselves of racialized baggage and move from black writing to writing black, the rhetoricity of race must be stressed" (1999, 64). Holmes' arguments apply to standard English as well: standard English is not something that belongs to white people more than people of color; if we are to unpack the racialized baggage we carry about whiteness, the rhetoricity of whiteness must be stressed as well.

Re(per)forming Pedagogy

In his recent article documenting the fundamental grammatical differences between Ebonics and standard English, Arthur L. Palacas continues to express the hope that demonstrating the difference of Ebonics will create respect for it, and thus finally "motivate and support a positive change in attitudes" (2001, 331). As tempting as it is to argue that the antidote to negative feelings about Ebonics is more contextualized discussions of grammar and error, more efforts to consider Ebonics rhetorically, and more consideration of the contexts in which Ebonics is used, our experiences suggest that we need to do more than this if we are to succeed in reschooling emotion. There is, in fact, more than thirty years of scholarship that documents the linguistic sophistication and rhetorical situation of Ebonics (Baldwin 1979, Baugh 2000, Green 1998, Labov 1972, Palacas 2001, Rickford 1998, Smitherman 1985). But *feelings* about Ebonics have not radically shifted because of this voluminous scholarship. And in light of the classroom experiences we have described and our engagement with critical race theorists across the disciplines, we are less convinced that changing attitudes or feelings about Ebonics should be our only goal.

The field's intervention cannot be only to learn and teach the grammar of Ebonics along with standard English. Rather, the performance of whiteness and white supremacy needs also to be challenged, which means stepping out of familiar rhetorical poses. Because remaining silent about our own performances of whiteness reinscribes our values and language as normative, we have begun to consider how we might reperform our whiteness in ways that disarticulate it from authority and order.

Feminist theorist Chela Sandoval draws on Roland Barthes and Franz Fanon to conceptualize whiteness as a set of poses that constitute a rhetoric and to develop her own alternative poses that can serve to recompose whiteness. Fanon, according to Sandoval, defines whiteness as a "mythology, a set of learned behaviors called up within a specific rhetoric and its categories" (1997, 101). In order to describe these "learned behaviors" that compose the mythology of whiteness, Sandoval extrapolates a series of poses from Barthes' *Mythologies*, poses that compose a rhetoric of white supremacy. We see the poses Sandoval extrapolates falling into three categories. The first category includes poses that serve to reduce the threat of the racialized Other: "innoculating" ourselves against the threat of difference by taking on and domesticating individual language acts or behaviors that signify difference; separating cultural objects from their context and making them commodities for white consumption; and equating all differences. The second category consists of poses that serve to make white experience normative. This is done by making the dominant culture's truth Truth, its history History, and so on; by assuming white experience inherently conveys authority; and by asserting white reality as if there is no other. The final category consists of a single pose, the pose of emotional detachment, which serves to deny the possibility of change (Sandoval 1997, 88–94).

Sandoval argues for five resisting technologies to upend this rhetoric: "reading the signs of power," "deconstructing them when necessary," "remaking signs in the interest of renegotiating power," committing to remaking signs to equitably distribute power, and mobilizing the above on a large scale (1997, 101). These five resisting technologies can become a part of our regular classroom practice. Student's written texts, the written texts we assign and discuss, and the cultural texts that write students and teachers are all sign-rich texts that can be used to identify and challenge white supremacist poses, or the rhetoric of whiteness.

In an effort to begin to mobilize resisting technologies, Donna has become particularly interested in making the racializing performances of emotion visible to teachers. In her work with new teachers of composition, Donna has been reminded of the anger and confusion that new teachers often experience as they first encounter student "error." Their reactions are not unlike

Mina Shaughnessy's initial response to the writing of her first SEEK students, which she found "so stunningly unskilled," "alien," and "disturbing," with their "tangle of errors and puzzling incompetencies" (Shaughnessy 1977, vii). While we can suggest, as Joseph Harris recently has, that our culture needs to "lighten up" when it comes to error, such a suggestion does little to disrupt the deeply entrenched emotional response to error. Shaughnessy's strategy, of course, was to find the "logic" of the error, a strategy that led to a number of studies advocating the pedagogical utility of error analysis and that was important in leading teachers to recognize the intelligence behind writing students' errors. However, as we found in our experiences with teaching Ebonics, *knowing* the logic of a nondominant language does not necessarily lead to a different way of *feeling* about the nondominant or the dominant language. While error analysis is a useful pedagogical strategy, our experiences suggest that it may not go far enough: understanding the intelligence of error does not necessarily change the way a person feels about the error. In fact, the word "error" itself suggests a negative feeling toward deviations from the standard.

With the goal of offering a space in which future teachers might begin to feel differently about grammar, Donna made "emotion" a central topic of inquiry in an advanced grammar class that she recently taught.[4] The members of the class included both undergraduate and graduate students, most of whom either were planning to teach in public schools or currently were working as teaching assistants in the English department. In addition to treating traditional topics in language study—syntax, semantics, and the like—she dedicated the central part of the course to the question "why is grammar such an emotional issue?" Among the topics covered were the relationship between identity and language, feminist critiques of language, and the "language panics" brought on by the Oakland Resolution and the Official English and English Only Movements. Because the emotional work of grammar was an explicit focus, students were less able to maintain an unquestioned emotional response to "correctness." One student, for example, admitted that she generally supported the idea of Official English, but confessed that she felt repelled by the antiethnic prejudices expressed in the writings of Official English supporters. Many students regularly used "emotion" as a basis for analysis in their online discussions and response papers for the class.

But in addition to *talking about* emotion and correctness, Donna also wanted to try to disrupt her own potentially racialized performance—to try to at least trouble the immediate articulation of her performance as a teacher of English with standard English and whiteness. Her strategy was to "come out" as a native speaker of a nonstandard dialect. And while she didn't feel comfortable speaking a dialect she rarely uses around anyone but her family—and even then it's an imperfect performance, marred by her own schooling in shame—she shared some of her favorite phrases from that dialect ("fixin' to," "y'all," "might could"). She described some of her own confusion as she was being schooled to take on an emotional relationship to standard English and to her home language. The point was to perform—at least for a few moments—a disarticulation of whiteness from standard English. Neither of us is under any illusion that this sort of performance answers the question of how to reschool emotion. In fact, unless it is accompanied by critical discussion, it can lead to the assumption that "everyone has to learn standard English," that there's nothing particularly distinctive at stake for speakers of racialized languages—an assumption that participates in one of the familiar homogenizing poses of whiteness. We offer Donna's performance, then, not as a model, but as one rhetorical moment intended to disrupt the racializing effects that articulate emotion and order.

Emotion is a powerful technology that connects language, morality, and order, producing a highly racialized sense of self. Rather than simply schooling students to understand grammar and to reproduce "correct" usage, teachers of writing need to examine how our classroom performances may uphold white supremacist logic. But we want to be clear: we are not arguing that teachers of writing abandon discussions of grammar in the classroom. In fact, we feel that *silence* about grammar with our students, particularly the students we have talked about here—basic writers and beginning teachers of writing—is an act of collusion with a colonizing white consciousness. Our hope is that other teachers will join us in efforts to understand "correctness" as a pedagogy of emotion and to work to perform in ways that question assumptions about language, emotion, and whiteness.

Notes

1. Throughout this chapter, we use "grammar" primarily in the popular, prescriptive sense of a set of rules for producing "correct" sentences.

2. See Boyd (1995), however, for an insightful exploration of the psychic and cultural forces at work in nineteenth-century grammar handbooks.

3. Linguists generally refer to the language used by many African Americans as "African American English" or "Black English" (O'Neil 1998). However, this language has also been called, variously, "Black English Vernacular," "Black dialect," and "Ebonics." All names, it seems, carry with them certain implications that we would like to avoid—implications that the language belongs essentially, rather than culturally and historically, to African Americans, or implications that the language is a dialect of English, an implication that is contested by linguists (see Palacas 2001). Because of the currency of *Ebonics* in popular culture, and because it is often preferred as a "nonpejorative label," we have chosen to use that term (Smith 1998, 54).

4. The design of this course was inspired by grammar courses described by Okawa (2000) and by Hagemann and Wininger (1999).

Chapter Seven

Conflict and Kitsch

The Politics of Politeness in the Writing Class

Wendy Ryden

Citizens of free societies do not preserve their freedom by pussyfooting around their fellow citizens' opinions, even their most cherished beliefs. In free societies, you must have the free play of ideas. There must be argument, and it must be impassioned and untrammeled. A free society is not a calm and eventless place—that is the kind of static, dead society dictators try to create. Free societies are dynamic, noisy, turbulent and full of radical disagreements. Skepticism and freedom are indissolubly linked. . . .

—Salman Rushdie, "How News Becomes Opinion, and Opinion Off-Limits"

I found the university . . . clean and noble, but I did not find the university alive. I found the American university had this ideal as phrased by a professor from the University of Chicago: 'The passionless pursuit of passionless intelligence'—clean and noble, I grant you, but not alive enough . . . And in this reflection of this university ideal I find the conservatism and unconcern of the American people. . . .

—Jack London, *How to Take an Exam and Remake the World*

Kitsch is a German word born in the middle of the sentimental nineteenth century, and from German it entered all Western languages. Repeated use, however, has obliterated its original metaphysical

meaning: kitsch is the absolute denial of shit, in both literal and figurative senses of the word.
—Milan Kundera, *The Unbearable Lightness of Being*

The concessions of politeness always contain political concessions.
—Pierre Bourdieu, *Outline of a Theory of Practice*

In the wake of the attacks of September 11, the following excerpted exchange took place on a listserv comprised largely of graduate students living in the New York metropolitan area.

> At the risk of starting the biggest fight on this list since last November's elections, I want to say that I would hope that the message on the flyer that Ann posted—WE STAND UNITED—WE WILL NOT TOLERATE TERRORISM!—means that people will also be taking a stand against American government-supported terrorism. . . . Yes, what happened at the WTC was a crime against humanity, but I find the assumption of American innocence and virtuousness that's behind the public discussion extremely disingenuous, to say the least.
>
> Let's see: this country is the largest supplier of military weapons on the planct.
>
> Whether or not Osama Bin Laden is responsible for this atrocity, he's certainly been responsible for numerous others. Yet, we trained him! How much reporting has there been about the fact that when the Soviet Union invaded Afghanistan, the CIA—under George Bush, Sr.—trained, armed and organized Islamic resistance. We funded Bin Laden for years. But at that point, he was a "freedom fighter." When he turned against us during the Gulf War, he became a "terrorist."
>
> We have killed—and continue to kill—thousands of innocent civilians in Iraq. We killed innocent civilians in Belgrade. In the Sudan. But that's called "collateral damage."
>
> We support military dictatorships around the globe that kill thousands of innocent civilians (e.g, Serbia, Colombia, Indonesia, Peru, Guatemala, Chile). But that's called "supporting our allies" or "maintaining stability."
>
> We have unconditionally supported 34 years of repressive Israeli occupation of the West Bank. Yes, we should mourn all those innocent people who were

> killed on Tuesday. Yes, there should be justice. But it seems to me that true justice should include public soul-searching and discussion of U.S. foreign policy and why so many people in what is euphemistically called "The Third World" hate us.
>
> And when we light our candles, point the finger at George Bush and every other American politician who has initiated and/or supported U.S.-sponsored terrorism for far too many years.
>
> Reminds me of how the Puritans came here, took more and more land away from the natives, and then called them agents of Satan when they rose up against them. I guess some things don't change.

This post elicited many responses, including the following two:

> In my opinion, this sort of politicking is inappropriate for (this) list.

and

> Hi all,
>
> I don't normally respond to the stuff I read on the listserv, but I must say I am saddened and offended that this forum is being used, AT THIS TIME, for politician-bashing and partisanship. Frankly, I don't CARE whose fault it is! As a "Third Worlder" myself, I am hurting so much for the people who died and are still dying as we speak, and who will continue to die in the weeks ahead, PEOPLE FROM ALL OVER THE WORLD, that finger pointing and blame-making seem uniquely pointless, and even tactless. Can't we just mourn?
>
> I teach in a NYC public high school, and my concern is that we, adult intellectuals, are not rearing enough human beings who know how to mourn for others, and who can therefore offer no comfort to others. And right now, I need comfort, don't you? I don't think it's too much to ask that we come down from our intellectual podium to weep with the hurting, and to comfort them in meaningful ways!

As the initial writer predicted, his email did indeed begin a "fight." The excerpts I have selected fairly represent, I believe, the parameters of the debate. I have referenced this email debate to focus attention on the place emotion has in intellectual exchange and how such emotion is tied to, and often modulated by, discourses of politeness and propriety. Many of us are familiar with similar debates that took place on other listservs and in other forums following September 11. These debates, I think, have allowed us to understand, in a way we don't often glimpse, the strength of emotions, particularly anger, in our intellectual activity and our writing and, by extension then, the complex role such emotions play in our classrooms and our students' writing. If we are often baffled by our students' resistance to engage in intellectual and political debate, we might remind ourselves of how difficult it was to have such discussions in the wake of September 11 and imagine that the discourses of our classrooms might also often contain these potent, but undertheorized, emotional dimensions.

The writer of the first email prefaced his remarks by acknowledging his fear that he would start a "fight," a hyperbolic synonym for argument. His word-choice underscores the breach of etiquette he intuited he was about to commit. What preceded his post were mostly outpourings of seemingly apolitical solidarity, concern for well-being, and inquiries about how to help. Overwhelmingly there was a feeling of unison and consensus, of people feeling, or presumed to be feeling, all one way. When that unanimity was threatened with a political objection, the writer, rather than challenged for his politics, was charged with being "inappropriate" and "tactless." The language of manners reveals the rhetorical mechanism through which the political commentary was meant to be contained and managed. While others wrote supporting the political position espoused by the first writer, objectors, who seemed quite angry at having to be angry, continually couched their dissatisfaction in propriety, suggesting that to be political was to be impolite in light of the disaster.

The way in which etiquette functioned in this email debate as a technology of consensus extends into our classrooms from the larger American cultural landscape that fosters a quelling of dissent. President Bush's post-September 11 "for or against us" declaration is not simply a response to an unprecedented disaster but a consistent manifestation of an already existing intolerance of rhetorical debate. Consider the use of the word "partisanship" in the above-mentioned email debate. While partisanship denotes concern with self-interest at the expense of true debate, the writer of the email invokes the term in order to stifle dissent as inappropriate. In the current political landscape, the term becomes a dirty word connected with disagreement and disunity, frowned on almost as if engagement in it were gauche.

The popular discrediting of "partisanship," as it is used on the listserv debate, for example, gains currency from a rhetoric of unity deadly to intellectual exchange. One of our Cold War legacies has been the stifling of intellectual dissent, as discussed by Frances Stonor Saunders. Saunders explains that as American intellectuals dealt with the blow of Stalinism, "their disillusionment was attended by a readiness to join in a new consensus, to affirm a new order. . . . The tradition of radical dissent, where intellectuals took it upon themselves to . . . disturb the complacency of power, was suspended in favour of supporting "the American proposition" (1999, 2). Indeed, an early 1950s *Time* cover story on the role of the intellectual proclaimed that "The Man of Protest has . . . given way to the Man of Affirmation" (Saunders 1999, 161).

This manufacturing of consent is what theorists of political kitsch ultimately see as the consequence of an idyllic cultural aesthetic that favors harmony over rupture. The linkage between kitsch and an aestheticized politics is most infamously exemplified in the Nazi banning of so-called "decadent art,"

art which irreverently showed a fractured reality not conducive to the idyll of fascism. As M. Kay Flavell notes, "in a totalitarian society . . . only idyllic art is tolerated. In an effort to draw the individual away from himself into a communal form of life that moulds personality along narrowly circumscribed lines, dictators tend to promote an easy, unproblematic art which suggests a serene and homogeneous world" (1985, 86).

The Czech novelist Milan Kundera follows a similar logic when he emphasizes the connection between kitsch and the appeal of totalitarian regimes, specifically Communist dictatorships. For him, the desire to belong feeds into totalitarian goals to suppress that which disturbs the perceived ideal and to eliminate deviation, vulnerability, insecurity, uncertainty, or incompleteness—in essence to eliminate a culture's critical rhetoric, specifically through a rhetoric of community.[1] Emotions play a vital role in such scenarios, as Ellen Quandahl points out in this volume: "dominant regimes work partly by determining . . . acceptable emotions."

In her book on kitsch, public policy, and education, Catherine Lugg also relies on this view of kitsch and emotion and the effect on public discourse. Kitsch is defined as suppression of difficult truth in favor of a more palatable, superficial aesthetic of consensus. Throughout her work, Lugg notes the political utility of kitsch and claims that fundamental to the nature of aesthetic and political kitsch is the avoidance of "complex, painful realities" (1999, 106). In considering the contemporary American political scene, Lugg notes the generic nature of kitsch and its tendency to work in terms of a master narrative: "kitsch aids the storyteller by providing a form of rhetorical shorthand" (119). It "condenses history, cultural mythology, and emotionalism into a simplistic symbol for ready and pre-digested consumption by the public at large" (120).

Lugg acknowledges here the role of emotions and their manipulation in producing consensus. Kitsch operates "as a condensation symbol rooted in bad art" that "combines elements of history, cultural mythology, and syrupy emotionalism to shape the direction of the political environment" (119). I read Lugg's "syrupy emotionalism" as sentimentality, an "emotionalism" of consensus that relies on an uncritical conception of community. Kitsch, paradoxically, is connected to both the invoking/manipulation and suppression of emotion. This paradox displays itself in the earlier-cited listserv exchange in the disqualification of (what might be politically productive) anger and the simultaneous promotion of seemingly apolitical unity through this "syrupy emotionalism." This functioning of kitsch relies on a sense of bourgeois politeness to foster its hegemonically compliant subjectivity.

Kitsch eliminates the dissent and difference absent from the dystopian "calm" and "eventless place" mentioned by Salman Rushdie (1996) in the epigraph to this chapter. Kitsch relies on and produces saccharine notions of community, disqualifying discord and anger as rude intrusions. In *The Book of Laughter and Forgetting*, Kundera (1980) uses the circle as an image of joining to describe the suppression of individuality and skepticism that occurred in

Eastern European communism. The circle is a symbol of the idyll, a metaphysical "place" where anger and conflict are replaced by harmonious joining that, according to Kundera, we all crave.

Rushdie's claim that societies ought not be "calm" or "eventless" is a claim that they ought not be governed by an uninterrogated consensus that results in the loss of critical rhetoric. What he says about "societies" ought to be true of the writing class or any intellectual environment. Such places ought to be filled with the democratic tumult of a "free" society. In principle, most of us might agree. But in a quotidian reality we have a much less idealized reaction to conflict. Most of us become uncomfortable when conflict, and its accompanying emotion of anger, are no longer academic and abstract, when they become concretized to exceed the limits of polite, bourgeois conversation surrounding dead and static texts, when they spill into our lived practices in palpable ways. This kind of conflict is "personal"; it disrupts collegial discussions of politics and is silenced through appeals to politeness; it threatens the teacher's authority to run a smooth, predictable, safe class; and it is inescapably accompanied by anger, hurt, fear, frustration, and alienation. The writing classroom is a place where such emotional conflict often occurs and perhaps should occur if we are to avoid the kitsch of the calm and eventless place governed only by propriety, unity, and syrupy emotionalism.

Critical pedagogy might well pay more attention to the rhetorical and social function of emotions, in particular anger. In Composition, however, concern with emotion has often been subsumed under "personal" writing and relegated to what Bartholomae has described as "sentimental realism" (1995, 67). The emotional is seen as part of the wrong-headed, depoliticizing trajectory of writing instruction that the turn towards rhetoric, such as Berlin's (1987) social epistemic, seeks to check. As Alice Brand explains, "Emotions seem to be there, but composition theory (and writing courses) apparently shouldn't much bother with it" (1991, 400). Thus in its laudable emphasis on political engagement, the field has moved away from the "soft" rhetoric of emotion, understood in the kitsch sense of manipulation and syrupy sentimentality.[2] By privileging an intellectualized rhetoric that makes short work of "inappropriate" emotions such as anger, we have embraced another aspect of kitsch.

However, contemporary revaluations of Aristotle stress the primacy of emotion to the *Rhetoric* (see Quandhal's essay in this volume) and to current understandings of rhetorical theory. William Grimaldi, for example, argues that, through the enthymeme, Aristotle "recognizes that person speaks to person not only with the mind but with the emotions and feelings as well" and that "rhetoric. . .makes the act of knowing a total perception of intellect, emotions, feelings" (1972, 17). Grimaldi draws our attention to Book I, 78a 20–21 where Aristotle asserts the power of emotions in intellectual activity: "The emotions are those things through which men alter and change their decisions."

The suspicion over emotion no doubt stems from its colonization by psychological and therapeutic discourse. This concern has been an abiding issue in writing. Emotions are marked for the personal sphere and are not valid areas of public knowledge to be tampered with in the classroom. But, as Wendy Bishop (1993) points out, despite the reluctance of writing instructors to take on the personal and emotional components of their students' responses, they are in fact continually negotiating this territory with them.

Anthropologists Abu-Lughod and Lutz question the popular understanding of emotion as "natural," *de facto* and *a priori,* and therefore part of a private realm not appropriately subject to public scrutiny: "Tied to tropes of interiority and granted ultimate facticity by being located in the natural body, emotions stubbornly retain their place . . . as the aspect of human experience least subject to control, least constructed or learned . . ., least public, and therefore least amenable to sociocultural analysis" (1990, 1). They argue for a discourse-oriented view where "emotion is social, cultural, political, and historical" (18). "We should view emotional discourse as a form of social action that creates effects in the world, effects that are read in a culturally informed way by the audience for emotion talk" (12).

Also working from a social constructivist perspective, Stearns and Stearns assert that emotions are not unmediated states of being but indeed can be understood as historical, diachronic phenomena. An "examination of emotional standards and expressions . . . reveals power relationships otherwise partially concealed" (1986, 14). Stearns and Stearns coin the term "emotionology" to refer to cultural standards of emotion as distinct from individual experience. They suggest that experienced emotion is inflected by reigning cultural standards. Peter Stearns' study excavating the history of workplace anger in America is important because "the evolution in workplace anger may be a key ingredient in larger changes in American life, in areas as seemingly diverse as protest behavior and personality formation" (1986, 141). I am interested in the implications of this for understanding conflict in the classroom, where the internalization of cultural attitudes toward the appropriateness of that emotion often manifests itself in the teacher-student, as well as interstudent, dynamic.

In general, Stearns traces a trajectory of anger control and intolerance for emotion in the American workplace, which he situates in a larger American social context of increased standards of anger control. "In preindustrial society," claims Stearns, "anger and work were common companions. . . .there were no clear standards regulating. . .the expression of anger" (124). But in the twentieth century,

> The dictates . . . of new competition for consumers, the smooth functioning of corporate bureaucracy, and reduction of class conflict at work all suggested growing attention to the articulation and enforcement of anger control standards. . . . the goal was, without equivocation, a limitation of anger expressed and, as time went on, even felt as part of the work experience. (129)

Concomitant with this trend was "a central emphasis on reshaping authoritarian styles" (132) of management, a velvet-glove approach to promoting the goal of the anger-free work environment for "middle and lower middle-class employees" who "were the principal targets" of this reform (131).

Stearns' observation about the increased censoring of anger is consistent with a kitsch ideal of America, a conflict-free zone where politeness reigns and anger and dissent are regarded suspiciously as the modus operandi of rabble rousers and troublemakers. Moreover, some of the trends Stearns identifies in the workplace run in interesting parallel to developments in writing pedagogy. The reduction in "authoritarian" management styles resembles the move of Composition pedagogy towards the decentered authority of the writing instructor. Likewise, the feminization of the workplace, a factor Stearns cites as contributing to the change in anger emotionology (127), charts a course similar to the feminization of Composition and the tendency to avoid angry conflict in favor of harmoniously cooperative writing communities.

Stearns and Stearns' caveat about the value of examining emotional discourse to discover concealed power relations may be applicable in this context. There is no Composition theory that doesn't at least pay lip service to the expression of difference; even the heavily normative collaborative learning paradigms of Ken Bruffee allow for the possibility of dissent through "agreeing to disagree" (1999, 41). We have, however, in recent years heard calls for a more rhetorical Composition theory: for example, one that provides for "a model of political conflict and negotiation" (Jarratt 1991, 42). But, as Thomas West (2000) comments, there are few that adequately account for the place of emotion in the discourse of difference, specifically that of anger. bell hooks suggests that loudness, anger, emotional outbursts are deemed vulgar disruptions of classroom social order and that "bourgeois values in the classroom create a barrier, blocking the possibility of confrontation and conflict, warding off dissent" (1994, 178). Lynn Bloom (1996) has shown us just how bound up our first-year writing programs are in the inculcation of "middle class" values. To what extent are suspicion and modulation of anger part of this middle-class "enterprise" that encourages, according to Bloom, "decorum/propriety" and "moderation/temperance"? At what cost do we allow such gentility to dominate the discourse of our classrooms?

Politeness may pave the way for the disqualification of "passionate" emotions in the discourse of the classroom, and it may not only curtail dissent but also camouflage important dynamics that warrant attention. But in order to hold the discussions that produce knowledge, don't we need the order of civility to enable our rational discourses? Stephen Fishman and Lucille McCarthy (1996) voice concern about conflict-based classrooms, advocating instead a Deweyan model of cooperative inquiry: politeness produces the dialogue necessary for social change. McCarthy and Fishman consider conflict in a holistic way that accounts for not just the intellect but feelings. Still I wonder if they are not relying on an assumption about rational rhetoric—that when someone exhibits the illogic of, say, racism, or sexism, or homophobia, the way to dispel it is by bringing light to darkness; calm, rational truth is thus seen as an antidote to passionate, irrational hatred. This definition of rationality is embedded in and generated by bourgeois discourses of propriety; reasonableness begets reason.

I have often followed this formula in teaching, such as when a white male student vehemently informed me that his research paper would be an argument against affirmative action policies that allowed "unqualified minorities'" admission to colleges. Rather than attend to that student's emotions, I encouraged him to pursue his study with the idea that doing so would help him "manage" his anger. That this student eventually modified his position substantially as a result of his research suggests that there is merit in allowing reason to run its course. But rational argument may be an insufficient rhetoric to produce an informed understanding of the student's investment in this project. Would a consideration of the emotionology that accompanies such declarations yield insights into the student's location within the straw logic of such a debate? For we might say of the affirmative action "argument," as James Baldwin said of the "argument" about Black English, that it "has absolutely nothing to do with the question the argument supposes itself to be about" (1995, 42). Rather, the student's anger here points to his own confusion and feelings of disempowerment, frustration, and alienation that embroil him in racist discourse effectively camouflaged as academic debate.

I am not suggesting attention to affective response solely for the sake of providing individual therapeutic support that effects psychological transformation. While I by no means discount the pedagogical significance of such a process, I am interested in the larger project of what emotional responses can teach us about the context and discourses of our classrooms and our students' writing and our positions as instructors. Particularly, I think it is important to consider outlaw emotions, such as anger, which have been heavily modulated by intellectualization and propriety, to look for the "power relationships otherwise partially concealed" that Stearns and Stearns (1986) suggest are embedded in emotional discourse. I believe, as West suggests, that it is profitable "to understand anger in social and political terms, rather than in just psychological ones" (2000, 44) or, perhaps more accurately, to look to the interstices among those said terms.

In that spirit, I now revisit a situation where anger revealed itself as a potent force in the classroom dynamic. While I did not attempt to block the expression of that anger, my impulse was to quash it through reason, to reintegrate it into polite, rational discourse. This response prevented me, I think, from adequately reading the collective anger that had surfaced in the space of the writing classroom and from learning something about the social and political dimensions of that anger.

The class in question was a first-year, writing-about-literature course offered as part of a required sequence in an urban community college. I chose as one of our texts the coming of age novel *Way Past Cool* (1992) by Jess Mowry, a book that depicts male urban gang life in a fictionalized Oakland and the economic and social realities of a post-Reagan inner city drug economy.

Rather than a belletristic approach to literature, I chose this book as a means to begin an inquiry into politics and cultural criticism. I assumed we would do so in a cooperative, polite way. I did not choose the book with the goal of provoking clash and confrontation, yet that is exactly what happened. I was not prepared for the anger that this book elicited.

To begin, I arranged us in the customary circle of cooperation used to facilitate discussion. I think now of the pejorative association that Kundera's theory of kitsch imputes to that formation: the closed structure that disallows dissent by promoting a sentimental unity. In this case, one student initiated, or should I say, short-circuited the discussion with the opening comment: "What did I hope for this class to learn by reading this book?" I was smart enough to know that this was not a real question, but more like the kind teachers usually ask students, one that has an agenda. The "question" was an indictment of my book choice, and my initial reaction was an emotional one: to feel hurt and defensive and nervous. With trepidation but a faith in rational discourse, I asked this student to elaborate on her question, which allowed her to voice the unspoken statement it contained: there wasn't anything at all to be learned by reading this book, that, to use her phrase, it "belonged in the trash."

The student was a woman in her mid-thirties, and several other "older" women joined in as well. Prompted by my logical inquiries to elaborate, students initially couched their criticisms in objections about the language of the book, what they termed its slang and profanity. As one woman put it, she better not hear her kids talking like that. A young woman from Germany declared that she wanted to read books that would improve her English, and this book wasn't going to do that. Neither the language nor the content were a fit subject matter for an English class, some of the students went on to declare. The class split with regard to the merit of the book. People were shouting at each other across the circle, and hand-raising was a slow-paced luxury. One young man, who was enthusiastic, remarked that he thought he had made a mistake and bought the wrong book and worried his mother might see that he was reading about gangs and drug-dealing. The woman who began this discussion boldly asserted that she had no interest in reading about gangs or drugs: who cared about these people anyhow? She said this book was giving a false impression of what African American culture was, and, stammering, she explained that she was disturbed that people "from other countries" were getting the wrong idea.

I remember that moment vividly now because, looking back, it should have been a key point in revealing the failure of rational discourse to address the implications of the students' anger. To quell the chaotic atmosphere, I asked students to write down their thoughts. But what, I wonder, would have happened if I had asked people to write down not what they were *thinking* but rather what they were *feeling*? What shift might that have produced in our collective understanding of what was transpiring? Students read out loud what they had written. One woman was offended not by the book but by people's dismissal of it as insignificant. The experiences of the characters were her experiences. The neighborhood she had grown up in was similar. Another young man wrote that maybe this book wasn't part of all African American experience, but it was certainly part of his and it was wrong for people to pretend it didn't exist. One young woman did write about her feelings. She didn't want to read this book because it was too sad; it reminded her of a life that she worked so hard to get away from.

As our sessions progressed, I wrote letters to the class summarizing what I thought had been taking place in our discussions (similar to Shoshana Felman's [1995] response to her class' "crisis" upon hearing holocaust testimonials). I photocopied these letters and asked students to write responses. Often they told me that I had it wrong, and a dialogue about a variety of issues emerged, ranging from the role of police in the community, the political potential of gangs, to what is considered appropriate subject matter for a college English class, and what makes standard English Standard. Rather than writing about the novel itself, several students wrote papers chronicling the debate as it had emerged in the classroom, analyzing what was contentious and why and placing their own views in relation to those expressed in class.

While I think this process was qualifiedly successful in producing a critical discourse, I have since come to question the way I read, or failed to read, the class' initial responses of anger. I responded to pathos with logos, and forced students and myself to frame emotional responses in terms of rational debate. As some of the students were trying to tell me, I got it wrong. Lacking a sufficient rhetoric of emotion and fueled by a desire to salvage decorum from an unruly class, I ignored what that anger might have told me about racism, my position as a white-identified instructor in a multiethnic classroom, and the imposition of this text. Had I paid attention to that anger, I might have seen sooner what I have since concluded: some students experienced this novel as a weapon that I, the white teacher, was using against them to expose painful experience to public scrutiny and to perpetuate a degrading stereotype about African Americans. This crucial subtext never found full expression in the "critical" dialogue that I tried to promote.

Shoshana Felman argues that teaching "takes place precisely only through a crisis: if teaching does not hit upon some sort of crisis, if it does not encounter . . . vulnerability or . . . explosiveness . . . it has perhaps not truly taught: it has perhaps passed on some facts, passed on some information . . ." (1995, 55). Felman's statement acknowledges implicitly the importance of emotion in rhetoric, for I would argue that the crisis Felman speaks of is at least in part an emotional crisis, one that defies the neat containment of polite, rational discourse. It is this emotional component that moves us from what Felman calls the "cognitive" to the "performative" and creates the teachable moment. "The question for the teacher is, on the one hand, how to access, how *not to foreclose* the crisis, and, on the other hand, how to *contain it*" (1995, 56). I think my class experienced such a crisis of vulnerability and explosiveness, but in seeking to *contain* the crisis, I did not adequately *access* its emotional dimension.

The result of this failure, then, was the production of a rhetoric of kitsch, one that enfolded messy anger into normative rationality and civility. The class's awareness remained at a *cognitive* level, only partially *recognizable*, to use Felman's terms.

Does Felman mean that crisis should be courted in the classroom? A slippery term, I take "crisis" to mean not so much that crisis should be induced but rather responded to. I'm not sure that crisis should or even can be manufactured, but when it occurs we might need to resist the urge to contain it too handily through an evisceration of its emotional component. An expanded understanding of rhetoric might lead us to a praxis that would recognize and do justice to the primacy of emotion in intellectual exchange.

Notes

1. Kundera's views of kitsch and its social and political implications can be gleaned from *The Book of Laughter and Forgetting* (1980), *The Unbearable Lightness of Being* (1984), and *The Art of the Novel* (1988). For Kundera the concept of kitsch is closely connected to belief in the idyll, which for him explains the cultural success and duplicity of the Czech Communist Party:

> People have always aspired to an idyll, a garden where nightingales sing, a realm of harmony where the world does not rise up as a stranger against man nor man against other men, where the world and all its people are molded from a single stock . . . where every man is a note in a magnificent Bach fugue and anyone who refuses his note is a mere black dot, useless and meaningless, easily caught and squashed between the fingers like an insect. (*Laughter and Forgetting* 1980, 8)

2. Consider Lester Faigley's critique of a student essay about letter writing, where he convincingly demonstrates the writer's—and teacher's—dependence on a middle-class aesthetic of polite sentimentality (1992, 122–26).

Chapter Eight

"Containing Creatures We Barely Imagine"

Responding to 'Bad' Students' Writing

Piper Murray

In Richard Haswell and Min-Zhan Lu's *Comp Tales* (2000), Chris Anson tells a chilling story:

> It goes like this: At one college somewhere in the U.S., a senior professor has a strange method of returning his students' papers. First he places each successful paper in front of its author. . . . Then he retrieves from his briefcase the papers of the students who haven't done well. These students get, deposited humiliatingly on their desks, a zip-lock plastic baggie containing the shredded contents of their paper. (175)

Even if we have not heard Anson's tale before, there is something strikingly familiar about it. For one thing, we all know—or feel like we know—such a "senior professor." His character cuts a familiar figure to readers inside and outside the academy alike: the professor who enjoys tenure but not teaching, who would rather be off somewhere reading Milton than teaching students how to write great, much less mediocre, works of their own. The living embodiment of just the kind of current traditionalism that compositionists of all critical stripes have labored to put behind us, he treats his students' less successful work literally like shit, turning it into waste products and depositing it on their desks in plastic baggies.

But the story does not end there. For while Anson initially frames it as an urban legend, the climax of the tale as he tells it in *Comp Tales* comes when he describes retelling it to a colleague over coffee. Upon hearing the story, his colleague "gasped, spilling her coffee, and looked at [him] in amazement." She knows this "urban legend"—*personally*. Legend or not, he is also a real, live "senior colleague" in her department, a man who "had earned a reputation" for "tortur[ing] developing writers with acts of shame and humiliation" (176). Upon discovering that this terrible teacher actually exists, Anson finds himself "equally stunned" (175). But again, Anson's shock—and our own—quickly takes on an air of familiarity, as he goes on to comment on what this story means to him and his own teaching. He explains that he used to tell it in his graduate Composition theory courses as an example of a bad scenario on which to base a case study: too unbelievable and one-sided to yield much reflection. "Now," he tells us, "I use the story as a case—a case that's symptomatic of an unresolved problem happening out there in the teaching world. It's called hateful teaching. The question is: what are we going to do about it? The discussion can last for years" (176). Anson's own discussion ends there, however, with the effect that this harrowing tale of hateful teaching has gone, in the space of just a few words, from tale told out of school to call to arms.

Anson's tale presents us with an extreme, a kind of border case that can serve only to highlight the differences between those who are a part of this "unresolved problem" and those who are a part of its potential solution. On the one hand, by framing it as a problem going on "in the teaching world," Anson's tale would seem to set this story firmly within the boundaries of the field of Composition. After all, in the business of both teaching writing and researching the teaching of writing, Composition is every bit, if not more, a part of "the teaching world" than any other academic subject. On the other hand, by locating this problem not simply "in the teaching world," but specifically "*out there* in the teaching world," Anson's commentary also fortifies the boundaries between Composition Studies and other teaching subjects even as it collapses them; you're either "out there" engaging in "hateful teaching" or you're in here discussing it over coffee—as a problem. It is as if, so "strange" are this professor's hateful methods to the kind of classrooms that Composition envisions, that the thought of actually employing them becomes unimaginable.

Yet, as our continuing fascination with (and collection of) such tales might attest, the thought is not *entirely* unimaginable. Indeed, while none of us would ever think of actually returning student papers shredded up and stuffed into plastic baggies, how many of us have not had those days, those semesters, when we would have indulged in at least the fantasy if we had thought of it? Likewise, while few of us are likely to see ourselves as engaging in anything we might call "hateful teaching," how many of us have not found ourselves extremely annoyed by a stack of papers filled with random punctuation, convoluted passages, "awk" sentences, clichés, and vapid conclusions? For my own part, I have to confess that, however much I have always loved the *idea* of responding to student papers—of coaching, encouraging, and questioning my students toward more powerful communication and more critical thinking—that love has often been lost on the fifth paper in a row that began "in today's society," or even on the first paper that bore no resemblance to the one I *thought* I had assigned. At such moments, what begins as a labor of love can quickly become an exercise in self-censorship.

And guilt. For while I've heard enough conversations among teachers walking down hallways and standing in office doorways to know that I'm not the only one who finds herself occasionally frustrated or disappointed or annoyed by her students' papers, I still can't shake the nagging feeling that I *know better*. If I know, for example, from reading theorists like Bizzell (1991) and Berlin (1991) and Bleich (1990) that students often resist pedagogies that ask them to think critically, then why feel offended beyond all reason by their failure to do so? Or, if I know from reading Shaughnessy (1977) and Williams (1981) and Bartholomae (1985) that error and incoherence have a logic and a phenomenology of their own, then what business do I have feeling angry when I encounter them in my own students' writing? In fact, let's face it: in the bright light of all we know about how students learn to write, how we actually feel about student writing often seems to make *less* sense, not more.

I think Charles Bazerman speaks to such questions when he writes,

> The truths of how we read student papers have remained secret and obscure, hidden in unexamined private experience. How we comment on student essays is an easier subject, visible and open to inspection. . . . But how we read student papers is a deep uncharted ocean, containing creatures we barely imagine until they come into our view. (1989, 139)

For Bazerman, this appears to be a classic case of theory versus practice, in which certain creatures, "barely imagined" as they are by Composition theory, only ever come into view in our practice—in, that is, the actual process of responding to student writing. But if the deepest and darkest of these "truths"—the depression, anger, annoyance, frustration, fatigue, and boredom we sometimes feel in the face of student writing—have really remained so untouched by Composition theory, how do we account for the fact that, when it comes to actually experiencing them, we get the distinct feeling that we *know* better, and that we ought to feel otherwise? Or, even more to the point: what is our relationship to our theories about student writing that they should find us—those who find ourselves both "out there in the teaching world" and at the same time very much "in here" in Composition—more easily embarrassed by the "truths" than some surly senior professor, who clearly knows nothing of such matters?

In her essay "Writing Theory: :Theory Writing" (1992), Susan Miller describes the pleasure and the power that early "writing theory"—theories about how writers write—brought to a whole generation of frustrated practitioners. What these first "pleasurable and powerful explanations" of the writing process offered, first of all, was the much-needed

> hope that we might revise the 'workbook and whip' and the 'shout at foreigners' approaches in which immediate frustrations and a long history of elitist social traditions around written texts had installed in us. But they also evoked less practical pleasures, assuring us that others shared our problems and that we could, in print, discuss them. (1992, 66)

As Miller goes on to suggest, however, the simple pleasures that writing theory brought to her generation turn out to be far less simple, and a lot less innocent, than we might be tempted to think. In fact, when it comes to assessing the difference that writing theory actually made, she cautions us against reading "the knowledge and pleasure that it created" (67) as the clear sign of "cool progress" that this "grand narrative" implies. "Separating two forms of composition teaching historically and oppositionally," Miller explains, "as product both before and *versus* process, suggests that two 'grand theories' have sequentially controlled the teaching of writing. Yet if a claim is made that a new theory replaces an old one, it is fair to ask . . . how extensive the change accomplished really was" (70). In other words, whatever pleasure we might take in the powers of writing theory, it remains an open question for Miller whether those powers have made themselves felt in the one place where it really counts—in our classrooms.

Perhaps we have always known that this story was too good to be true, at least in any objective sense. No matter how much pleasure we may take in its telling, few of us entertain any illusions that the writing process movement really brought the revolution in the teaching of writing that we like to think it did. At the very least, tales like the one Anson tells serve as a reminder of what we already know: that there are still plenty of people "out there in the teaching world" who, for whatever reason, know little of either the powers or the pleasures of writing theory. Rather than framing her doubt as a question of who "has" writing theory and who does not, however, Miller pushes us to make a much more subtle distinction, and one that makes the boundaries between "out there in the teaching world" and "in here" in Composition a lot fuzzier: the distinction between, as she puts it, "the theory we *say* we have" and "the theory we *actually* have" (68). That is, confident though she is that most of us would identify ourselves firmly in the present, i.e., on the "right" side of the divide between product and process, Miller suggests that the past might live on—not, as so many of our stories suggest, in some other institution or in someone else's classroom—but *in us*, in what we do if not in what we say. It is perhaps little surprise, then, that when it comes to the question of *how* we determine whether we really do have the theory we say we have, it is to that part of our practice that remains, as Bazerman puts it, most "hidden in unexamined private experience" that Miller turns—and that she finds most telling: namely, how we read and, perhaps an even touchier subject yet, how we *feel* about student writing. Miller puts it this way: while "the theory we *say* we have determines many other, largely professional, interactions, . . .[t]he theory we *have* determines whether frustration and blame—or interest and analysis—follow our reading of 'bad' student writing" (66).

Here Miller would seem to give the grand narrative of writing theory one more twist, and one that, I would argue, has important implications for how we read our own responses to student writing. For, as suspicious as Miller finds our tendency to "separat[e] two forms of Composition teaching historically and oppositionally, as product both before and *versus* process" (70), here we find that the *responses* associated with each form do indeed break down into fairly oppositional—and fairly telling—terms: frustration and blame clearly belonging to one grand category, interest and analysis to another. In questioning the idea of "cool progress" from one theory to another, Miller does, of course, leave open the possibility that we might experience "mixed emotions" (e.g., feel both frustrated and interested), or that we might take a mixed approach (e.g., at once analyze and blame), toward "bad" student writing. But the clear distinction she draws between the two pairs suggests that the presence of conflicting emotions would indicate that we are operating under conflicting paradigms, not that conflicting emotions or approaches could be prompted by one in the same paradigm. Thus, at the same time as Miller exposes as a fantasy the idea "that two 'grand theories' have sequentially controlled the teaching of writing" (70), it would seem that she ultimately preserves that fantasy—if only as an ideal—when it comes to how we respond to "bad" student writing. In fact, by drawing an imaginary line between the theories we say we have and those we actually have, Miller calls into question, not the "grand narrative" of writing theory, but rather the confidence with which we plot our own progress *in relation to* that narrative. Meanwhile, if we find ourselves filled with frustration or blame, or if we ever feel like stripping the scare quotes from the "bad" in "'bad' student writing," we can take those feelings as a sign that we have not made the kind of progress we like to think we have made—not *really*.

Considering how troubling Miller seems to find them in theory, not to mention how embarrassing we find them in practice, it seems worth asking just what it is, after all, about frustration and blame that make them so old paradigm in the first place. While she does not address this question directly, Miller implies what makes frustration so anathema to writing theory is that it betrays our continuing investment in the very powers and privileges, the very "elitist traditions," that that theory was supposed to put behind us. For if "bad" student writing frustrates us so, then we would seem more interested in upholding the standards of "good" student writing than in empowering our students to write better. Unlike interest, which concerns itself with the way things are, i.e., in how students *actually* write, frustration suggests a simple desire that things were otherwise, i.e., that students simply wrote better. And unlike interest, which is the product of what we already know and what we want to know, desire is often thought to operate in *spite* of what we know. More the stuff of wishful thinking than writing theory, then, desire just seems too self-serving, not to mention too troubling, to be conducive to the kind of interest and analysis that careful attention to the writing process requires.

Still, it is one thing to say that whatever frustrations we feel in the face of "'bad' student writing" might be at odds with, and might even upset, our interest in analyzing that writing. But does it necessarily follow that those frustrations signal a return of the repressed powers, privileges, and other "unselfconscious claims" that "a long history of elitist traditions installed in us"? Or, on the contrary, might our frustration suggest a shift in the balance of power in the other direction? After all, frustration is what we feel when we do *not* have the power to get what we want. To be frustrated is to find ourselves powerless over both what we want and over our ongoing desire for it. For while frustration and blame betray a violent desire to "workbook and whip" our students into shape by exercising the privilege and the power that "a long history of elitist traditions installed in us," they also find us potentially overcome by that very desire, subject to *its* will rather than to the writing theories that would make that desire a thing of the past. Even for Miller, for whom frustration is clearly associated with the teacher who guards his own power and privilege, it also signifies a kind of lack: a lack of the kind of "pleasurable and powerful explanations" that brought so much relief to a field of frustrated practitioners.

Blame, especially as *opposed to* analysis, puts us in intimate touch with similar paradoxes. On the one hand, blame represents an attempt to reestablish order after it has been disrupted or challenged. On the other, it is also a kind of last resort, an admission that whatever wrong has been done cannot be righted. Perhaps even more importantly, whatever other baggage it may carry, blame also assigns a certain degree of agency in a way that analysis does not—indeed, that analysis may even deny. For while analysis functions by treating its subject as an object—as, that is, an objective phenomenon—blame treats its object as a subject, as an agent capable of being assigned responsibility for his or her actions, as someone with the power to have done otherwise. Thus, by treating the question of blame as irrelevant, there is a way in which writing theory, ironically enough, seems actually to usher in a structure of feeling in which students and teachers both are seen to have less agency rather than more—hardly what we expect from the body of "powerful and pleasurable explanations" that writing theory represents. In all these ways, at least, frustration and blame both might be said to be the effects, not of power, privilege, or omnipotence but of *impotence*. As such, they might be read less as a return of the repressed and more as a sign that we may not, after all, be feeling quite as powerful as writing theory seemed to promise we would—a sign, in fact, that writing theory may have "created" more knowledge and pleasure than power.

Writing theory may have done away with the idea or "theory" that students ought to be faulted for writing "badly." But as our ongoing frustration and blame continue to assert—in spite of all our wishful thinking that it were otherwise—writing theory cannot do away with the *feeling* that at least some "bad" student writing is, after all, the product of bad students. In other words, we may indeed know and believe in our heart of hearts that this is not the case, but we cannot prevent it from *seeming* so. And the fact that writing theory is supposed to make errors appear less "bad" may only make their *seeming* "badness" all the more frustrating, that much more of a reminder of our own powerlessness to make every "bad" student paper make good sense. Perhaps, then, what really make frustration and blame such an embarrassment to writing theory is their ability to remind us of the uncomfortable fact that we may not, after all, really have in practice all the power that we have "in theory." For to cast frustration and blame as a thing of the pretheoretical past is to claim absolute power for writing theory, to claim that "writing theory," if we *really* have it, gives us the power never to meet a piece of writing that frustrates us, never to want to blame a student for failing to follow the assignment or for mistaking clichés for critical thinking. To confront frustration and blame as a thing of the present, however, means confronting the ever-present limits of that power, of *our* power.

By regarding even the worst student writing with the kind of interest and analysis usually reserved for literature, writing theory seems to leave little room for frustration, blame, or, indeed, any of the other strange "creatures" (Bazerman) that lurk just below the surface of our responses to "bad" student writing. Yet, as we have also seen, our awareness of these "secret and obscure" creatures *as* secret and obscure reminds us of the ways in which, far from falling outside the realm of writing theory, such creatures are in fact central to our understanding of what it means to "have" that theory—or not to have it. In fact, considering just how familiar they are as strange creatures, they seem less to lie outside the realm of writing theory than to form what Judith Butler (1993) might call its "founding repudiations": all the more powerful—and all the more present—for their repudiated status.

To say so, however, is not simply to admit that frustration and blame might creep into our responses once in a while, *despite* all we care about the writing process. It is also to face the ways in which such feelings are in fact integrally and intimately related to the very interest and analysis that writing process theory calls for. The ways, for instance, in which the "interest" we take in "bad" and "good" student writing alike (and, indeed, in "bad" and "good" students) is fundamentally different from the kind of interest we take in any other kind of text. The ways in which the interest we find in "bad" student writing may *necessarily* entail frustration and blame. The ways in which writing theory in fact introduces a whole new set of hopes and pleasures and desires—for good student writing and for power over bad student writing—that the "conservative teacher" like the one in Anson's story might never know. And, finally, the ways in which the interest and analysis that follows our reading of "bad" student writing, rather than being opposed to frustration and blame, may necessarily entail them. Indeed, getting in touch with these strange creatures requires us, finally, to ask whether they really represent a lapse into the repressed past, or whether, on the contrary, they might actually point to the other—and very present—side of writing theory's most ambitious project: namely, to encounter all student writing, and perhaps *especially* "bad" student writing, as the object of our desire, as more than merely "interesting." It also means asking whether interest and analysis, to the exclusion of frustration and blame, are really the best responses to any and all texts worthy of our attention—or whether it is only a "long history of elitist traditions" that make us continue to think so.

We might ask, finally, where those desires for less bad writing leave us in relation to the writing theory they threaten to embarrass. As we have seen, such questions, if they come up at all, are usually framed as one more casualty of the conflict between theory and practice. And yet, as the combination of fascination and repulsion with which we respond to (and tell and retell) stories like Anson's suggests, how we really feel about student writing may simply refuse to be explained away by the theory-versus-practice, past-versus-present structures against which we plot our progress. After all, the reason we find stories like Anson's "plastic baggie" story appalling is precisely the fact that, while we may on occasion *feel* like doing so, the fact is that none of us would ever *actually* return our students' papers to them in plastic baggies. On the contrary, I would be willing to bet that the more we may feel like lodging accusations in our students' margins (cliché! overgeneralization! awk!), the harder we work to prevent those accusations from actually making their way anywhere near our students' writing—the more careful we are, for example, to carefully transform such impulses to do so into expressions of interest rather than frustration, analysis rather than blame ("could you be more specific?" "this seems interesting; could you develop it further?" "not sure what you mean here. . ."). In other words, while our frustration and blame may make us *feel* as though we do not have the theory we say we have, our actual practice, i.e., the comments that we *actually* write on student papers or utter in classrooms or conferences with students, would probably find us more in line with our theory than we think—or feel. Thus it is not, after all, either in what we think we should do (our theory) or in what we actually do (our practice) that the seeming contradiction lies, but rather in what we *want* to do: in, that is, the space where we may indeed entertain the many "creatures" that compete for our attention without actually believing in those creatures "in theory" or letting them come into view in our practice.

How, then, might we view such "creatures" in a way that allows them to speak to our theory and our practice, if not through the familiar lens of theory and practice? Alison Jaggar has written that, "rather than repressing emotion in epistemology it is necessary to rethink the relation between knowledge and emotion and construct conceptual models that demonstrate the mutually constitutive rather than oppositional relation between reason and emotion" (1989a, 156–57). Similarly, I want to suggest that rethinking the relation between what we know about student writing and how we feel about it asks us to explore the emotions and fantasies and desires that trouble our thinking as "mutually constitutive rather than oppositional." It asks us, in other words, to read those feelings not as "random and perverse manifestations" of our own ignorance but instead as *structures of feeling* in the sense that Raymond Williams (1977) means that phrase: as reasons not to reinforce but to revise the very structures that fail to contain them; as signs, not simply of what we already know, but also of what we might know; and, finally, "not feeling against thought, but thought as felt and feeling as thought" (127, 132). Viewed in this way, the fact that there seems to be no ready place for our fantasies or frustrations in *either* our theory *or* our practice suggests that they call, not for greater commitment to the theories we say we have, but instead for new ways of thinking about both, as well as the relationship between the two. In other words, reread as a structure of feeling, the dissonance we feel between interest and analysis on the one hand, and frustration and blame on the other, might be taken, not as a sign that our theory and practice are often at odds with one another (which is news to no one), but instead as a sign that there are aspects of our experience that remain in tension with *both* our theory and our practice.

This does not, of course, mean that we uncritically accept every feeling as somehow more in touch with the truths of "bad" student writing. But what it does mean is that, rather than prompting us to cry out for a more perfect fit between our theory and our practice, such feelings (if we let them) might refer us instead to a kind of third space between the two, a space *between* how we think we should respond to student writing in theory and how we actually respond to student writing in practice. And that this space refuses to be contained by the stories we tell about either writing theory or student writing—and perhaps even plots against them—makes it, to me, the place where those stories might begin to get *really* interesting.

Chapter Nine

Manufacturing Emotions

Tactical Resistance in the Narratives of Working-Class Students

Janet Bean

I live in the former rubber capital of the world, where industry and civic identity are inextricably intertwined. In the winter my family sleds down the hills of Goodyear Metro Park on a prototype toboggan we bought at a Rubbermaid engineer's yard sale; in the summer we watch the Ohio Ballet at the city park in Firestone Heights. Woven into my everyday life are reminders of the manufacturing roots of the city. The university athletic teams are the "Zips," named after a popular zip-up rubber boot that was manufactured in the city in the 1930s, and the most striking building on campus is the glass-encased Goodyear Polymer Science Building. When I sit on my front porch, I sometimes hear a distant hum. "It's the blimp," I call to my children, and they run across the yard, faces turned skyward to see the *Spirit of Akron*.

Our house was built at the height of the prosperous 1920s, and although we're on the west side, downwind from the rubber factories, the grout between the bricks is stained dark from decades of pollution. I'm told that the people grew accustomed to the pervasive odor of sulfur in the air. "It's the smell of jobs," they used to say, before factory after factory closed in the late 1970s—Firestone Plants 1 and 2, Goodyear Plant 2, General Tires, Mansfield Tires, Mohawk Rubber Company, Sun Rubber Company. Between 1975 and 1985, Akron lost 35,000 manufacturing jobs, eliminating virtually all major rubber production in a city that once manufactured two-thirds of the nation's tires and half of the world's rubber goods (Rodgers 2001; Love and Giffels 1999, 188).

Most of my students are from Akron and neighboring towns, and most were born during the economic downturn of the late 1970s and early 1980s. The decline of the rubber industry, coupled with the struggling steel industry, affected all of northeast Ohio. Many students remember the strain of living in uncertain times: the "For Sale" signs dotting the yards in their neighborhoods, the stress at home as Mom somehow dodged yet another round of layoffs, the silence of fathers at the dinner table, the family from West Virginia that lived next door one day and was gone the next. Yet, if these students were born in uncertain times, they also have lived most of their lives during the longest period of sustained economic growth in American history. One of my students writes, "I have seen the death and rebirth of Akron," and he, like many others, credits the city's phoenix-like renewal in part to the university and the "flow of educated people" it produces.

In 2001, *Newsweek* magazine listed Akron as one of the top ten "new tech" cities in America for its preeminence in polymer engineering, citing The University of Akron's research facilities as instrumental in the city's industrial success (Rodgers 2001). Even as companies have moved production facilities elsewhere, many, including Firestone and Goodyear, have maintained their presence in the city, replacing blue-collar jobs with white-collar jobs in research and development. New companies have emerged, such as The Plastic Lumber Company and Advanced Elastomers Systems, which take advantage of polymer technology. Akron's history—as it is commonly told—follows the plot of the American success story: it has faced adversity and prevailed, pulling itself up by its bootstraps by developing its brainpower. In shifting from a manufacturing to a more diversified economy, the city has not only survived but also moved forward.

I hear the story of Akron's success echoed in the narratives of my students, many of whom are the first generation in their families to attend college. They are the truck driver's son studying engineering, the hair stylist's daughter on a full academic scholarship, the steelworker's son who finances his education by working third shift at UPS, the mother who does her homework at the kitchen table with her children, the army veteran who plans to go to medical school, the sons and daughters of immigrants from Laos, Vietnam, and India. They write of jobs at Target and OfficeMax and Subway that pay for their tuition; of sacrifices made by parents so they can attend college; of hard work in high school classrooms and athletic fields that have led to scholarships. In telling stories of hard work that brings rewards, challenges that build character, and futures that are bright, they are tapping into one of the master narratives of our culture—the story of upward social mobility. A university education plays a central role in this narrative, signifying entrance into the middle class. It is not surprising, then, that students bring this deeply embedded cultural narrative into their college composition classrooms.

Composition scholars have become skeptical of master narratives, especially narratives of the self, as a form that reinforces cultural hegemony. The narrative of upward social mobility is particularly suspect because it focuses attention on individual agency and promotes an ideology of meritocracy that can obscure the effects of class, race, ethnicity, and gender. As cultural studies has become part of the mainstream of Composition Studies, pedagogies have emerged that attempt to provide students with tools to critique social codes and analyze the relationship between power and discourse. Not all first-year composition students, however, want to see their cherished beliefs recast as cultural "myths." Groups that have been historically disadvantaged in the education system—working-class students, African Americans, and children of immigrants—are often the staunchest supporters of "bootstrap" ideologies of individual opportunity and responsibility. These students are understandably drawn toward narratives that provide a sense of agency; by casting themselves in the role of hero in a narrative of meritocracy, they affirm their ability to control their lives.

Despite the popular appeal of bootstraps narratives (and perhaps because of it), composition teachers do not always welcome them in the classroom. In addition to preventing students from engaging in the kind of explicit cultural critique increasingly expected in first-year composition, narratives of meritocracy encourage the use of clichéd language and concepts. My students, for example, write and enjoy reading essays with sentences such as "If you work hard, even if you don't enjoy it, there will be a positive outcome"; "Life is what you make of it"; and "It all rests in your imagination." Thomas Newkirk points out the tendency for composition teachers to view this kind of student optimism as "shallow, naïve, and unsophisticated," as an "irritant" rather than an admirable quality (1997, 37). Before we judge students' narratives of upward social mobility as evidence of a failure to think critically or simply dismiss them as bad writing, however, we might consider the possibility that the very persistence of these narratives, their use by thousands and thousands of individuals, signals a more complex relationship between writer, culture, and power than is readily apparent. In focusing on how the master narrative supports hegemony, we may be forgetting to ask an essential and pragmatic question: how are individuals *making use* of narratives of meritocracy?

In *The Practice of Everyday Life* (1984), Michael deCerteau challenges the common assumption that "users" are passive and governed by rules established by the dominant culture. He argues that the opportunistic and clandestine creativity of groups and individuals collectively form a "network of antidiscipline" that prevents society from being reduced to the "grid of discipline" imposed by the dominant cultural economy (xiv–xv). In everyday practices—walking, storytelling, talking, cooking, reading, using urban spaces, remembering, reusing—lie the arts of resistance. DeCerteau is particularly interested in what he calls tactics, the subversion of discipline by the weak: "A tactic insinuates itself into the other's place, fragmentarily, without taking it over in its entirety, without being able to keep it at a distance. . . . Whatever it wins, it does not keep" (xix). Without ideologies or institutions of their own, tactics remain concealed within dominant structures; they evade, erode, and confound, yet in their multiple and ever-changing forms cannot be rooted out and disciplined.

When students make use of master cultural narratives to tell the story of their lives, they do not simply act as passive receivers and transcribers. Their reconstituted texts offer "readings" of the master narrative that may involve an infinite number of transformations. DeCerteau explains that "users of social codes turn them into metaphors and ellipses of their own quests" (xxi–xii). Readers "poach" on the text of another, insinuating their own histories into it, making it "habitable, like a rented apartment" (xxi). To understand the power of renting and poaching, we need only think of the transformations of college dorm rooms each year as students temporarily make these institutional spaces their own through acts of makeshift creativity. Likewise, students may practice in their writing the "subtle art of 'renters' who know how to insinuate their countless differences into the dominant text" (xxii). Our students' narratives of meritocracy may contain tactics of resistance that we, like administrators who are unaware of illegal lofts and unauthorized paint in dorm rooms, have been unable or unwilling to see.

I'd like to turn now to a classroom moment that illustrates how tactics of resistance can reside within the cultural commonplace of the American success story. Emotion, I will argue, can function as a powerful tactic when introduced into academic discourse because it opens up a rhetorical space for ambiguity and disrupts—at least for a moment—the privileged position of rationality. Last fall, I asked my honors composition class to read Harlon Dalton's essay "Horatio Alger," which is anthologized in the popular cultural studies textbook *Rereading America: Cultural Contexts for Critical Thinking and Writing* (Colombo *et al.* 2001). Dalton argues that ideologies of meritocracy, exemplified by the Horatio Alger myth, blind us to the deeply ingrained structures of racism in our society. The discussion was progressing somewhat tentatively, as discussions about race often do, when Sarah burst out angrily, "I hated this guy." In a rush of words, she told us about her life—how as a child she lived in government-subsidized housing, how her mother worked to find a better neighborhood for them to live in, how she was a latch-key kid who spent hours and hours alone with her sister while her mother worked, how she devoted herself to excelling as a student. The longer she talked, the more uncomfortable the class became. As students looked at the floor and fiddled with their pens, embarrassed by the raw anger and declaration of poverty, she told us of her dedication to her schoolwork and her determination to go to college. "He can't tell me I got my scholarship because I'm white," she said, her cheeks flushing and voice rising.

This incident stays with me because it demonstrates the power of emotional expression and our limited understanding of its rhetorical force. It would be easy to focus on how Sarah doggedly holds on to the ideology of meritocracy and avoids engaging Dalton's argument on intellectual terms. She appears to be a prime example of the kind of student resistance to cultural critique that has frustrated many teachers of critical pedagogy and been the subject of much scholarly debate (see, e.g., Fitts and France 1995; Hurlbert and Blitz 1991; Durst 1999). Yet there is another kind of resistance at work here, I believe. Hers is not the resistance of the privileged but the resistance of the weak, a tactic that operates within the structure of dominant discourse even as it transgresses this structure. Her anger is a complicating rhetorical move, one that asks us to hold contradictions in mind: we must affirm her individual achievements while at the same time acknowledging her class identification, recognize the impact of poverty on her family while supporting a reward system based on merit. Although Sarah operates within a framework of meritocracy, her experiences cannot be completely contained in its structures. Her identification with her mother's struggles and her expression of class consciousness put pressure on the ideologies of individualism that underlie meritocracy. Her expression of anger allows her to occupy conflicting positions within the dominant narrative of upward mobility.

To understand Sarah's anger as a tactic of resistance to cultural hegemony rather than simply as an act of resistance to Harlon Dalton or cultural studies pedagogy, we need a theory of emotion that takes into account the role the affective plays in the development of critical agency. It is not surprising that emotions have been undertheorized in Composition pedagogy. Feminist ethnographers have pointed out that "the primary Western narratives about emotion portray them as an 'internal,' interior space tied to the 'natural' body and functioning as a universal 'fact' of biological existence" (Boler 1999, 12). Simon Williams notes a strong tendency for "social theorists. . .to define human actors in largely 'disembodied' terms as rational agents" (2001, 2). According to Bryan Turner, this theoretical split between mind and body creates an impasse that limits our understanding of resistance and agency. He writes, "the mind is seen to be the causal knowledgeable agent and the body is regulated to an object or an environment that is subtly manipulated by consumerism or regulated by disciplines. Despite constant talk about resistance, Foucauldian bodies are merely objects of medical and political discourses" (1992, 138). To develop an effective theory of human agency, argues Turner, we must replace Cartesian dichotomies with a more dialectical understanding of the relationship between mind and body, reason and emotion, public and private.

Anthropologists Lila Abu-Lughod and Catherine Lutz (1990) argue that emotion and discourse should not be viewed as two entities, one private and interior and the other public and social. Locating emotion in the politics of daily life, in speech acts and discourse, they define it as a construct tied to both sociability and power relations. Emotion is "a form of social action that creates effects in the world, effects that are read in a culturally informed way by the audience" (12). It is crucial, then, to examine "the many ways emotion gets its meaning and force from its location and performance in the public realm of discourse" (7). If we accept Abu-Lughod and Lutz's theory of emotion and discourse as mutually constitutive, rhetoric becomes a powerful analytical tool for understanding the role of feelings in our culture: the study of emotion *is* the study of rhetoric. In the following sections, I use this rhetorical model of emotion to examine how feelings of obligation, gratitude, anger, and nostalgia function as social action in the narratives of working-class students.

Obligation and Gratitude: Representing Parental Pain

Children of factory workers understand the physical toll of work on their parents' bodies, from the daily strains of fatigue and stress to more debilitating conditions such as ruptured disks, carpal tunnel syndrome, and arthritis. Moreover, as witnesses to their parents' suffering, they understand its relation to their own material comforts; they know that the food on their tables and their college educations are purchased through their parents' pain. Often, this pain is surrounded by silence—the stoicism of mothers and fathers, the quiet of a son trying not to disturb his father's rest on the sofa, the watchfulness of a daughter who sees the effort it takes for her mother to sew. In *The Body in Pain: The Making and Unmaking of the World*, Elaine Scarry explains that "pain is not only itself resistant to language but also destroys language, deconstructing it into the prelanguage of cries and groans" (1985, 172). Thus, to put the experience of pain into words is to challenge its destructive force. The very act of writing pain brings into existence a language of resistance. Scarry argues that "a great deal . . . is at stake in the attempt to invent linguistic structures that will reach and accommodate this area of experience that is normally so inaccessible to language; the human attempt to reverse the de-objectifying work of pain by forcing pain itself into the avenues of objectification is a project laden with practical and ethical consequence" (1985, 6). The representation of the body in pain has a political dimension, for what cannot be verbally expressed will not be politically represented (12). When students represent their parents' pain within narratives of meritocracy, then, they challenge prevailing discourses of success that insist on a disembodied view of work. Expressions of emotion, particularly those of obligation and gratitude, become tropes through which children can acknowledge their parents' suffering, attribute meaning to bodily pain, and offer critique from within dominant narratives.

The American work ethic, which is grounded in ideals of self-constraint, discipline, sacrifice, and delayed gratification, emphasizes bodily control and emotion management (Williams 2001, 20–21). In the narrative of upward social mobility, the pain of the body is transmuted into an ideal of self-sacrifice. This sacrifice works across generations: the hard work of the parent pays off in the child's advancement, which, in working-class families, is often figured as a university education. Karen writes, for example, that her parents "cared about our education, encouraging us constantly to succeed and become someone far from who they had to be and to do something that required thinking."[1] Following the script of the dominant cultural narrative, parents manage and control the physical pain that comes with factory work so that their children can move up in the world.

Students' narratives, however, often complicate the code of silence and sacrifice. Greg explains that he knows very little about his father's work in a steel mill: "When I asked my dad what it was like to work in a factory, he said very little in reply. . . . In all my eighteen years, I have never heard him talk about what he does at work." In writing his essay, Greg interrupts the disembodied narrative that his father—and society—has constructed about work. He makes the body central to *his* narrative, opening his essay with a commonplace from his childhood: "'Work with your brain, son, not with your back.' My father said these words to me more times than I can remember." The words "brain" and "back" serve a dual function here: while they are conventional symbols of white-collar and blue-collar work, they also define work as an activity that cannot be separated from the body. Furthermore, the use of the word "son" creates a powerful emotional appeal to intimacy, reorienting what could be a motivational cliché by shifting emphasis away from an exhortation of meritocracy to the bond between father and son. In keeping the body present and visible, Greg refuses to transmute physical pain into an ideal of self-sacrifice. He writes the desire for upward mobility through his father's body, in suffering and revulsion: "He has been breaking his back in a factory job for nearly twenty-five years now, and the idea of his son following in his footsteps is a sickening thought to him." For Greg, the act of attending college to get an engineering degree repays a debt he feels to his father. It is this rhetoric of obligation that allows him, in deCerteau's terms, to "inhabit" the dominant narrative of upward mobility. By locating his college experience within the particular and embodied context of his father's work, he operates within hegemonic discourse yet eludes being completely defined by it.

There is enormous power in the image of the parent's body at work. Indeed, many children of factory workers can recall the moment that they first saw their mother or father on the job site. Antwan, son of a steel worker, describes how disturbing this experience was for him as a child:

> When my dads company had an open house my family and I attended. As we went through the tour I noticed how dangerous it is in there. The way the factory was set up, if you got seriously hurt somewhere in the factory there's a chance you would [not] get any help because some places there's no one there. That was a bad thought because you could die in there and no one would know.

Seeing a parent in danger or pain inevitably evokes an emotional response in a child—fear, anger, helplessness, perhaps even a sense of responsibility. Antwan's fear of the dangers in his father's workplace were justified: "My dad broke his wrist, dislocated his shoulder, broke a bone in his jaw, and sustains a back injury all from work." Still, like Greg, he frames the physical hardships of his father's job within an ethic of family obligation. He explains that his father continues to do dangerous work in order to provide for his family, specifically to create opportunities for him and his sister. Within this framework, the risks and pain of factory work create an obligation that Antwan must reciprocate.

A rhetoric of obligation is a consistent feature in the narratives of working class students who recount their parents' physical pain. Karen, the daughter of

Hmong immigrants, has seen the effects of factory labor on both her parents. Unlike Greg's and Antwan's fathers, her mother does not have the benefits of a long-term, union job: "Working in places like plastic factories and sewing sweat shops, she skipped from job to job." Karen describes the kind of work that the women of the Hmong immigrant community do:

> My mom and aunts mostly worked in plastic factories making molds of toy cars or factories in which they had to glue a small chip to another, using tweezers and pliers. My mom now works in a store, hanging up clothes all day; it is almost like assembly-line factory work because she and other workers stand alongside of a table in the back and place the clothes on hangers, while others come and take the full racks to put out in the store.

Because of the repetitive fine-motor motion required by these jobs, her mother suffers from arthritis that limits her ability to work. Karen's father has been working as a tool inspector for seven years, but too often the "money would leak out of [his] pockets like water," creating financial hardships for the family. Through images of tedium and pain, Karen's narrative creates a view of factory work as dehumanizing and calls into question dominant ideologies of self-sacrifice and delayed gratification. "My mother and father were like robots," she writes, "which were only programmed to be able to do factory work." In pursuing a college education, she hopes to fulfill her parents' desire that she "become someone far from who they had to be."

Despite elements of resistance in these essays, I want to make it clear that they *do* operate within the general plot of the upward mobility narrative. My students believe in hard work and merit-based rewards; they want to get a college education and make their parents proud; they want more prestigious jobs and entrance into the middle class. The experience of witnessing their parents' pain creates an ethic of obligation and gratitude, however, that complicates the motive of upward social mobility. Antwan's rationale for a college education makes his family's motives explicit: "My dad is in bad physical health due to the lifting of steel for thirty years. He strongly disagrees with me working for a factory even if it's just for a summer job. That's why he wants me to go college; he wants me to avoid the stressful work of factory labor." For these students, what drives them to success is not simply a desire to move upward; instead, they are striving for work that will prevent them from repeating their parents' life of pain.

Anger, Loss, and Nostalgia: Representing Working-Class Masculinity

Working-class men who attend college often feel ambivalence about taking on a middle-class work identity because it means turning away from models of masculinity endorsed by their communities and families. In *Ragged Dicks: Mascu-*

linity, Steel, and the Rhetoric of the Self-Made Man, James Catano argues that middle-class and working-class masculinities are constructed through quite different rhetorics. While middle-class masculinity locates agency and self-making in upward mobility and individualism, working-class masculinity emphasizes agency through workplace independence and class identification (2001, 121–123). For many young men, attending college can feel like a betrayal of deeply rooted identities. Anger becomes a tactic for resisting the hegemony of middle-class masculinity, as is clear in Greg's narrative:

> My father being a working class man has instilled certain values in my entire family. I have found that I have far more respect for the blue-collar worker than for the white-collar worker who makes twice as much money, simply because the blue-collar worker has to work ten times harder in order to provide for his family. Ironically, I am going to school to become one of those white collar executive types who ultimately puts people like my father out of work. I hate the idea of becoming part of the system that I hate so much, but if I don't roll with it, it'll roll right over me. I guess my driving force is seeing my dad on the couch with his back out of place, saying, "Work with your brain, son, not with your back." I will remember those words for the rest of my life, and someday I will be very successful because of them.

This paragraph, which concludes his essay, turns the narrative of success in on itself: respect is inverted, with blue-collar work privileged over white-collar work; a vision of an executive job loses its power as it is juxtaposed with an image of blue-collar layoffs; and the meaning of success is undercut by the irony of the final sentence, which is a lament as much as a prediction. Moreover, the defining characteristic of dominant middle-class ideologies of success—individual agency—is reversed, leaving a hero no choice but to fall in line. Through a rhetoric of anger, Greg creates a powerful argument about class injustice, even as he takes his place at the university to become a member of the managerial class.

Mark, son of a trucker, enacts a similar tactic of resistance as he recounts the tension between working-class and middle-class masculinities. The emotion that motivates his narrative, however, is loss rather than anger. Although he has a passionate interest in cars and trucks, he knows that changes in the industry make it impossible for him to follow in his father's and grandfather's steps as an independent trucker. In an essay about the summers he spent on his father's tractor-trailer rig, he explains the importance of his connection to male role models in his family:

> I stood where my father once stood, near our father's trucks. My grandfather, like my father, owned his own truck, and my father traveled with him like I do. My father followed in my grandfather's footsteps. Trucking was my father's only interest, and almost only mine, but I would break the father-son tradition to later go to college.

College, more than a gateway to upward social mobility, represents separation and betrayal of family. In the following passage, it is clear that Mark resists giving up the sense of identity he has cultivated through family bonds:

> As my father chained down his load with his ratchet binders and flung his tarp over the aluminum bows to cover the cargo, I stretched the rubber straps and hooked them onto the trailer's rub-rail. As I did my small chore to assist my drowsy exhausted father, I saw my hands were dirty. This was not just any dark dirt; it was my shining pride. My father grew up in the steel industry with his father, just like I did. This place—this enormous, filthy, dangerous place—gave me the feeling that I knew where I came from, and no one could take that away from me.

A profound respect for physical labor is central to working-class views of masculinity. Mark sees the dirt on his hands as his "shining pride," a symbol of solidarity, just as Greg had a greater respect for those who work with their backs. There is a note of defiance here: he knows where he came from and "no one could take that away." He is aware of the irony of taking an identity from an "enormous, filthy, dangerous place," but he takes it anyway, out of love for his father. From this same love comes the motive to risk his chosen identity: by attending college, he can make father proud and repay an ethical obligation.

With the shift away from a manufacturing economy, young men who might prefer blue-collar work are forced to consider middle-class pathways to success. Bryan grew up in the Ohio Valley, where dozens of steel mills line the Ohio River from Wheeling, West Virginia, to Pittsburgh, Pennsylvania. For his entire life, he has witnessed the male members of his family face uncertainty in their steel jobs, and he foresees "certain doom" for the factories and small towns in the Valley. He writes:

> It is just hard to believe that a company that needed so many workers at one time would hire my grandfather at the age of 15 write out of the 10th grade, and now hasn't hired a new employee in over 20 years. "At one time you didn't have to think about were you could find a job all you had to do," says my grandfather, "was walk down the street and to the main office of Wheeling Pitt and tell them that you wanted to work, and just like that you had a job making enough money to support a wife and five kids." Wouldn't it be nice to be able to find jobs like that today? I couldn't even imagine what that would be like. I know that I wouldn't be in college today if I was able to get a job that easily, and make that kind of money.

Nostalgia can be viewed as sentimentality in its worse form, a cloying desire for a past that has been sanitized of unpleasant realities. Yet in this essay, nostalgia has the force of cultural critique. For Bryan, who loves hunting, hometown football, and physical work, the economic imperatives that have led him to college are unwelcome and unfair. The upward narrative of social mobility is a story of loss, as the tortured syntax of the final sentence of his essay suggests:

"All I can do though is pray that by the time the mills do go under and the 50,000 plus people lose their jobs that I no longer live in the Valley even though I will always consider it my home no matter how bad things get their." Even as Bryan writes himself into the narrative of upward social mobility, he makes it clear that the price of success—measured in the devastation of community and family—is too high.

Conclusion

It has been my goal to show that resistance can reside not only in the explicit cultural critiques of Marxism, feminism, and postmodernism but also in rhetorics of emotions and lived experience. This is not to say that academic rhetorics and everyday rhetorics produce the same kind of resistance; there are, in fact, important differences between the practice of intellectual theory and the practice of vernacular theory, which Thomas McLaughlin defines as the questioning of dominant ideologies by "those who lack cultural power and who speak a critical language grounded in local concerns" (5–6). In affirming obligation and gratitude to their parents, in announcing and solidifying class and family identification, in expressing nostalgia and a sense of loss, working-class students employ tactics that challenge the dominant ideology of social mobility even as they make use of it. Because these tactics necessarily operate within the space of a powerful other, the act of resistance is always complicit with hegemonic discourse. Practitioners of vernacular theory do not distance themselves from the local; they use languages of the particular, of the body and emotion, to inscribe heterogeneity into the systems they inhabit. In contrast, academic strategies of resistance are grounded in the ability to distance oneself from cultural practices and ideologies. In this view, critical resistance develops in a self-consciousness and self-reflexivity that can be achieved only through detachment.

From the perspective of academic critical theory, it is possible to interpret the narratives of upward social mobility I have examined above not as resisting, as I have argued, but rather as uneasily resigned to the status quo. What matters in the end, some might say, is the fact these students had no choice but to concede to the dominant ideologies of individualism and meritocracy. I will grant that there is a limited perspective in the tactics of these students, a blindness, as deCerteau puts it, that results from "combat at close quarters" (38). Yet it would be unfair to say these students become objects of the dominant discourse because they ultimately do not find a way to stand outside it. The *trajectory* of their narratives is evasive and disruptive; even as they remain within the structures of the dominant discourse, they are not fully contained by it. McLaughlin argues that "the fact that vernacular theories. . .do not completely transcend ideologies does not make them different in kind from academic theories" (5). If there is a blindness that comes from maintaining a connection to local concerns—to emotion, to the body, to one's kin and community—then I would argue there is also a blindness that comes from holding oneself at a distance from these things.

To recognize emotion and connection as a potential means through which students might generate critical resistance, we need to discard binaries that oppose feelings and reason. We might question our own reluctance to acknowledge emotion as intellectual work and consider whose interests we are serving when we exclude representations of pain, anger, obligation, and love from academic discourse. Martha Nussbaum explains that "[e]motions are not just the fuel that powers the psychological mechanism of a reasoning creature; they are parts, highly complex and messy parts, of this creature's reasoning itself" (2001, 3). If we do not allow students to engage their emotions in the intellectual work of our classrooms, we are cutting off a powerful means of making sense of the world. "Part of ethical thought itself will be omitted with the omission of emotions," argues Nussbaum (3). When students use emotions in their writing, they often open up spaces that call for interpretation and exert pressure on dominant ideologies. Emotional rhetoric can allow the writer—and the reader—to occupy conflicting positions within a text. There is pedagogical power, argues Megan Boler, in learning to "inhabit ambiguous selves" because it is in ambiguity that we develop the capacity to change (1999, 197).

If we want students to understand and critique cultural uses of power, we must acknowledge the ethical work they are already doing as they render their emotions and experiences in words. We need to make room in our composition classes for rhetorics that engage emotion and experience, and we need to become better readers of student texts. Expressions of personal experience and emotion create tactics of resistance that disrupt the dominant cultural narratives in which they reside. If we read student texts looking for the logic of these tactics, we may discover that working-class students are neither mystified because they use narratives of meritocracy nor anti-intellectual because they reject ideological critiques of that meritocracy. Instead, we might see that our students are pragmatic agents of tactical resistance.

Note

1. I would like to thank my students for allowing me to use their essays, which I have quoted here as they were written, and for teaching me to be a better reader. I would also like to thank Lance Svehla, Julie Drew, Alan Ambrisco, Jinny Marting, and the reviewers of this essay for their valuable commentary.

Chapter Ten

Collaboration, Ethics, and the Emotional Labor of WPAs

Alice Gillam

The challenge of feminist writing program administration, then, is not just to change administrative structures but also to foreground the inevitable resistance and conflict that result and to make critical reflection about that resistance and conflict as much a part of the program as a new syllabus or new teacher training workshops.

—Amy Goodburn and Carrie Shively Leverenz,
"Feminist Writing Program Administration"

During the 1998–99 school year, we who form the writing program administrative team at the University of Wisconsin-Milwaukee conducted a self-study of our collaborations.[1] Throughout the year, we wrote about our experiences, shared our writing, read articles about collaborative administration, and discussed a range of issues. Among the important issues to emerge were the emotionally laden ethical dilemmas we faced as WPAs, two of which I discuss in this essay: 1) how to negotiate between institutional demands regarding first-year writing instruction and our own individual and collective goals; and 2) how to acknowledge the differing emotional investments we had in the program when some of us, the graduate WPAs, were "temporary" labor while others, namely me, were "permanent" labor. The first receives greater attention in the present essay because it is the one I have pondered over the longest. However, it is the second dilemma, raised by the graduate WPAs, which has brought home to me the truth of Goodburn and Leverenz's (1998) assertion that critical reflection about resistance, conflict, and, I would add, our differences must be as much a part of our work together as planning the general syllabus or new TA orientation (289).

But before discussing the insights that resulted from our grappling with these two dilemmas, I'd like to comment briefly on the tendency in writing program administration discourse to idealize collaboration as democratic and equitable and to associate it with feminism. In "Decentering the WPA," Jeanne Gunner (1994) argues that a horizontal model of program administration allows for democratic decision making on the part of the teachers involved in the program. Unlike the top-down WPA-centric model that often disenfranchises the very people who teach most of the first-year courses, the decentered model "places power in the hands of *all* faculty, giving them the means to influence the direction of the program they form" (14–15). Similarly, Marcia Dickson (1993) argues that collaborative administrative practices are not only democratic but also "feminist": "A feminist model . . . is more concerned with doing away with hierarchies than with perpetuating them. The feminist form of administration I envision allows for the blurring of the lines of authority and control. A feminist administrator becomes one of a group of instructors" (148).

In Composition Studies, there has been a rather thorough-going critique of collaborative learning pedagogies from scholars representing a diverse range of perspectives. Since most readers are no doubt familiar with this decade-long critique, I will summarize it only briefly. Donald Stewart (1988) and David Smit (1989) argue that the goal of consensus encourages conformity and stifles individual creativity, while Greg Myers (1986) and John Trimbur (1989) contend that collaborative learning often masks the workings of power structures that serve to privilege certain voices and silence others. John Schilb (1992) reminds us of the dystopic meaning of collaborate, as in "to cooperate treasonably as with an enemy occupying one's country" (106), and Evelyn Ashton-Jones (1995) argues that portraying "collaborative pedagogies as pedagogies of equity . . . perpetuate[s] and collude[s] in the silence that helps to conceal the reproduction of gender ideology" (17). Empirical studies such as Gail Stygall's (1998) confirm Ashton-Jones' charge. Unless "the feminist teacher explicitly teaches and models new forms of talk," asserts Stygall, "unstructured collaboration . . . jeopardizes participatory learning for women students" (253–54).

However, it is only recently that writing program administration scholars have begun to consider the dystopic meaning of the term *collaboration* and to question the idealizations of collaborative administration as democratic and equitable. Molly Wingate (1995), for example, in "The Politics of Collaboration: Writing Centers within Their Institutions" urges us to remember that the collaborations that occur within writing programs are shaped by the collaborations that occur between writing programs and the larger institutions in which they reside. Further, several contributors to the 1998 special issue of *WPA: Writing Program Administration* devoted to collaborative writing program administration point out the discrepancies between the utopian ideals that underwrite collaborative administration and the complications that are inevitably entailed in practice (Harrington, Fox, and Hogue, 52–64; Schell, 65–80).

The unquestioned link between collaborative models of administration and feminism has also begun to be challenged. Louise Wetherbee Phelps (1995), for example, offers a sometimes harrowing narrative of her attempts to implement feminist approaches to writing program administration. And in their previously mentioned essay, Goodburn and Leverenz argue that structural change alone is insufficient in enacting feminist principles of "nonhierarchical collaboration, shared leadership, multiple sources of authority" (1998, 290). It may be that feminism and collaborative administration share certain democratic ideals and emancipatory agendas, and it may even be that women are more attracted to collaborative approaches to leadership than men because of sex-role socialization. However, collaborative administration does not automatically or necessarily have anything to do with seeking a more just social order for women. Indeed, like the assumption that collaborative pedagogies are always already equitable, the assumption that collaborative administrative practices are always already equitable can, as Evelyn Ashton-Jones reminds us, "perpetuate and collude in the silence that helps to conceal the reproduction of gender ideology" (1995, 17).

In this essay, I would like to extend both strands of the emerging WPA conversation about collaboration—that is, the strand that considers the institutional collaborations entailed in WPA work and the strand that offers a more complex picture of intraprogrammatic collaborations. Specifically, I draw on feminist theories of emotional labor and ethics to interpret my experiences with both types of collaboration.

Institutional Collaboration and the Ministration in Administration

From the mid-1970s until 1997, the University of Wisconsin-Milwaukee prided itself on having a writing proficiency requirement for all graduates. Mandated by the Faculty Senate, this requirement in its various forms—impromptu essay test, large-scale portfolio assessment—aimed to certify graduates' writing proficiency and to reassure the community that our urban campus, though it may have a more or less open-door entrance policy, did not have an open-door exit policy. Although the method of certification varied, two characteristics were consistent: impartial, standardized assessment and universal application. That is, judgments of writing proficiency were "external" to the classroom, and all students were subject to the requirement—those with high ACT scores, those with As in second-semester composition from another institution, all students. Both aspects of this requirement were deemed necessary to ensure "fairness" and maintain "standards," and, not surprisingly, both aspects generated a great deal of controversy and anger.

In 1993, I assumed the position of Coordinator of Composition, one year after the method of proficiency testing changed from an impromptu essay exam to portfolio assessment. It had taken my predecessor seven years to accomplish this reform, and it was welcomed as a major victory. Unlike the free-standing impromptu essay examination, large-scale portfolio assessment tied the proficiency requirement to course work and instruction in that the portfolio essays were produced as a part of first- and second-semester courses. As expected, this more enlightened approach had a number of benefits—it accounted for the writing process and encouraged revision, it required constant discussion of student writing among teachers, it allowed the teacher to be a "coach" rather than a "judge," and it promoted fruitful exchanges about teaching and debates about what constituted passing essays.

Nevertheless, controversy continued to swirl around the previously mentioned hallmarks of this requirement—its standardized assessment and universal application—as well as around a new source of controversy, our supposedly "politically correct" set of course readings. Transfer students resented our refusal to waive the requirement based on prior course work. Students on the left suggested that portfolio assessment disadvantaged minority students, a charge not borne out in statistics, and students on the right objected to the curriculum. A sample of the nearly weekly attacks in the conservative campus paper reads, "It should come as no surprise to anyone on this campus that the Composition Program is run by Socialists, feminists, and queers. . . . They teach how heterosexual men are evil and how multicultural sensitivity means agreeing that all whites are evil too."

So from the outset, my tenure as WPA was marked by crisis and controversy—threatened sit-ins, command appearances before various tribunals appointed to review the new requirement, emergency meetings with central administrators, angry phone calls from community college deans and parents, you name it. In May of 1997, the Faculty Senate decided to take the "teeth" out of the proficiency requirement by allowing students to fulfill it through transfer credits. With this "defeat" of sorts came emotional depletion and time for much-needed reflection.

At first glance, it would appear that my role in leading the battle to preserve and implement the new requirement called for the kind of masculine agency described by Ed White in "Use It or Lose It: Power and the WPA" (1991); aggressive and decisive action, tough talk, and strategic, preemptive moves. And indeed the situation did at times require those behaviors, but I've come to realize that the appearance of agency masked the real nature of my role. In fact, my role was primarily that of caretaker, the "minister" of proficiency in the sense that the OED defines *minister*, as "one who acts under the authority of another, who carries out executive duties as the agent or representative of another." After all, I was appointed not to make policy, but to manage and "care for" an already-formulated policy, one deeply imbricated in the local cultural ideal of certifiable writing proficiency for all. I was acting under its authority and executing my duties through its agency. Of course, none of this was clear to me at the time, so caught up was I in day-to-day triage.

Not incidentally, this local cultural ideal of "proficiency" was often described and defended in masculine terms—the requirement was "tough," "rigorous," and "demanding"; its assessment practices were "objective" and "impersonal"; they "maintained standards." Even the program's most virulent critics never questioned the idea or value of writing proficiency. Indeed, their attacks were always prefaced by mantra-like homages to the necessity and importance of writing proficiency and accompanied by the claim that they supported a writing proficiency requirement, just not this one.

In retrospect, I have come to identify my work in defending and implementing my program's proficiency policy as a kind of emotional labor that can be instructively read through feminist theory, specifically through the theories of sociologist Arlie Russell Hochschild and philosopher Sandra Bartky. Although their work often focuses either on commercial caregiving jobs like those of airline attendants or caregiving in the context of intimate heterosexual relationships, their discussion of both the emotional and ethical costs exacted by such caregiving resonates with my experience.

In her groundbreaking study *The Managed Heart: Commercialization of Human Feeling* (1983), Hochschild defines emotional labor as requiring "one to induce or suppress feeling in order to sustain the outward countenance that produces the proper state of mind in others" (7). For example, the flight attendant simulates pleasure and enjoyment for the benefit of the airline passengers to whom she's serving food and drink. Conversely, the bill collector suppresses empathy for the debtor in order to carry out the job of collecting on the debt. "Whereas flight attendants do emotion work to enhance the status of the customer and entice further sales by their friendliness," Hochschild explains, "there is another side of the corporate show, represented by the bill collectors who sometimes deliberately deflate the status of the customer with distrust and anger" (16). In both cases, the pretense or "trained management of feeling" can be costly for the worker: "it affects the degree to which we listen to feeling and sometimes our very capacity to feel" (21).

In my role as "minister" or caretaker of the proficiency requirement, I often felt compelled to induce certain feelings and suppress others. For example, I felt pressured to express an unequivocal enthusiasm for the requirement publicly lest any suggestion of doubt give fuel to opponents' fire. I felt a need to constrain my sympathies for distraught students who failed portfolio assessment lest too much sympathy instill false hopes that I would reverse the readers' decision. And I felt a need to suppress my own defensive anger in response to hostile students or parents who became strident or verbally abusive lest I compromise my credibility and authority.

While most jobs require some management of feeling, Hochschild contends that if we are too successful in censoring private feelings and publicly performing contrary ones, we risk "losing the signal function of feeling" (21).

Drawing on Freud's notion that feelings perform a "signal" or epistemic function in revealing inner perspectives and external realities, Hochschild writes, "[l]ike hearing or seeing, feeling provides a useful set of clues in figuring out what is real" (30–31). As the above examples suggest, my ministration of the proficiency requirement produced what seemed like irresolvable emotional conflicts. In order to defend and care for the requirement, I felt I must suppress doubts and emotions that threatened my ability to carry out my job successfully. To deal with this discomfort, I developed a certain myopia in which I focused on carefully orchestrating my verbal and emotional responses to the crisis of the day, thereby forestalling the larger ethical questions about the value of the requirement and its material impact on students' lives.

Particularly useful to me in understanding these deeply mixed feelings and the resulting loss of perspective has been the work of Sandra Bartky, who extends Hochschild's analysis to consider more fully the consequences of emotional labor for women caregivers. In "Feeding Egos and Tending Wounds: Deference and Disaffection in Women's Emotional Labor" (1990), Bartky argues that female caretaking puts an epistemic and ethical "lean" on the caretaker's perspective. Bartky claims that caretaking involves epistemic risks for the female caretaker in that she "accepts uncritically 'the world according to him'" and has "corresponding difficulty in constructing a world according to herself" (110–11). This assumption of another's perspective, this overidentification with the other, Bartky says, is "part of the caretaker's job" (111). Similarly, the ethical risks in caregiving are that one adopts the other's values along with the other's view of reality. In short, an "ethical lean, like the epistemic lean may rob the caregiver herself of a place to stand" (113).

I'd like to expand on Bartky's analysis a bit here by considering the differing but related meanings of the homonyms *lean* and *lien*. The term Bartky uses is *lean*, "to bend or slant away from the vertical," "to incline the weight of the body so as to be supported," "to exert pressure." Metaphorically, Bartky suggests that the pressure or weight of supporting another psychically and emotionally bends or hobbles the posture or position of the one serving as the ballast or support. But it seems to me that the term "lien" is an equally suggestive metaphor. A "lien" is, of course, an economic and legal hold on one's property, a proprietary claim on one's material status. In the examples of caretaking cited by Bartky—marriage, service jobs—the obligation that binds the caretaker to the husband or job is material as well as psychological.

Similarly, I realize in hindsight that I felt there was a "lien" on my title as Coordinator of Composition, an unspoken prior obligation to carry out the agenda of the dean, who appointed me and who avidly supported the proficiency requirement, who was, indeed, a key architect of the "new" version of the requirement. That is, I felt that my professional status and material condition—recognition as a successful coordinator, future promotions, merit raises, etc.—depended upon my ability to implement the new requirement.

Although I was well aware that others understood the term *proficiency* differently than I and that its popular meaning entailed repressive notions that I wanted to resist—gate-keeping and surveillance; positivistic measurements of writing performance; stable, overly simple definitions of "proficiency"—I believed that I could appropriate this term for critical pedagogical ends. That is, by instituting a more progressive form of assessment, defining proficiency in ways that valued critical thinking and intellectual risk-taking over formal correctness, promoting critical pedagogies, and creating a progressive curriculum, I thought I could disassociate the program from the conservative pull of this cultural ideal. In the end, I believe I was appropriated by it. As Bartky explains, the need to "cheerlead" for the other requires one to construct "elaborate rationales that aim, by reconceptualization to make the [other's] failures less terrible or . . . not failures at all but rather problems to be solved within the given economy of meaning" (103).

What I could not see at the time was the way in which my perceptions—that is, my identification of problems and my construction of solutions—operated within a restricted "economy of meaning" shaped by the proficiency requirement. The adjustments that I and my colleagues made in response to problems, and there were many, all preserved the essential features of the requirement: standardized assessment and uniform application. So caught up in defense and repair of the requirement was I that I was literally unable to formulate an independent standpoint from which to assess the situation and act. Epistemically, this lean/lien shaped how I accessed my disciplinary knowledge about writing and writing instruction. Ethically, it resulted in my rationalizing that the uniform requirement that allowed no exceptions was "fair" and turning a blind eye to the ways in which it was inevitably "unfair," failing as it did to accommodate individual students' extenuating circumstances.

Although this narrative of institutional collaboration is clearly local and context-bound, I think it has some broader implications. First, I think that all writing program administration involves ministration or service in the name of other agencies and agendas and we ignore this or are blind to it to our own detriment. Second, I think that overidentification with an idea, principle, policy, or programmatic model can lead to the kind of epistemic and ethical "lean" Bartky discusses even if the idea or principle is far more enlightened than the notion of certifiable proficiency for all. In other words, caretaking of even noble principles can be blinding and can work against self-critique.

Further, I think that women administrators may be more vulnerable to overidentification. Part of this comes from our socialization to attend to and defer to others and to doubt our own epistemic authority, and part of this comes from others' perception that we are "wedded" to our work. In their 1996 *WPA* article, for example, Wendy Bishop and Gay Lynn Crossley recount an incident in which a senior English faculty member said to Gay Lynn shortly after she had become a WPA: "It must be hard to be you. You are your work"

(75). The summer after the Faculty Senate effectively eliminated the proficiency requirement, I had a similar, and even more chilling encounter with this perception. At a luncheon following a meeting of advisors, recruitment officers, and others planning summer orientation for new freshmen, the Director of Recruitment turned to me and said, "I hope you will think this is funny but when I told someone who all was coming to this meeting and I mentioned your name, he said, 'Oh, I heard she died.'"

Intraprogrammatic Collaborations and the Ongoing Need for Critical Self-Reflection

Since the demise of the proficiency requirement, which happily did not also result in my demise, I have experienced an enormous sense of relief and liberation. Since that time, our collaborative administrative team has worked energetically to accomplish numerous programmatic reforms: gone is the anonymous large-scale portfolio assessment and in its place is small-group portfolio assessment in which teachers can discuss their students' writing and appeal other group members' decisions; gone are the formulaic, arhetorical criteria for assessment and in their place are criteria tied to the newly articulated, rhetoric-based program goals, which, although developed independently, echo those articulated by the Conference on College Composition and Communication's Outcomes Task Force. In addition, we have begun a peer mentoring program for new TAs, and two of our graduate WPAs have launched a series of Brown Bag workshops for sharing teaching ideas among new and veteran teachers. And in addition to all this, we have reconceived the first- and second-semester curricula and restructured the basic writing curricula. In short, we have been very busy and very task-oriented.

With some of these initial reforms completed, with the reflection prompted by our self-study, and, truth be told, with the writing of this essay, however, I have begun to wonder to what extent my preoccupation with and enthusiasm for these programmatic changes blinded me to the "lean/lien" (in both senses) our collaboration placed on the graduate WPAs. How free have they felt to challenge my ideas about program reform? Have they sometimes felt compelled to defend or act as cheerleaders for programmatic policies that they didn't necessarily endorse? What do their differently situated relationships to the program mean for our relationship and work together?

I owe these self-reflective questions to the graduate WPAs, who began to raise my consciousness about the significance of our differently situated roles in the program in the context of our self-study. As I reviewed their reflective writing and recollected our conversations, I began to see a connection I had not heretofore seen between the emotional labor I had expended in "caring" for the institutional proficiency requirement and its attendant ethical costs and the emotional labor and ethical costs entailed in being a graduate WPA collaborator.

While I certainly cannot answer the above questions from the perspective of a graduate WPA, I can suggest some of my own recent insights. Before our self-study, I had not considered sufficiently the relationship between our different positions in the program and the resulting differences in emotional investment and labor, but the reflections of the graduate WPAs have prompted me to do so. As Laura Micciche, a graduate WPA at the time of our self-study, explained, "the very real material differences [in our locations in the academy] have an affective structure that is worth mention. . . . Non-official administrators like graduate students are generally invested in their work as a form of professional development and not necessarily as a 'career.'" For them the work was "temporary," for me more "permanent"; for them it was a form of professional development that might or might not be a part of their later careers; for me, it was a career choice, at least for the time being. Despite my sometimes very mixed feelings about being a WPA, I was deeply invested in succeeding at this job. By contrast, the graduate WPAs were understandably ambivalent toward this work.

On the one hand, graduate students are told that administrative experience improves their chances of landing a tenure-track job in Rhetoric and Composition; on the other hand, they are warned against accepting a job that involves WPA work before tenure. The collaborative nature of the administrative work they do as graduate WPAs is touted as good job preparation, yet as job candidates they need to be able to claim individual credit for achievements. They are encouraged to invest time in expanding their curriculum vitae with professional development activities such as WPA work, while at the same time they are told that all this is a distant second to their scholarly performance, which is ideally verified by pre-job-search publications. And finally, they are expected to make commitments of time and energy to the long-term well-being of a program of which they are only temporarily a part and for which only the "official" administrator will get most of the credit and material rewards.

In our work together, however, I often failed to consider the differing emotional investments that quite naturally follow from our differently situated positions in the program. Because we made many decisions together and shared in the design of curricula and assessment procedures, I assumed that the graduate WPAs felt the same way I did when some aspect of the program succeeded or failed, was praised or criticized, and this expectation, in turn, required of them a form of emotional labor. Unintentionally, I often put subtle or not-so-subtle pressure on them to induce or suppress feelings that mirrored my own and that affirmed my reading of a given situation. Moreover, I looked to them for camaraderie and emotional support in a department that seemed largely disinterested in my work. I frequently turned to them to seek advice or to rehearse a difficult decision in the hopes of gaining their affirmation: "We understand; what else can you do?" To challenge my perceptions or the legitimacy of my affective response was obviously uncomfortable, if not risky, for them. After all, in addition to being their administrative supervisor, I was also a member of many of their dissertation committees. In short, I have come to realize that collaborative administration between faculty and graduate WPAs, especially when it seems to be working well, can create for the faculty WPA a false illusion of equality, one that does not acknowledge adequately differences in status nor the epistemic and ethical lean/lien such differences can create for graduate WPAs.

Like the earlier narrative of institutional collaboration, this account of intraprogrammatic collaboration is local and context-bound, shaped by particular personalities and relationships. However, here too, I would argue that the insights gleaned have broader implications. Plainly, the critical self-reflective work that Goodburn and Levernz call for in the epigraph to this essay is vital to a collaboration that would respect differences in position and allow for differences in perspective and emotional response. Without the critical self-reflection entailed in our self study, it is unlikely that I would have come to understand how some of my behaviors place emotional and ethical strains on the graduate WPAs with whom I work. For starters, then, it is crucial that collaborative teams build in time for this kind of ongoing individual and collective critical self-reflection. Beyond this, I think we need to hear more narratives from the perspective of graduate WPAs, and we need to address issues of status difference, conflict, and emotional labor explicitly in our training of graduate WPAs.

To date, few graduate students have written about their ambivalent relationship to this form of professional development or about their complex feelings toward the faculty WPAs with whom they collaborate. Rather, most narratives by graduate writing program administrators have focused on the emotionally fraught relationships with peers, the fellow graduate students they supervise (see Brown 1999; Jukuri and Williamson 1999). An exception is Goodburn and Leverenz's "Feminist Writing Program Administration: Resisting the Bureaucrat Within." While their emphasis is on their own failure to "recogniz[e] and reflec[t] on [their] inscription in dominant and dominating ideologies of labor and management" (277), they also discuss their conflicts with the faculty WPA (284–85, 287–88). Not only are narratives like Goodburn and Leverenz's useful in raising the consciousness of faculty WPAs but also they provide instructive reading for new graduate WPAs.

Finally, however, the greater ethical responsibility to engage in ongoing critical self-reflection lies with the faculty WPA who is the one responsible for the design and implementation of a particular program's collaborative arrangements. While I do not agree with Sheryl Fontaine, who argues that we should abolish the practice of appointing graduate WPAs since it fosters competition and exploitation, I do agree that we need to rethink how we do so. Specifically, I think we need to devote far more attention to the training of graduate WPAs and to providing them support for this often emotionally demanding work, perhaps in the form of a mentor who is a former grad WPA.

Conclusion

All writing program administration, I would argue, involves not only institutional collaboration but also intraprogrammatic collaboration. No matter how independent a program may seem, there are always institutional constraints and "liens," and no matter what the formal administrative arrangements, WPAs cannot accomplish much if they do not enlist the help and support of those who teach in the program. Yet the work of such collaborations generally and the emotional dimensions of this work specifically are invisible in a material sense and largely untheorized. In academic culture, argues Bruce Horner (2000), the labor that is valued is intellectual labor that can be commodified in the form of a single-authored scholarly text (2). In these terms, the emotional work entailed in the collaborative writing program administration is simply not work at all. By definition, it's not intellectual, not commodifiable as a product, and not the work of a single person. Mara Holt and Leon Anderson (1999) refer to the emotional labor of writing program administration as "disappearing" work because it is work that is "in" people and therefore invisible.

Despite the invaluable contribution of the WPA position statement on "Evaluating the Intellectual Work of Writing Administration" in validating WPA work, it reifies the distinction between intellectual and emotional labor and ignores the less visible and commodifiable aspects of our work. While I am not suggesting that we add an addendum to this document on emotional labor, I am suggesting that scholarly work like Laura Micciche's recently published "More Than a Feeling: Disappointment and WPA Work" (2002) is sorely needed. For, as I trust my narratives illustrate, attention to the affective dimensions yields new knowledge and raises important ethical questions.

Note

1. As a research team, we wish to thank the Council of Writing Program Administrators for the grant that partially funded this research. Additionally, I wish to thank Virginia Chappell for her invaluable comments on earlier versions of this essay.

Chapter Eleven

No Hard Feelings

Downsizing and the Limitations of Pathos in the Academic Workplace

William W. Wright

When I first heard that I was to be downsized from my job as an assistant professor at a small college in New York State, I got angry. I had bought the ethical argument that we would do well if we did good, I had believed many of the encomia to community, and now I was out of one job and in a somewhat unexpected and desperate search for another. "This must be a mistake," I thought, "or worse, a conspiracy." Like a lot of small colleges, College X had its share of budget shortfalls, generational tensions, and political intrigue. It should have come as no surprise then that the best plan to align a vaguely deficient budget was to dismiss a number of their best junior faculty. Despite how easy it was to understand and interpret the college's actions, losing a job hurt. I was at turns angry, sad, pitiful, and funny.

The discourse of and around our downsizing took two forms. The official discourse of letters, meetings, and pronouncements embraced logos and either avoided the pathetic appeal entirely or employed it to anticipate counterargument and build ethical appeal. "No hard feelings," which we were told more than once, came to mean "no feelings at all," at least not for us. No one said, "This is going to hurt me a lot more than it will you," but that paternalistic anticipation of the ethical appeal of suffering was present in every comment about how difficult it was to proceed with the plan.

Downsizing by its nature resists any individual ethical interpretation or response on the part of the downsized. Institutions cut positions and ignore people. Outside of indignation, we are not allowed much room to respond. "It's not about you" was both the justification for firing us without reference to our record and a line of comfort from our friends, and it served to reduce those of us dismissed to objects rather than agents of discourse. Pathos, the rogue and trickster in Aristotle's trivium of appeals, was reduced as well. Any indignation, righteous anger, sadness, or love that we might have expressed in resistance to the turn of events was ignored or employed in service to the inexorable and passionless arguments from logos.

The unofficial discourse of coffees, emails, and conversations was much more, and more often, pathetic. Colleagues both supportive and dismissive cried, expressed disappointment at what seemed to them a broken covenant, worried over their own jobs, or manufactured false hopes for a positive resolution. Students expressed anger, surreptitiously passed petitions and gossip in class, and told jokes. I was teaching Business Communication at the time and working hard to encourage the students to examine and critique the rhetorical and material conditions of business discourse. The course is one that bridges the gap between theory and practice and between college and community. Nevertheless, we did not take up my situation as a topic for exploration despite the fact that all the students knew. They addressed the topic indirectly in class and passionately in their evaluations. What was interesting about both the official and unofficial discourse was how little of it those of us directly involved produced. We became sites where feeling could privately be expressed, where pathos could be vented or employed in support of arguments from ethos and logos.

Outside of shame and anger, the pathetic appeal carries little weight in the academic workplace. Should it? If the dismantling of a college's community and hobbling of its future are not an occasion for pathos, what is? Critics of the academy, such as Megan Boler (1999), have pointed out that the emotions are most often employed and encouraged as a means of teaching self-control. In *Feeling Power: Emotions and Education*, Boler uses the term "pastoral power" to identify the means by which the emotions are employed to produce "individuals [who] are policed and disciplined through modes of internalized control" (1999, 21). She has also suggested that our witnessing of the "politics of anger and fear" can offer a site for resistance to that control. I want to offer a discussion of the limitations of pathos in the academic workplace by addressing the contact zone between institutional, logos-based versions of my own downsizing and individual, ethos-based versions. From there we will turn to the more difficult task of setting out a theory of workplace pathos that I think will be of use to many of us who study rhetoric and work in the academy.

Logos and Ethos in the Discourse of Downsizing

The details of our pending dismissal were simple. Finding himself between the rock of a limited or overcommitted budget and the hard place of a top-heavy and graying faculty, the vice president for academic affairs (AVP) cut seven positions from a faculty of roughly 200. Three of those seven were junior faculty entering their fourth, fifth, and sixth years of service to the college. The college community was prepared for these cuts in the following manner. Rumors of a budget crisis and lost jobs began to circulate early in the fall, producing fear and its attendant reflection. A faculty meeting was held in mid-October to address budget concerns and to put down rumors that the trustees had recommended that all junior faculty be dismissed. For many of the faculty present, this was the first we had heard of such rumors. The college treasurer offered an historical tour of the numbers of faculty and students, and then the AVP stated that cuts in the faculty were likely though not in the numbers that had been suggested unofficially.

Unconsciously and rather artfully, the unofficial discourse had raised anxieties through pathos while the official discourse sought to lower anxiety through logos, and the administration reaped the ethical benefit of telling us that things were not as bad as we had been encouraged to fear. Following questions about the advisability of cutting junior faculty and the availability of monies from the endowment and other sources, the AVP sought to reassure the tenured faculty that this trimming was nothing like the major cuts of the 1970s nor the publicity disaster visited on a sibling institution for cuts it made in the 1980s.

Those of us affected began to hear that we were going to be dismissed about one week before individual meetings with the dean made it official. This period of time allowed or forced us to calm down, to apply reason to our imaginations, and to school our emotions. If anything, the unofficial discourse made official actions seem only ceremonial, a recognition that the time for rhetorical deliberation had passed. As if to reinforce the now arhetorical nature of the situation, the first words out of the dean's mouth were something to the effect of, "I suppose you have heard about the job cuts." At the meeting, the dean assured me that she was sad to see me go, that she was disappointed in the dismissal of efforts to suggest an alternative plan for encouraging early retirements, and that she was certain that the college would carry on without us. She also told me I would be receiving an official letter from the AVP.

That letter was just one of the many rubber balls of comment and response that bounced quietly around the campus over the next ten months. In it, the AVP argued that regardless of our possible value to the college, he was recommending that we receive terminal contracts in the spring so that the budget could be "brought more into line." The appeal to numbers was meant to echo the claim of "no hard feelings." Logical appeals work best, as Aristotle points out in both the *Rhetoric* and the *Poetics*, when they can project an aura of inevitability. Nothing projects inevitability better than a budget. My invited response to that letter made a case for the continued commitment to innovation that junior faculty represented, argued for the need of experts in rhetoric and cultural studies, and suggested that my dismissal would inadvertently sanction the unethical behavior of a few colleagues in my own and another department.

Outside of self-righteous indignation, there was little pathos in my letter or in the responses of other terminated faculty. While we evidenced our indignation and righteous anger, we did not mention the personal and particular situations that might have inspired pity or moved us back into the position of agent—the new child in the family of one us, for instance, or the immigrant parents who depended on the salary of another. In those letters and in our other official actions as teachers and community members, we practiced a pathos of absence. We did not speak out officially, in part to maintain the ethical high ground of victim, and in part because our situations were already and unofficially well known.

The institutional version of these events is made up of budgets and systems. There were no evil agents, only discursive practices that necessitated dismissal and limited debate. Logos reigned supreme. The outcome of events became inevitable regardless of individual activity. In *The Postmodern Organization* (1993), William H. Bergquist offers the pendulum and the fire as the modern and postmodern metaphors for contemporary organizations. The modern organization works with what Bergquist calls first-order changes. These changes are actions that occur within the conventional system and which are easily reversed if the need arises. In our case, the pendulum of budget expenditures was beginning to swing too much in one direction. Much like adjustments in the prime lending rate by the Federal Reserve, our dismissals were a proactive adjustment meant to push the pendulum back the other way. Emotion was either absent or hidden, and the assumption was that we could be hired back with no hard feelings.

Apart from the mix of anger and embarrassment that comes from being marked for termination, the surprising and frustrating part of the experience was how quickly those of us facing dismissal moved from agents to objects in the discourse of downsizing. The accumulation of student petitions, appeals, committee reports, letters of explanation, and sympathetic comments served to catch us up in the discourse of insignificance and absence. We were mourned even as we continued to work and teach. Our profiles on campus increased but only in so far as others made us larger objects of discussion. Expressions of sympathy and interest tended to reinforce the claim in the official discourse that this wasn't about us, that our dismissal was an issue of numbers rather than talent.

Systems made certain outcomes more certain. Tenure and our lack of it, for instance, served to drive a wedge between older faculty and younger faculty on how the college should best proceed and what the place was for seniority on campus. On the other hand, the fact that most of the affected faculty were long-serving offered a different argument on seniority to the younger faculty. There was nothing cumulative about our years of service, nor would there be for theirs. We were no safer or more vested than when we had first arrived. Pathos followed logos. This turn of events served to frighten rather than enrage the newer junior faculty and so limited any attempts at collective comment or action.

The individual version of the story, with all its evocation of ethos and its comfort in conspiracy theories, is more fun to tell. A traditional reading might begin with villains and heroes. The potential villains in this case are many. The AVP's credentials include failing to seek faculty input on the budget crisis, the seeming heartlessness of singling out long-serving junior faculty, the scuttling of faculty senate attempts to revise the grievance procedure and policy for dismissal, the limiting of appeals committees to comments on budget numbers only, rejecting the advice of deans and senior faculty, and being a hatchet man for the president of the college. The president's candidacy for villainy rests largely on his indifference and silence. He spent the bulk of his time fiddling with the physical plant while the budget burned. He failed to respond to appeals from across the campus. He alienated independent thinkers in the administration to the point where they left for other jobs. He was shameless in sending out spokespersons to be conveniently misquoted in the local media.

Some of the minor devils might include the chair and old guard of the English department who knew just enough about cultural studies to engage in a self-righteous campaign of secret meetings and character assassination, program directors who benefited from but did not defend the administrative work of junior faculty, and those few members of the faculty who cultivated a compliant ignorance and silence to the workings of the college. For them, questions about the status of junior faculty were as pointless as questions about the salaries of departmental adjuncts or the secretarial staff. None of these groups sought to instigate our downsizing, but their discourse directly and indirectly led to it.

The potential heroes in this case are few. Again, the AVP might qualify for taking painful action in a budget crisis, deflecting criticism of the president, and setting up an appeals process. The various faculty and administrators who offered alternatives and resistance would also qualify because of their interest and hard work, as would the students who put their faith and energy in petition and complaint. Those of us affected were heroic only in our inaction, in the silence and diligence with which we went about our teaching, in the grace with which we accepted sympathy, praise, or anger. We were tropes employed by others, serving other arguments, heroic only in so far as we made a good show of our inevitable martyrdom. The only expression of agency we were offered was to concur, gossip, or, in my case, quit.

An institutional version of the ethos story is likely to concentrate on the attractions of powerlessness and the dangers of empathy. The trope of victim, which we might assume is available only to the terminated individuals, leaks and spreads. It was difficult to keep clear the space between agent and subject, victim and victimized. Everyone involved in the discourse of this particular downsizing could seek out sympathy by claiming, unofficially, to be a victim. We were told repeatedly by administrators and their advocates that their hands were tied. "It's the system," they would say sadly. The college was presented as a victim of rumor and false information. Public attention or intramural condemnation did not result in anger at the college's actions so much as it did sympathy for the college's suffering. Students were victims of misinformation.

When such misinformation turned up in the local paper or when students congratulated us on the false rumors of our pardon, we would seek to correct them, and as often as not, they would express hurt at the correction. The lack of any admitted agent to the misinformation and the sense that somehow the college was now the victim made it impossible to ascribe ethical responsibility and made it seem mean-spirited to demand retraction.

Throughout its history, rhetoric has had to find a place for pathos, and more often than not, that place has been in service to logos. Throughout their histories as well, philosophy and psychology have also had to come to terms with the affective domain. Mary M. Garrett (1993) has argued that Western rhetoric, as presented to us in Aristotle, has tended to subjugate pathos to the service of logos. As she puts it, "To the extent that the emotions are regarded as irreducible to the cognitive they are irrational, uncontrollable, potentially dangerous phenomena" (1993, 20). Aristotle himself in the *Rhetoric* suggests that arousing "emotions has nothing to do with the essential facts, but is merely a personal appeal to the man who is judging the case" (1354A, 17–19). Western rhetoric, philosophy, and psychology continue to struggle with the tension between mind and body. Emotions have been consigned to body and defined as physical conditions that we should seek to control with the mind.

The popularization of the emotional intelligence movement can also be seen as an attempt to gain control. Daniel Goleman's *Emotional Intelligence* argues that our failure to recognize, accept, and reflect on emotions is responsible for much of the individual violence in our culture. His last chapter is called "Schooling the Emotions," and in it he says this: "The bedrock of character is self-discipline; the virtuous life, as philosophers since Aristotle have observed, is based on self-control" (1995, 285). Megan Boler has offered a critique of Goleman that compares his discussion of self-control with early twentieth-century discussions of mental hygiene. She suggests that emotional intelligence is social control and that the emotional agent in Goleman is "still the *man* of reason" (1999, 60) whose job it is to get control of feelings in service to success. Boler concludes her discussion of Goleman by pointing out this contradiction: "emotions are simultaneously explained as neurobiological processes beyond our individual control, which we are nonetheless expected to control through our industry and education" (64).

In our own work as teachers and in our own workplaces, pathos is circumscribed and sanctioned. Any tears and anger over our dismissals were expressed unofficially or within the confines of the dean's office. Pathetic appeals to the particular conditions of the terminated were discouraged. Those of us affected were scrupulously careful to avoid them. In our celebrations and condemnations of expressivist and postexpressivist classrooms, we are also circumscribing the role of pathos. Mary Louise Pratt (1991) suggests that the classroom in the contact zone is a "safe house" where each of us can see and hear our culture(s) objectified and resisted. The safe house of a composition classroom might allow for tears and intuition, but in doing so it sets out the boundaries for their expression. One way to read the new workplace of casual Fridays, company retreats, video games, and climbing walls is to suggest that institutions are recognizing the affective domain by sanctioning it and, indirectly, controlling it. If we cannot stop pathos, better to design a way to purge it.

The Limitations of Pathos

At this point, the limitations of pathos should be clear. When pathos is employed in the academic workplace, it is employed in service to logos and ethos. When pathos is not of use to arguments from logos and ethos, it is schooled, vented, or disciplined. When it cannot be adequately disciplined, it is marked off as unofficial or embraced by everyone. And whenever pathos is present, whether as servant, student, or deviant, it tends to objectify the subject of the discourse and limit the space for rhetorical action.

Plato's charioteer allegory presents a model of pathos in service to logos and ethos. Logos is the clearheaded charioteer resisting the madness of appetite embodied in the disobedient horse. In Socrates' retelling of the myth of the origins of writing in the *Phaedrus*, we have a model for the schooling of pathos. The god Thamus dismisses the invention of writing with the complaint that it "will produce forgetfulness in the minds of those who learn to use it" (275A 1–2). Socrates adds to the complaint with the claim that written texts are mute, that they will not respond to queries, and that, "if you question them, wishing to know about their sayings, they always say only one and the same thing" (275D 9–10). In the discourse of downsizing, pathos is fixed on paper, whether in the self-righteous letter or the earnest petition. And once fixed on paper, the argument does not lend itself to repeating officially. Our written texts are both eloquent reminders and instruments of control. Why repeat an argument that you have made more clearly on paper? Why repeat the pathetic appeal when the audience for that appeal says, "I know. You've said that already" or "I feel bad about this, too"? The problem or lesson here is not that these written texts are incapable of being interrogated. The problem is that they can be filed and forgotten. They contain pathos both in that pathos is in them and in that it cannot easily get back out.

Toward a Theory of Pathos in the Academic Workplace

Despite these limitations, pathos still has something to offer us as we examine the rhetoric of the academy. In developing a theory of pathos in the academic workplace we should ask what we want beyond the industrial or utopian models of the college community, and what we want from the power of feeling in addition to anger, distress, and discomfort. That theory will have to attend to the idea of love and will need to address the concepts of pleasure, wholeness, recognition, transgression, and kinship.

If we are going to celebrate pedagogies of anger and distress and discomfort, and we should, then we must also recognize the place for pleasure, even joy, in those pedagogies. Teachers and students can stay angry and uncomfortable only for so long and to limited ends. Logical appeals to the political benefits of anger as a way to resist hegemony and ethical appeals to distress as the noble condition of learning will not, by themselves, move us to the places in the future where we would hope to go. As human beings, however we construct the term, we remain more than simply logical and ethical. If there is one central tenant to a theory of pathos in the academic workplace, then this is it: if we take pleasure in the things we do, in the discourses that we employ, then we are likely to keep doing them—not as a means of social control or self-policing but as a way to social action. Ignoring pleasure is finally to ignore and subjugate pathos all over again. There are plenty of bad feelings available in the academic workplace and in the discourses of downsizing. The downsized are allowed distress at the reification of the system; administrations are allowed distress at the accusations of heartlessness and at their untenable positions; the community is allowed distress and fear over broken covenants and future disappointments. All the more reason to explore and embrace the pleasures provided in recognition and love. To be happy does not necessarily mean to be atomistic, complacent, or complicit.

A theory of workplace pathos should begin with whole people and the methods for treating them as such. When we divide rhetoric into parts, the idea of wholeness is lost, and pathos suffers most from the division. We need to reunite pathos to its more successful siblings, logos and ethos. Such a theory should force us to recognize the place for pathos in the local decision-making processes of educational institutions. We should also recognize that the decisions, actions, and discourses of an academic institution suffer when they fail to attend to the whole that is rhetoric and the whole person that is an employee. This focus on practice echoes Thamus' complaint in the *Phaedrus* about the invention of writing. He is concerned that the presence of a disembodied discourse will force learners to concentrate on the collection of reminders rather than on the practice of memory. This complaint should be familiar to any of us who have struggled to define academic disciplines by their methods rather than, as is commonly done, by their contents. Socrates' concern that writing will not answer to dialectic extends the complaint. The thing that is missing from the mute discourse of writing for Socrates is the whole person, the pathetic agent.

Academic workplaces need to attend to their practices as well as to their memories, traditions, and systems. We often take the history of a discipline for the discipline itself and the memory of its contents for the practice of its methods. Socrates' critique of writing and his celebration of love as an act of recognition reminds us that, at their best, doctors and rhetoricians treat the whole person at a specific point in time. Emotions are a local phenomena and the pathetic appeal is the local appeal, the one most dependent on the moment and the relationship between audience and speaker. The pathetic appeal is also the most rhetorical in that it cannot be understood without its context. Rhetoric, we tend to forget, is first and foremost the art of speaking, the gathering and moving of an audience. A letter of logical disagreement over the rationale for downsizing is transferable. The tears, laughter, anger, or joy that downsizing might produce are both more powerful and more fragile because of their contextual nature and their brief shelf life. Our understanding of the whole person is not a function of knowledge but of treatment. This is particularly true of the rhetorician, for she is a necessary generalist and is expected to move the soul. Treating the whole person demands recognition and attention to pathos.

A theory of workplace pathos cannot ignore the necessary and quotidian pleasures of recognition. We need to speak out and to speak to one another. In his discussion of movement in the *Rhetoric*, Aristotle recognizes a relationship between recognition, pleasure, wholeness, and the soul: "We may lay it down that Pleasure is a movement, a movement by which the soul as a whole is consciously brought into its normal state of being" (1369B 33–35). A theory of workplace pathos must recognize the need to move and the pleasure that comes in that movement. If that recognition takes place, there are consequences for how we create and maintain positions, curricula, and programs. That recognition is also not simply something that happens to us. It is a conscious act, something we do to and for others. It is a process of pathetic contact. A passionless academy would be, according to Aristotle's claim, abnormal. Reducing the academic workplace to a logos-centered enterprise or an ethos-sanctioned list of worthy participants or to a site for the production of official paper begins to suggest serious consequences. In the academic workplace, recognition or the lack of it should be a site for inquiry.

Next to the pillars of wholeness and recognition in this theory of workplace pathos, we should add the idea of pleasure. Aristotle has already reminded us that pleasure is movement, for him the movement of the soul into its natural state. Pleasure is also, of course, pathos. It is the recognition of the whole person, what Aryeh Kosman (1976) calls "coming to recognize the *beauty* of another." Boler both warns us against the easy and often gendered embrace of empathy and suggests empathy as a way to revise our classrooms and ourselves (1999, 206). Pleasure is also, finally and most importantly, rhetoric. We can establish that most clearly in a response to the condemnation of rhetoric in Plato's *Gorgias*. In the *Gorgias*, rhetoric suffers from Socrates' analogy to medicine. According to that analogy, rhetoric is cooking, the poor imitation of philosophy's more noble medicine. Rhetoric is makeup to philosophy's gymnastics.

Whatever their ethical orientation, rhetoric, cooking, and makeup are local and effective because they are pleasurable. The artful and social benefits of cooking are not to be underestimated. In the vocabulary of discourse analysis, cooking provides the occasion for an encoder, decoder, and text to interact pleasurably. The opportunities to play at a variety of selves in the use of makeup, to make one's self up, is also pleasurable. The frustration of being downsized is that one is given only the one face to wear again and again. The figure, the turn of phrase that marks much of rhetoric's long history, is pleasurable, even glamorous and enthusiastic in the dangerous Greek senses of those words. At their best these are acts of the highest form of pathos, love, for they are directed at both the self and an other. We cook and make up and turn phrases for both our own pleasure and for the pleasure of others. Any theory of workplace or classroom pathos will have to recognize that fact by way of assignments, service work, release time for students and teachers, and at the level of food, performance, and play. Pedagogies of discomfort ask us to be ethical, to do the right thing regularly. Pedagogies of pleasure, however suspect, ask us to be pathetic, to do the enjoyable thing regularly. If it is a contest between the two, then pedagogies of pleasure are going to win out. Pathos will not trump ethos, but it will remain more attractive.

For our purposes in this book, the most attractive characteristic of pathos is its awkwardness, most specifically, its ability to make a rhetorical situation awkward. However it is packaged, controlled, silenced, or ignored, pathos does not fit. It does not easily belong in the business meeting, the busy classroom, or the official work of the academy. And when it turns up in these places, it makes us uncomfortable, impatient, and, finally, thoughtful. The lesson of Plato's *Phaedrus* is that pathos transgresses. It is the disobedient horse that moves the soul toward beauty, despite fierce discipline on the part of the charioteer and disinterest on the part of the obedient horse. Pathos breaks the rules of behavior and, we would hope, exposes the assumptions upon which those rules are based. Exposing those assumptions helps us both to cross them and to bridge them.

The fact that pathos is an act of transgression and the fact that it is out of place in the academic workplace should give us some hint of its power and uses. When pathos disobeys and escapes service to logos and ethos, it exposes the foundations and divisions of our actions. Our colleagues in the business world might laugh to hear it, but the contemporary academic institution is based upon the idea of efficiency and divided into three groups of employees: those who administer budgets, those who make knowledge, and those who do physical labor. Unofficially we recognize the need and benefits of inefficiency and we cross those boundaries in the division of our labor. Officially we see these divisions as the neutral and practical way to proceed.

In making a theory of workplace pathos we need to recognize kinship in our rhetoric and in our workplace. In our rhetoric we can choose to see how logos and ethos can serve pathos. In the discourse of downsizing, for instance, logos can serve pathos by identifying when pathos can be most disruptive and by reminding us of the very practical need to repeat ourselves. Ethos can serve pathos by demanding the timely publication of emotion and by reminding us that rhetoric is a process of "recognizing the *beauty* in another." In our workplace we can recognize kinship across the lines of status, discipline, position, and ideology. We can structure classrooms, principles, and communities that choose to recognize pathos. In the discourse of downsizing, that recognition would include seeing the humanity of the people involved, making a space for downsized and downsizer to express pathos, encouraging official and unofficial oratory, and drawing the workplace community into the decisions of the college, with the recognition that these actions will make those decisions more difficult. In the everyday work of the academy, that recognition would include seeing and reaching across the divisions of labor and epistemology. None of this should be easy. If anything, increased attention to pathos in our classrooms and workplaces should make our jobs more difficult.

Rather than make our classrooms and academies into what Pratt has called a "safe house," we should recognize how and why we might choose to make them unsafe. It should be harder to fire employees once we recognize their humanity. It should be difficult to grade students if we love them. It should be disturbing to ignore our colleagues when we recognize a kinship. It should be more difficult to accept and encourage the neutral rhetoric of Lysias when we choose to value the inclusive rhetoric of Socrates. This is not to say that we should not fire each other or grade student work or encourage a variety of discourses from students. The point is to use pathos to keep ourselves humble in those firings, gradings, and encouragements. We should be nervous at our efficiencies and our successes. The cicadas of doubt should trouble our uncritical acceptance of economic models of the academic workplace and economic metaphors of academic discourse. Perhaps as rhetoricians we can hire ourselves out as inefficiency experts, ever ready to complicate an elegant logical conclusion.

As the title of this book suggests, the purpose of rhetoric is to move. Sometimes that movement is a transgression, a gesture across boundaries and categories, a re-seeing. The mirth, anger, and sympathy we construct in response to the discourse of downsizing allow for the possibility of movement in transgression. I got passionate enough or lucky enough to move from one job where I was not happy to another job where I work with colleagues and students for whom I have great affection. The presence of pathos in unexpected situations is itself a kind of motion. Emotions in the classroom and the workplace are often seen, and sometimes dismissed, as transgressive, as violating both rules and boundaries. Rhetoricians can choose to see the expression and repression of emotion in, for example, the discourse of downsizing as deliberate rhetorical acts. Exploring those acts and theorizing from them can allow us a means to bridge the gap between official and unofficial discourse in the academy and between logos and ethos in the larger culture.

Chapter Twelve

An Anatomy of Radical Anger in Writing Program Administration

Brad Peters

Situating a Definition of Radical Anger

In this volume, Ellen Quandahl closely examines the association between emotion and ethics in Aristotle's corpus. I'd like to build upon her useful insights by reiterating, in particular, Aristotle's stipulation that anger is a just response—"a desire accompanied by pain, for a conspicuous revenge for a conspicuous slight at the hands of [those] who have no call to slight oneself or one's friends" (*Rhetoric* 1378a 31–33). As such, the philosopher insists that anger is "thought not less human than reason," and that the good-tempered person tends "to be angry in the manner, at the things, and for the length of time, that reason dictates" (*Nichomachean Eihtcs* 1111a 1; 1125b 35–36). Accordingly, Aristotle asserts that "acts proceeding from anger are rightly judged not to be done of malice aforethought; for it is not the man who acts in anger but he who enraged him that starts the mischief"—and for Aristotle, it follows that "Anger is always concerned with [directed toward] *individuals*" (*NE* 1135b 26–27; *Rhetoric* 1382a 4–5, emphasis added). Those individuals may be construed as social or political inferiors, equals, or superiors; indeed, a difference in power relations may well account for the slights that induce anger. Even so, Aristotle says, "it is not easy to define how, with whom, at what, and how long one should be angry, and at what point right action ceases and wrong begins" (*NE* 1126a 32–34).

Here is the point at which I have found that anger often causes problems while teaching in and administrating a writing program. Whereas such documents as the *Students' Right to Their Own Language* (1974) suggest writing programs can become something of a social movement for providing many otherwise "unprepared" students with a means for accessing postsecondary education, we know much of our scholarship also indicates that such programs, ironically, have become structures of entrenched inequity for teachers (e.g., S. Miller 1991 and Schell 1998, "The Costs"). Consequently, writing program administrators (WPAs) sometimes have to deal with what I call a *radical* anger—often expressed by teachers in training—that interferes with students' access to education. This emotion inevitably constructs WPAs as the representatives of entrenched inequity, challenging them to seek ways to cope with the disruptions that radical anger causes without reifying the inequity.

What is radical anger? In *The Human Condition*, social theorist Hanna Arendt identifies a kind of anger that "is a natural reaction of those whom society has tried to cheat of their strength" and may contain a "vehement yearning for violence" (1958, 203–4). It is akin to what Kathleen Dixon and William Archibald call an "*outburst* . . . a response to a conflict that expresses a person's orientation to [a] conflict and to the social and political conditions that underlie it" (1998, xi). Laura Micciche notes that such anger can even become "a necessary response to inequity . . . that, historically, has functioned as a catalyst for collectively organized social movements" (2000, 34). But this anger can become radical when it also spurs an individual to act in a prolonged, extremely disruptive public manner against a policy, a practice, or often, another person whom she feels *symbolically represents* the social or political conditions that put her at a disadvantage. Just so, in our discipline, radical anger may lead a person in a writing program to the edge where her actions against something or someone constrain WPAs to respond unsupportively, even while they clearly see—and may well empathize with—the reasoning and justifications that drive her.

Let me illustrate with a specific incident that occurred at a west coast campus in a state university system, shortly after the 1997 Ebonics controversy that the Oakland School Board precipitated (see Baugh 2000). Arendt's categories of historical contexts for work (mass society, the household, and the *polis*) will help me explain some of the complex origins and motivations behind this incident, demonstrating her assertion that notions of work in the public and private domains—derived from ancient Greece—remain embedded in our postmodern expectations of how people at work should live together. My narrative begins with state legislators, who had recently decreed that the state system had to cut back all "remedial" courses in writing by 90 percent. The legislators intended incrementally to withdraw the funds for such classes until, after a six-year period, students' "preparation" for the state university underwent a sea change. Community colleges were expected to shoulder the task of teaching basic writing instead, although it remained unclear what funds would be reappropriated for that purpose. Many, including me, suspected the legislators envisioned a society whose utter diversity would be tidily sorted by its educational institutions and, to borrow Arendt's words, would be "seen under one aspect and . . . permitted to present itself in only one perspective": its categories of commercial "productivity" (1958, 58). The legislators seemed to be influenced by the notion of a writing program as an instrument of enforcing such productivity.

The legislators' decree understandably caused agitation on campus. Faculty in an ethnic studies department got out in the quads to denounce the situation over loudspeakers to the students as they passed to their classes. The faculty also selected students from their courses to perform rap lyrics that protested how those from "nontraditional" ethnic backgrounds and social classes were having their rights to an equal educational opportunity taken away. The faculty had other compelling reasons to make their concerns public. For one thing, the 90 percent reduction of basic writing would, in effect, choke the lifelines of support for the ethnic studies departments, which shared the "service responsibilities" of the English department, and like the English department, used basic writing as an effective means of recruitment as well as literacy education. But more disturbing (again Arendt's words prove useful), the ethnic studies faculty feared the legislators' attempt to alter the university curriculum (and in a larger sense, a commonly shared—but multiply perceived—world) through "the destruction of the many aspects in which it presents itself to human plurality" (1958, 58).

Although I certainly didn't oppose this agitation, it came home to me unpredictably. Our writing center hired a tutor who was an African American graduate student recommended by faculty in ethnic studies. As the semester progressed, the tutor—whom I'll call Jeanne—overtly criticized many professors' assignments as racist, deliberately avoided working with white students, and antagonized her fellow tutors. She seemed to be influenced by the notion of a writing program—and the writing center, in particular—as a *polis*, where members of the university could speak and act upon the current political situation. I became aware of as much while teaching a preservice seminar in writing instruction for teaching associates (TAs), whom I asked to visit the writing center to observe what went on and design a brochure for their future students.

When one TA (a Chicana woman) went to observe another tutor she already knew (a white woman), Jeanne asked the TA what she thought she was doing. The TA started to explain, but before she could say much, Jeanne insisted that the TA observe her instead, so the TA could "get the facts straight." The TA politely but firmly answered that she intended to finish her observation of her friend first. Jeanne berated the TA loudly for "acting white" and disrespecting people of color. She became so hostile that others—the TA, the tutor she was observing, and several students—hastened to leave.

The TA came to my office in tears the next day. Although I did not recognize it at the time, I *reacted* (an emotional response, in Arendt's terms) as if I was influenced by the notion of a writing program as a private household of which—as director of Composition in the English department—I was head. As such, I felt the urge to *re-act* autocratically (a political response, as Arendt puts it), to protect people in "our" program. I asked the TA to write a detailed account of the incident. I then telephoned the writing center administrator, with whom I enjoyed a good working relationship. My colleague told me of similar incidents that had happened. She had already tried several times to talk with

Jeanne, and Jeanne had toned down her actions temporarily each time. But the complaints did not stop, and Jeanne's anger grew increasingly defiant. Even so, my colleague feared reprisals from a number of campus sources, if she dismissed Jeanne. Her official status as "part-time" faculty (although she usually worked a 40–50 hour week) provided her with small defense against charges of racially motivated actions. And if she *did* act upon the situation, how could it *not* be racially motivated?

Given as much, I asked if the time had come for a strongly worded letter from me, advising my colleague to dismiss Jeanne, even though no reporting line existed between my colleague and me. If anyone questioned the action, I suggested that we combine the TA's written experience with the other examples my colleague had cited, to provide evidence of Jeanne's unprofessional conduct. I said I'd send a copy of the documents to our college dean. My colleague felt extremely uneasy about going this route. So did I. Besides looking as if I pulled rank on a "subordinate," I knew that anyone—faculty in ethnic studies, the Affirmative Action office on my campus, supervising administrators—could interpret my response as egregiously crossing the lines of my own untenured authority. But I followed through, believing my colleague had done all she could in her limited administrative role, leaving me to push the limits of mine. The resolution, if indeed I could even call it one, seemed fraught with inequities and provided no one with a sense of having successfully resisted those inequities—leastwise Jeanne, whose radical anger kept her from articulating an effective challenge against the much larger social issues bearing down upon, and leading to, her dismissal.

Nonetheless, there were no reprisals.

I have not begun with an edifying tale. Rather, I have chosen to do a cultural analysis that not only recounts the perpetuation of angry reactions but, as anthropologist Pierre Bourdieu might observe, also shows how institutions tend to "reproduce the objective structures of which they are the product . . . determined by the past conditions which have produced the principle of their production" (1977, 72). An objective institutional structure, I infer, is a thing that necessarily helps to organize large numbers of people, but a thing not necessarily negative or positive in and of itself. Jeanne's radical anger—rising from how she interpreted the objective structure of the writing center—constrained the situation, in Bourdieu's terms, to become "dependent on the decrees of the consciousness which creates it and hence totally devoid of *objectivity* . . . moving because the subject chooses to be moved, revolting because [s]he chooses to be revolted," where her "emotions, passions, and actions are merely games of bad faith" that, in turn, played a racially imbalanced system against itself (74). As a result, I see myself as having used other objective structures of the university—e.g., its hierarchy and my position in it—to punish Jeanne for not conforming to expectations, regardless of her sense of injustice. Arendt would most likely see this outcome as a species of "vengeance, which acts in the form of re-acting against an original trespassing, whereby far from putting an end to the consequences of the first misdeed, everybody remains bound to the process, permitting the chain reaction contained in every action to take its unhindered course" (1958, 240).

In the discussion to follow, I continue turning to Arendt as a source of important insights that I believe can help teachers and administrators consider radical anger as a force that should make WPAs re-act ethically in times of unpredictable transition. In so doing, I will reflect on one more instance where administrative reactions to radical anger led to a more promising understanding of how the emotions can affect our professional relationships and lives, as well as the objective institutional structures within which we interact. Then I will revisit the narrative I've detailed above, to consider alternative responses that a wiser WPA might have taken.

Radical Anger and Ethical Response

Let me preface my other instance of radical anger—which took place in another institution—with some extended observations. Radical anger is monomaniacal in its focus, yet megalomaniacal in its aims and search for all available means of persuasion. Its very zeal to assert its sources of pain demonstrates a compelling ethic and logic that can sometimes win over others whose *sensus communis* is shaped by similar pain. The radically angry person may collar those others—usually peers—in intensely private talks, creating an audience that is then familiar with his particular source of pain when he speaks of it in more public settings. This profoundly intuitive move to cultivate a private and public audience gives the radically angry person a rhetorical leverage that someone merely prone to outbursts does not have, even though the zeal in radical anger can "advance one's cause, and set it back simultaneously" (Dixon and Archibald 1998, xi). This move also gives him staying power, even when many (if not most) of his peers do not accept his techniques.

Just so, dealing with radical anger requires a WPA to take account of the affected person's formidable rhetorical advantage, from the perspective—as Arendt puts it—of "the Aristotelian *phila politikē* . . . a kind of 'friendship' without intimacy and without closeness" and a regard "independent of qualities which we may admire or of achievements which we may highly esteem" (1958, 243). Arendt believes this approach restores the "modern loss of respect, or rather the conviction that respect is due only where we admire or esteem" (243). A WPA must assume such an approach by actively seeking points of empathy rather than points of contention with the radically angry person. If a WPA takes a more confrontational stance—as someone who feels personally vilified or attacked—she will undoubtedly substantiate herself as the symbolic source of pain, personifying *impersonal* social and political conditions much larger than she is.

I now want to bring these observations to bear upon my account of a radically angry TA in a private, southwest university where I was introducing a more coherent plan of teacher training. Although I had been hired as a "visiting" director of Composition with a temporary appointment of five years, I had convinced faculty of the English department at least to lend moral support to an experiment in programmatic change, requiring new TAs to come together regularly in an effort to formulate a consensus of various but effective pedagogical practices. I wanted this experiment to provide the evidence for establishing a credit-bearing seminar, so that TAs wouldn't be going pell-mell into their classrooms, essentially expected to master teaching in privacy, or even isolation, under the department's longstanding premise that to achieve "competence and excellence . . . isolation from others is the necessary life condition . . . being alone with the 'idea,' the mental image of the thing to be" (Arendt 1958, 161). I use Arendt's words to emphasize that this longstanding premise defined the work of Rhetoric-Composition as a loosely constructed model of *fabrication* (associating the teaching of writing with the historical notion of an apprenticeship), extremely problematic in its implicit emphasis upon TAs achieving "a mastery of things and material and not of [relationships with] people," rendering students as "'material' upon which to work . . . losing thereby their own intrinsic 'value'" until they were made over into acceptable academic writers, however the TAs might define "academic writer" as a product (161, 155).

A TA I'll call Charlotte interpreted the steps I was taking as a threat to the way she taught composition in this working context. In an early round of class visits to all TAs, I discovered that she spent much class time lecturing about Cicero or analyzing Shakespearean monologues, asking students to memorize and recite this material, and assigning five-paragraph themes about it. She also had them write about issues oddly adapted from the *progymnasmata*, such as whether or not she should marry. She regularly had students do rote exercises in grammar workbooks, and rarely provided instruction on anything beyond line-editing skills. She told them that "Auntie Charlotte" was the only teacher they'd encounter who could prepare them for what professors really demanded. She took great pride in her approach and clearly showed an intense emotional commitment to her students. I remarked on the latter to her, but also mentioned methods that other TAs were beginning to experiment with successfully.

Charlotte seemed to perceive teaching composition as a kind of *labor* (an even more problematic definition of work that Arendt historically associates with domestic slavery) and her classroom as a kind of household. Yet at the same time, she recoiled from my project of program development because she seemed to anticipate such a program—in terms that I borrow again from Arendt—as enforcing "The sameness prevailing in a society resting on labor . . . and expressed in its conformity . . . intimately connected with the somatic experience of laboring together, where the biological rhythm of labor unites a group of laborers to the point that each may feel that he is no longer an individual but actually one with all others" (1958, 214).

I intuited as much from the way Charlotte physically sat apart from all the other TAs when she attended a few group sessions. Discursively, she set herself apart as well, contesting any point that other TAs asserted—not in contrast to her own methods but in contrast to what she anticipated were my pedagogical biases. In this sense, when she disagreed, she made an appearance of disagreeing with me, not with her peers, but only in a way that did not challenge me directly. Outside of the sessions, I often saw her discussing her dissatisfaction with TAs toward whom she felt friendly. Shortly after midterm, Charlotte informed me she was simply too busy to bother with our weekly meetings on pedagogy, our rotating schedule of visiting one another's classes, our compilation of teaching portfolios, or our flirtations with technology. She took particular exception to the listserv I'd set up for everyone's ongoing discussion. Her whole face twitched with anger during one office visit, when she told me she'd have to leave that sort of nonsense to the *technoweenies*. As I had no means to constrain her to participate (a constraint she would have openly rebelled against, in any case), I could only empathize with the problems of time management she said she faced and encourage her to participate as often as she could because, I emphasized, our group needed to hear the different perspectives she had on teaching. And to be frank, I *did* find her command of Cicero impressive. But she assured me that the TAs knew her perspectives all too well.

After her first semester, Charlotte awarded all her students a grade of "A." During her second semester, her behavior became even more disruptive—and on a larger scale. She engaged in a battle with her faculty advisor about taking two required graduate courses unrelated to Composition pedagogy. She argued that she had to focus more on classical rhetoric and canonical literature, if she were ever going to meet her own degree objectives. She was also doing weekly private lessons in Greek and Latin. Moreover, she announced that the graduate program's inadequate system of remuneration was forcing her to work overtime to support herself. Although appointment as a TA stipulated that no one could teach courses outside the university, she had taken on an additional three sections of composition at a nearby two-year college. Charlotte's anger and her tirades against department administrators became so extreme that at one point, she threatened to sue her faculty advisor and the university and at another, she wondered sarcastically if she ought to get a gun. More to the main, however, she had very close relationships with a few adjuncts in the program, and she seemed to identify much more readily with their working conditions than with the TAs', probably because these women shared her age, social background, economic status, and multiple worksite assignments. Yet she also seemed to fear permanently ending up classified as "occasional faculty," as they were, and felt the program of study she'd set for herself would assure her of a different future.

After consulting with the university counseling center, a group of us—the chair, the director of graduate studies, and me—met regularly to strategize responses to Charlotte's continued episodes of "acting out." We located a faculty member whom she respected highly and had turned to as a mentor, who also suggested compromises to us on Charlotte's behalf. When under strong protest, Charlotte enrolled in one of her required graduate courses (a seminar on research techniques), the chair asked the professor to encourage her to integrate her interests in classical rhetoric and Shakespeare. The director of graduate studies reasoned with her to give up some of her teaching overload—two of the three community college classes. The chair urged Charlotte to attend a few more pedagogical sessions with the other Composition TAs, persuading her also to adopt some of the practices that would serve her students better, especially in terms of responding to and grading their work. Although the "acting out" episodes never abated, they became less disruptive, and this collective effort programmatically sustained Charlotte until she eventually left to accept a full-time position with a two-year college.

Although I fully recognize many ethical questions that my version of this incident reveals—above all, the consultation with a counselor and the assumption that Charlotte needed to be "normalized," or brought into conformity with the objective structures of the institution—I refer to Arendt's thoughts on interactions "between people who are different and unequal" that take place in a public realm such as a university: "The equality attending the public realm is necessarily an equality of unequals who stand in need of being 'equalized' in certain respects and for specific purposes" (1958, 215). Not I alone, but others who shared my administrative concerns, felt that Charlotte had taken a self-destructive path of action that would harm her professionally in the long term and influence other TAs and students adversely in the short term. I think we intervened as humanely as we could to keep her within the objective structures that determined our relationships with one another.

Just so, this incident exemplifies how a *collective* response to radical anger helps a WPA to humanize the objective structures of an institution, even as those structures evolve to meet administrative concerns about writing programs. In my collaboration with the chair and director of graduate studies, I was also able to clarify fairly dramatically the exigency for developing a more coherent and stable program of teacher training, underscoring the benefits that the department administration, as well as students and TAs, would receive. Furthermore—and I do not present this as a toss-aside remark—we also started a related discussion about creating positions that would provide for regular continuing employment in the writing program, rather than relying on the position of "occasional faculty" to staff a number of course sections. That discussion bore results after I left for the position at the west coast campus that I mention above—and it seems worthwhile to elaborate upon it in light of WPA scholarship that debates the concept of collaborative administration.

Bureaucratic Dynamics Impinging on Conflict Management

Roxanne Mountford might say Jeanne's story and Charlotte's both emphasize that WPAs must understand "that their actions and beliefs are imbricated in the overall intellectual and political trajectory of higher education" (2002, 51).

Harrington *et al.* would suggest finding the best way to re-act to radical anger also requires the WPA to decide whether the conflict is internal to the writing program, or external—and what kinds of partnerships are possible to build in the intellectual and political context of the institution (1998, 61). Jeanne's story falls under the category of an internal conflict, because it primarily had an impact on the day-to-day operations of the writing program per se and affected the operations of the writing center and the TA training program, without coming into any immediate contact with the other objective structures of the institution. The priority, then, and the problem, consisted of how to think ethically about re-acting to *her*, while remaining sensitive to the larger events that caused her to react so angrily—as tough a task as it sounds.

Although I must still postpone addressing how I now would prefer to have re-acted, I'll note at present that our re-action involved only a very limited kind of collective response to Jeanne's radical anger—limited between the writing center director and me, resulting in what WPA scholarship has called an "authoritarian consensus" that effectively creates no more than an imposed orthodoxy that erases difference (Harrington *et al.* 1998, 60). Kurt Spellmeyer would situate such consensus within the culture of concealment that an institutional bureaucracy promotes, a culture that works "at odds with the lived experience of almost everyone" and ultimately contracts "the domain within which our thoughts can be consonant with our actions" (1998, 175). Arendt, in turn, would associate authoritarian consensus with punishment—one of the few reactions that can "put an end to something that without interference could go on endlessly" (1958, 241). These dynamics indicate the pressures that accompany the idea of the "unitary WPA" which Harrington et al. assert is "a holdover from a simple and hierarchical notion of the place of a writing program in an English department" (1998, 63). Acting in response to urgency, what the unitary WPA gains in bureaucratic expedience, he loses in negotiated wisdom. All the same, I felt pressured at the time to act accordingly, believing that I would only draw out a bad situation or make it worse by consulting anyone in an anxious ethnic studies department, or a large and territorial English department (the biggest on campus), or a besieged university administration.

On the other hand, Charlotte's story represents an external conflict because it had an impact not only upon the writing program, but also on issues and policies of the English department—with implications for other departments that employed TAs, as well. I therefore couldn't act as a unitary WPA. At the same time, the collective response that occurred among the department chair, the director of graduate studies, others, and me facilitated a "pluralistic consensus" that in fact rewarded the emotion work of writing program administration (see Holt, Anderson, and Rouzie, this volume), because key partners came to see a greater good in reforming the writing program and at least some of its contingent labor conditions. This collaboration among partners meshes with Richard Miller's advice that WPAs acknowledge the "constraining forces that shape local labor practices" (1998, 9) and take advantage of the bureaucracy that maintains them as a potential agent of change—an agent that can make the "effort to engage rather than to erase difference," provided that WPAs seize the moment to work with bureaucracy in order to "create a rhetorical environment in which conflict can be fully explored" (Duffey *et al.* 2002, 81; Harrington *et al.* 1998, 61). Bureaucracy, in this sense, promises something much more than a culture of concealment and a schism between our thoughts and actions. It promises, in Arendt's words, forgiveness as "the only reaction which does not merely re-act but acts anew and unexpectedly, unconditioned by the act which provoked it and therefore freeing from its consequences both the one who forgives and the one who is forgiven" (1958, 241).

WPA scholarship does not explore the concept of forgiveness very much, for many concrete reasons—including the many unforgivable actions that our professional lore readily recalls of our dealings with bureaucracy. Yet I find evidence in Charlotte's story that when WPAs are able to deal with radical anger in partnership with a more local, more immediate, more invested bureaucracy, forgiveness can arise—according to Arendt—"directly out of the will to live together with others in the mode of acting and speaking, and thus they are like control mechanisms" that can undo what would otherwise doom us all to be "the victims of an automatic necessity bearing all the marks of . . . inexorable laws" (1958, 246). That's not to say that I'd be ingenuous enough to advise new WPAs that occasions of radical anger are generally—or even sometimes, or even rarely—occasions to seek out audience with the representatives of our institutional bureaucracies, to discuss needed reforms in the programs we direct. A sense of *kairos* must obviously guide us so that we can make apparent the connections between radical anger and the much greater problems that such anger doesn't articulate very well. We also need to know to whom we're explaining these connections and what vocabulary will draw their attention most artfully toward equitable resolutions. We also need to be certain that bureaucratic interests are as at stake as ours, are compatible with ours, and are debatable in such a way that punishment doesn't seem the better alternative (including punishment of WPAs who appear incapable of handling the situation, alongside punishment of the radically angry person). Real forgiveness, so it turns out, demands much more work than dispensing a wafer, waving a staff, or lapsing into permissive relativism, because it points to necessary changes in the conditions that brought about radical anger in the first place. But more important, such forgiveness also acknowledges the radically angry person on a personal as well as bureaucratic level. At a historical moment when nothing short of terrorism seems to cut through the bureaucratic culture of concealment, forgiveness may be the only re-action to radical anger that can rescue us all from consequences that we once believed unimaginable and unspeakable.

Having said as much, I circle back to the issue of addressing radical anger as an internal conflict. I'll venture that most of the excellent, recent scholarship on collaboratively managed writing programs still falls short of advising a WPA how to handle such a persistently disruptive emotion (e.g., see Duffey *et al.* 2002; Goodburn and Leverenz 1998; Rickley and Harrington 2002; Powell *et al.* 2002). The prevailing assumption (or hope) seems to be that when intense emotional disruption arises, collaborative efforts will keep its affects/effects at bay so that programmatic life will go on. This assumption sidesteps the fact that much of a WPA's internal power in a program can be as precarious as that of the contingent or inexperienced faculty she directs, grown mostly from her ability to provide, as Worsham calls it, "orientation and a sense of commitment to social change" for students, while the composition instructors she directs work in a context where even an intense emotional disruption of work "does not offer a resource for critical positioning or coalition building" (Worsham 1998, 234; 230). Moreover, when a coordinating committee replaces the unitary WPA, differences between the tenured/untenured Composition faculty on the committee and prevailing hierarchies elsewhere will still undercut the articulation of meaningful partnerships for change (see Harrington *et al.* 1998). Radical anger sniffs out such powerlessness, and in affect/effect, seeks quixotically to challenge it.

So what happens, Jim Corder has asked, "if a narrative not our own reveals to us that our narrative was wanting all along" and without pause "sends us lurching, stunned by its differentness, either alarmed that such differentness could exist or astonished to see that our own narrative might have been or might yet be radically otherwise than it is?" (1994, 416). How do we manage a disruptive, angry narrative without resorting to the bureaucratic punishment that we, too, would find so devastating if it were directed at us?

Reprise

The technique that Jean-François Lyotard calls telling "little stories" lends names and narrative particularities to the emotional phenomenon of radical anger, so that when these little stories are examined within Arendt's historical analysis of working contexts and definitions of work, I can justify that radical anger is not merely a public aberration of radically weird, dysfunctional, dangerous, or eccentric individuals (1988, 155). Rather, it is an explicable, recurrent action that fairly reasonable, but inexperienced people will sometimes take against shifting working conditions that they find socially or politically overwhelming. As such, WPAs need to pay attention to its emergence, to consider what re-actions are most appropriate both on the personal and administrative levels.

How then, might I have re-acted most appropriately to the instance I earlier recounted about Jeanne, whose radical anger so disrupted the work of teacher training and writing center operations? I turn here to Corder's interpretation of *phila politikē*, the Aristotelian term recovered by Hanna Arendt. Corder has suggested a number of re-actions I could have made—reactions that all WPAs might want to keep in mind. I'll list them here: WPAs must learn ahead of time the respect owed to a person overtaken by radical anger, so as to "extend every liberty possible to her"; WPAs must dispense with firm policies and set principles, "to pursue the reality of things only partially knowable"; WPAs must try "to abandon authoritative positions," seeking shared authority with strategically positioned, concerned colleagues *and* the radically angry person, uncomfortable as that may be; WPAs must remain open to invention, so as not to "foreclose on interpretation and argument" as radical anger construes it; WPAs must study why there seem to be "only a few ways of handling the conflict," so as to find viable alternatives; WPAs must develop and assert an ethos that holds a whole cadre of others in mind, viewing matters "both as [the radically angry person] sees them and as others see them"; WPAs must respond to radical anger with "the anecdotal, personal, and cultural reflections that will make us plain to all others," when we're called upon to make complicated decisions (1994, 425–28). This approach—though it is further from any of the professional discussions we've ever had about resolving conflict—will help us learn to hear and speak "a commodious language" that raises the possibility of forgiveness, torn and distraught as radical anger may render it (Corder 1994, 428).

Trying any combination of these re-actions might have helped me succeed where I failed with Jeanne. Or perhaps I would have failed, as Corder was fond of saying, at a much higher level. Jeanne's "little story" continues to remind me that as WPAs, we are not merely dealing with advanced students. We are creating future colleagues, who, in re-action to our dealings with them, will either embrace the ethical principles that make the work of our discipline worthwhile—or they will reject them—in which case, we most certainly won't be able to justify or sustain our discipline's continuity.

Chapter Thirteen

Making Emotion Work Visible in Writing Program Administration

Mara Holt, Leon Anderson, and Albert Rouzie

Scholars from a variety of fields in recent years have endeavored to clarify and reconceptualize the range of activities that characterize the labor of college and university faculty. Ernest Boyer's *Scholarship Reconsidered* (1990), for example, has provided a much needed alternative perspective on the relationship between research and teaching. Closer to home, an MLA task force published a significant challenge to current perceptions of intellectual labor in *Profession*, "Making Faculty Work Visible" (1996). Even more recently, the Council of Writing Program Administrators has published a document on its website titled "Evaluating the Intellectual Work of Writing Program Administration." The challenge in such efforts is to acknowledge academic work that has been missed, marginalized, or demeaned in academic discourse and practice.

Our goal in this chapter is to examine one particularly significant but largely invisible kind of academic labor, which sociologist Arlie Hochschild (1983) has termed in another context *emotion work*. We want to explore the significance of emotion work for understanding the institutional lives of writing program administrators and faculty more generally. Our scope includes the sociological literature on emotion work as well as material from qualitative research that Holt and Anderson conducted with Writing Program Administrators (WPAs) in 1995–97.[1] In both formal and informal interviews with WPAs, as well as in Holt's field notes, emotion work frequently came to the foreground in the labor of writing program administration.

Emotion work refers to responsive attention to the emotional aspects of social life, including attention to personal feelings, the emotional tenor of relationships, empathy and encouragement, mediation of disputes, building emotional solidarity in groups, and using one's own or others' *outlaw emotions* to interrogate structures. The challenges of emotion work lie at the fault lines of academic organizational culture, the places where theory and practice conflict.

For example, faculty members are hired to equalize the gender, race, and increasingly, sexuality imbalance without examining the structures of labor and reward systems that were built under circumstances that no longer apply.

When Holt entered her department in 1988, for example, most faculty were men with wives who supported them emotionally, cooked for them, took care of their children, helped to manage their schedules, and even edited their work. Partly due to the feminist movement, a generational and demographic shift has brought more diversity into the department, but discourse about the situations of new faculty members has been neglected. Simultaneously the pace of scholarly production has increased and with it expectations of performance for promotion and tenure. Prior to the shift, many women coming into the department—who were expected to do emotion work in addition to the standard faculty responsibilities—chose not to have children or deferred having a family. Women who did have children paid a high price in terms of their career; they are still far from qualified to apply for promotion to full professor. More recently, men and women who enter the faculty bring with them family responsibilities. Still there's no adjustment of expectations for scholarly or emotional work.

Fault lines represent change and opportunity for growth. Now is a fruitful time to recognize that emotion work can contribute to productive change. Too often, however, emotion work is at best made invisible, at worst, completely neglected, to the detriment of academic productivity and a humane work environment. Without emotion work, conflicts are harder if not impossible to resolve. The masculinist ethic that still prevails may prevent even those who are most culturally conditioned to do emotion work (women) from doing it, and it reinforces the division between working and taking care of emotions that is strongly inscribed in school and on the job. The structures and cultures of our departments work to maintain a gendered distinction that creates a disincentive for men to do emotion work. Women are damned if they do emotion work and damned if they don't. If they do, they reinforce the gendered separation, raise expectations that they will continue to do it, and their scholarship suffers. If they don't, they disappoint those gendered expectations, pay a price, and deprive others and themselves of needed emotion work. The way out of this dilemma is recognition of the importance of emotional labor in making work a less alienating activity for all involved and in redistributing the responsibility for all kinds of work. We propose that emotion work is not merely an energy-draining expectation, but that it is personally fulfilling, and that its value should be recognized and rewarded.

Writing program administration is at the nexus of several fault lines in the academy—all those we mentioned above and more. WPAs experience and represent much of the contradiction and ambivalence of the change in university and department cultures. Thus, WPAs experience and represent much of the contradiction and ambivalence of emotion work itself. After an overview of the sociological literature on emotion work, we will demonstrate the ways in which

WPAs perceive the importance of emotion work, the gender-based character of *feeling rules* in academic environments, the potential benefits of recognizing emotion work as valid intellectual labor, and some possible means for doing so.

Sociological Literature on Emotion Work

The climate that WPAs work in—emotion work performed but not acknowledged—isn't of course limited to writing program administration. When sociologist Arlie Hochschild developed the concept of emotion work two decades ago, she opened an immensely fruitful arena for sociological investigation. In *The Managed Heart* (1983), Hochschild explores the emotion work of female flight attendants for a large commercial airline, describing it as the suppressing of negative emotion (surface acting) or creating positive emotion (deep acting) on the basis of workplace expectations. Hochschild believes that although emotion work is vital in private life, when it is the result of corporate mandates in commercial settings the cost is alienation from self. In this she is following Marx, but substituting service work for physical labor, and for good reason, since the U.S. economy has shifted toward service work. Hochschild discusses what she calls the *feeling rules* of workplace organizations. We extend Hochschild's work by giving greater attention than she does to the issues involved in building and maintaining social relationships. On the one hand, problems result from the emotional dissonance that WPAs often experience when working at the intersection of institutionally marginalized members of the academy, such as adjunct instructors, and those with more power, such as chairs. On the other hand, we want to recognize a positive dimension to emotion work that is absent in Hochschild's analysis.

In seeking to map the experience and awareness of emotion work in writing program administration, we adopt the analytic strategy of standpoint epistemology particularly as Dorothy Smith has developed it in her books *The Everyday World as Problematic* (1987), *The Conceptual Practices of Power* (1990), and *Writing the Social* (1999). We seek to understand the *ruling relations* and conceptual practices of power that are revealed when we begin to examine the daily experience of emotional labor from the standpoint of women, the "local particularities of everyday experience" (Smith 1999, 73). We do not intend to essentialize gender. Not all women perform academic emotion work, and many men do. Nevertheless, emotion work is a profoundly gendered activity, because the culture expects it of women more than of men.

In *Gender Trials: Emotional Lives in Contemporary Law Firms* (1995), Jennifer Pierce explores the social reproduction of gender inequality in the legal workplace, focusing on the distribution of emotion work between what she calls *Rambo litigators* and *nurturing paralegals* in a large law firm. Pierce also examines the strategies female attorneys use to deal with the gendered expectations of their behavior—specifically, the expectations that they serve as emotional nurturers for the Rambo litigators and other members of the law firm staff. What happens when men do women's work? Christine Williams has researched nursing, social work, and elementary school teaching for her book *Still a Man's World* (1995). She concludes that when men do women's work, men are given more credit and advanced more quickly. This is borne out by Sally Barr-Ebest's study of WPAs (1995). In contrast to the *glass ceiling* so often used to describe women in men's occupations, Williams uses the metaphor of a *glass escalator* to describe men's advancement in women's occupations.

Arlene Kaplan Daniels' article "Invisible Work" (1987) helps explain why men get this occupational advantage. Daniels argues that men get more credit for certain kinds of invisible work—such as emotion work—that are seen as "natural" for women, but not natural for men. Women's emotion work is held to a higher standard than is men's emotion work, and women are sanctioned more severely when they don't meet those gendered expectations. Daniels cites, for example, Norma Wikler's study of teachers in which she found students to be harder on women teachers than men when an instructor is not readily available, supportive, or sympathetic to student problems. Part of the credit that men get when they do emotion work includes "the resources . . . to perform at their best advantage [and this includes staff, time, independence]" (1987, 409). Furthermore, Daniels argues that emotion work is absolutely crucial to the functioning of organizations. Work would not get done without it, she says (1987, 412).

In "Love and Knowledge: Emotion and Feminist Epistemology," Alison Jaggar (1989a) offers useful insights for understanding emotion in the academic workplace. First, related to what Hochschild refers to as *feeling rules*, Jaggar observes that the discounting of emotion works politically in favor of dominant groups. Using the dominant group's feeling rules to evaluate the significance of emotion, she says, can "blind us to the possibility of alternative ways of living" (1989a, 159). In this regard, she points to the importance of emotions that run counter to an organization's feeling rules. She writes: "People who experience conventionally unacceptable, or what I call 'outlaw emotions' . . . often are subordinated individuals who pay a disproportionately high price for maintaining the status quo" (1989a, 160). This applies to WPAs in their roles as activists dealing with inequities in the university. Jaggar notes that "[c]ritical reflection on emotion is . . . a kind of political theory and political practice, indispensable for an adequate social theory and social transformation" (1989a, 164).

The sociological literature on gendered emotion work, as well as the problems of "invisible work" more generally, suggests the importance of understanding the range of activities that are needed for an organization to work effectively. Anthony Giddens, British social theorist and senior advisor to Prime Minister Tony Blair, contributes to this discussion through his concept of emotional or *dialogic* democracy. This involves balanced interpersonal relationships and responsiveness and the breaking down of gendered emotion expectations. As does Alice Gillam in her essay "Taking it Personally" (1999),

Giddens links the personal, professional, and public spheres, arguing that balanced and responsive interpersonal relationships are necessary for productive work. He defines productive work as the achievement of material and socio-emotional well-being, as opposed to what he calls "productivism," or obsessive, ritualistic busywork, done for its own sake. An obstacle in the way of achieving meaningful work environments, according to Giddens, is that we don't have many good models of democratic relationships. In his books, *Beyond Right and Left: The Future of Radical Politics* (1995), and *The Transformation of Intimacy* (1993), Giddens offers as possible models 12-step groups and same-sex relationships.

Taken together, these writings on emotion and emotion work can offer insights into an often neglected dimension of work life, illustrating the centrality and necessity of emotion and emotion work, but also alerting us to the double-binds and costs often embedded in workplace organizations.

WPAs and Emotion Work

Daily emotion work is crucial to accomplishing the goals of literacy widely espoused in higher education. At our institution, for example, excellence in writing is the first goal of our president's 2002 mission statement. However lean may be the financial support for addressing literacy needs, as an educational value, literacy is beyond debate. But as sociolinguists and critics in the Ebonics movement have pointed out, what literacy entails is highly contested and inevitably personal, thus emotionally fraught. How literacy is defined is always changing, depending on the demographics of the college population, the sophistication of bringing new discourse into the academy (for example, Anzaldúa's *mestiza* rhetoric [1987]), and the implications of new technology. Even our basic writing students are literate in ways that often their teachers are not. Change incites conflict among various constituencies in English departments, in universities. WPAs are at the center of these conflicts, whether they want to be or not. WPAs *show empathy and give encouragement* to new writing teachers. WPAs teach this kind of emotion work to new teachers, who engage in it with their first-year students, who need it to gain the courage to write. WPAs *mediate conflicts* with confused parents who may think that alternative pedagogies, such as individual conferencing or computer classrooms, mean that the teachers aren't doing their jobs. WPAs must graciously explain to faculty senates why first-year students pass English courses and still don't write to please their engineering teachers. And WPAs engage in the complicated emotional and intellectual work of translating scholarship on literacy and rhetoric to their literary colleagues. The boundaries that WPAs—all rhetoric faculty by Theresa Enos' definition (1997)—negotiate are terrifying, exhilarating and sometimes excruciatingly tedious. Negotiating these boundaries—and helping others do so—requires a great deal of sophisticated emotion work, labor that is more often accomplished than acknowledged.

Most WPAs embrace a positive notion of emotion work in their roles of teaching writing and training graduate teaching associates. Encouraging students or new teachers to express themselves, to gain knowledge and confidence, can be fulfilling in itself, especially to social activists, who tend to be drawn to rhetoric in general, and administration in particular. The tending of relationships, the opportunity to practice love, as Susan Kirtley discusses in this volume, can be an enormously uplifting and regenerating activity. WPAs are socially situated in the university similarly to department chairs and graduate directors—central, important, and constantly called upon. What WPAs often have that other department administrators don't have is a group of eager, enthusiastic first-year teachers who are in graduate school to pursue their dreams, which usually involve teaching. WPAs are a part of the transformative process that new teachers go through. Though sometimes villainized, more often than not—especially if they're good at emotion work—WPAs get to be heroes to their students. In one of our focus group interviews, a community college writing center director talked about the students he tutors, stating:

> They're all very much lacking in self-confidence; through their high school experiences they've been beaten down, so to speak, told they're not good writers, they're here in college, they're carrying that baggage with them and I feel that's probably the first thing we need to do is develop that sense of confidence . . . that will carry them through the developmental courses into the required core curriculum. So my role is to facilitate that sort of environment.

Many WPAs, of course, spoke of enjoying helping their graduate students develop as teachers. This work includes resolving problems that occur with new teachers, much of which requires the emotion work of *mediation*. A male Director of Composition at a research institution spoke:

> Two weeks ago, Friday morning, eight o'clock, thirteen students at my door, teacher was sick that day. And they took that as the occasion to tell me all of their woes . . . and they probably were about fifty-fifty in terms of legitimate versus illegitimate claims. So I found the classroom and spent over an hour talking and listening. Wasn't on my calendar, is not something that you can report to the Dean, absolutely crucial and vital, absolutely frustrating because . . . this is a teacher who I want to be supportive of, who I think is generally a good teacher, but I also want to be responsive of students. And boy, that kind of thing on a less dramatic level happens continually.

As this comment emphasizes, while WPAs see such emotion work as "absolutely crucial and vital," they also recognize it as invisible—"not something that you can report to the Dean"—and very time-consuming. This is the overriding issue: *emotion work is crucially important, often fulfilling, but not officially recognized.*

Given the invisibility of emotion work, the inequitable distribution of power within Composition faculties that Theresa Enos has described is disturbing. In *Gender Roles and Faculty Lives*, Enos describes a hierarchy of WPA work in which male (or male-identified) faculty hold the jobs at the top of the hierarchy, while females "tend to handle the many details of day-to-day committee work and the nitty-gritty work with students" (1997, 66). Even women who hold the "real" titles are viewed as "program caretakers rather than innovators. . . . [T]heir recompense is inadequate and expectations often unstated. 'Lite' power, heavy duties is a pretty accurate description of the WPA, but even more so if the WPA is female" (1997, 77). Implicit and often unacknowledged expectations can plague collaborative writing program administration as well, as Eileen Schell has discussed in her 1998 article, "Who's the Boss?" Schell, who codirected a writing program with a male WPA, writes:

> [One of the things] that troubled me most about being an untenured WPA [in a collaborative setting] . . . was the ways in which I was singled out as the member of the co-directorship who was more 'approachable' and 'accessible.'. . . When an instructor felt upset about his or her teaching evaluations or when a teaching assistant had endured a bad class, I was often the first person they approached for advice and solace. Perceived as being more caring, understanding, and 'available,' I often found myself spending extra hours and sometimes days on my administrative work when I needed to be writing or preparing for my classes. Gender stereotyping played a role in the perception that I was more nurturing and approachable and . . . I participated in reinforcing that stereotype with my attentive care taking behaviors. (1998, 74–75)

Similarly, in her article "Becoming a Warrior: Lessons of the Feminist Workplace," Louise Phelps argues that "[t]he utopian vision of feminist administration doesn't provide a vision realistic enough to guide us through the minefield of ambiguities, complexities, and pain entailed in wielding power responsibly" (1995, 293). Phelps' concern, however, is the inverse of Schell's: the tacit preference among many women academics for indirectness, a sense that direct confrontation is inappropriate. We label as a *feeling rule* what Phelps states as "the tendency to consensus-building that may suppress productive eccentricity or 'crossness'" (1995, 301). We are reminded of Hochschild's airline attendants, who until very recently have been taught to smile in the face of confrontation, to defuse conflict and accommodate unruly passengers, rather than be direct or cross. The work performed with indirectness is a careful, deliberate strategy of saving the face of the other, whether it is student, new teacher, faculty member, chair, or dean. Those of us who have been socialized into this kind of indirectness, generally women, face the implicit cost of relinquishing self-expression, which can lead to a sense of powerlessness—Phelps' point. And yet what are the immediate consequences for women who take Phelps' advice to be assertive and direct? Do they garner the respect and tangible gain that straight, rich, young, white men ostensibly do? Or do they accomplish less, finding themselves discredited as troublemakers with whom no one wants to be associated?

Women WPAs in particular seem aware of the implicit feeling rules that prescribe and proscribe certain kinds of feelings as (in)appropriate for them, as what Jaggar calls *outlaw emotions* (1989a). Often, in fact, they may have these feeling rules pointed out to them by others in the university who wish to control their behavior. A female former Director of Composition at an urban university revealed that her dean publicly accused her of making her decisions emotionally, implying that her decisions were invalid. This hyperrational view of administration derives from a scientistic ideology that undergirds rules for what counts as valuable knowledge—the hard knowledge of the sciences versus the soft knowledge of the humanities. To maintain this narrative, emotion must be labeled as irrational and irrelevant; thus administrators who cross the line into emotion are represented as out-of-control.

While the expression of negative emotions is perceived as beyond the pale, nurturing is acceptable, even expected. Another female WPA at a large state university said:

> My chair is one of the loveliest men. I really care about him. He's a wonderful sensitive man and yet what he wants of me, 90 percent of the time, is somehow to care for him, to love him or somehow support him. I'm not sure whether it's a mother thing or whether he sees me sort of in a daughter role. He's someone I've known for many many many years. It's amazing to me because that's embedded in the work—and we work very closely together on the writing and university related things—but embedded in that is this care taking he wants of me.

Not all the feeling rules are necessarily gender-based. As one male WPA said: "I also think, like on my campus, conflict is really a dirty word. So if you're seen as somebody who isn't afraid of it that can be a bad thing."

But far more women than men in our focus groups spoke of the power of feeling rules to silence or distort their expressions of conflict or anger. One senior male WPA seemed to struggle to understand the differences in the expression of anger between male and female WPAs with whom he had worked:

> [Women] whom I've worked with . . . have had difficulty using authority in a way that I had no difficulty using it. And they also internalized criticism in a debilitating way. They might turn to tears and inaction and I would scream and throw something.

Recognizing the feeling rules that many women experience helps to explain what he finds inexplicable. What might be the consequences should a woman express feelings in his way? Strong, outlaw emotion is disciplined through the application of often unarticulated feeling rules that banish emotional expression and outbursts to private office spaces. This tacit understanding is reinforced through hallway and interoffice discourse rather than through a set of explicit codes. Arguably these codes are more powerful because they remain below the radar. Without a doubt, the standard of acceptable expression of anger is different for men than women. In one of our departments, more than one man is known for vituperative outbursts, which are then excused; women are pilloried for far less intense expressions of anger.

In addition to gender, class can play a role in emotion work, as Doug Hesse's article "WPA as Father, Husband, Ex" demonstrates. As a male with working class roots, Hesse writes, "I'm someone who feels every student complaint as a leak in the roof, every criticism of the writing program as a cough in the engine" (1999, 45). And he goes on to ask, "How do the feminized dimensions of being a WPA mutate in combination with certain class-bound masculine outlooks and practices? One result," he speculates, "is a crippling kind of alienation from both self and those others (wife, children, colleagues, friends) who might ameliorate that separation" (1999, 53). Neglecting one's emotions (the male model of the ideal WPA) is a form of emotion work that alienates one from oneself, much like the *surface* and *deep acting* of Hochschild's flight attendants, whose fake smiles eventually confuse them about what they feel and ultimately, who they are.

It is important to acknowledge that feeling rules are not unbreakable constraints. And many of the WPAs we interviewed found themselves experiencing outlaw emotions that went against the grain of their institutional contexts. One reason for the experience of outlaw emotions was the dis-ease that WPAs, especially women, often felt about the dominant feeling rules in their departments. As a west coast female WPA at a large state university explained:

> I'm trying to figure out how to do this without using the rules that, 'forgive me,' the men set up before I got there. Because I don't like those rules, I don't like the results of those rules and I don't play very well by those rules. . . . I don't think quickly on my feet so when I have these confrontations it's like, I'll be back in ten minutes and I'll give you the answer. Because I tend to talk around things. And they tend to do things like this. And so I'll take the conflict and go back to my office and ruminate and figure out what are the real issues here and how can I go about it.

It's important to point out that this kind of thing could happen to anyone, anyone, that is, whose confrontational style doesn't fit the tacit norm. In one of our departments, for instance, the norm is, as described above, explicitly confrontational, and some of the women, Asian men, and others feel disadvantaged. In the other of our departments, the norm has been indirect confrontation, such that assertive women and men are often seen as openly hostile.

WPAs find themselves experiencing outlaw emotions in relation to other kinds of perceived injustices in their institutions as well. For instance, most of the WPAs we interviewed experience the emotional dissonance of their roles of *company man* and *social activist*, particularly in regard to the supervision of adjunct faculty. A senior female at a research university noted:

> If you work hard for your part-timers or you try to change the curriculum or, no matter what you do to try to do your job well, my experience has been that that's regarded as a personal disloyalty on my part to my male boss. . . . A part-timer would come into my office and cry and I would talk to her and try to explain how things work and then you would discover that the reason why she was crying was that he had made her cry. Then she came into my office, then I'm in trouble. It's like the daddy-mommy thing. If daddy says you're naughty then you can go to mommy.

This WPA resisted the dominant feeling rules, but over time was so frustrated by the injustices she was expected to condone—and even support—that she eventually resigned from her position.

Outlaw emotions can also emerge from the awkward and ambivalent role that WPAs frequently must play as designated advocates for existing policies that they had no part in creating and with which they don't fully agree. So, for instance, Alice Gillam in "Collaboration, Ethics, and the Emotional Labor of WPAs" in this volume speaks about the spot she found herself in regarding a first-year writing proficiency requirement. Although she sought to tailor it to her own ideology, she found that its history and structure led to her feeling appropriated by it rather than being able to fashion it in a way she could believe in. She experiences this ministration in the name of others' agendas as a source of deep ambivalence—an outlaw emotion. Rather than dismiss her own or her coworkers' feelings, Gillam sets up a structure—in the form of reflective writing—that allows her to interrogate her own practice.

In her article "Taking It Personally," Gillam exposes the sexist structure of academic work when it strictly separates professional and personal lives—and codes the "ideal" WPA as male. She says: "This discourse sets up an economy of values in which the most 'public' professional acts are deemed most important and the more 'private' trivialized" (1999, 68). So, for instance, a woman WPA at a church-affiliated liberal arts college referred to her relational and emotion work as a WPA as "[t]hat kind of disappearing work that you do that's in the people that you worked with." Most WPAs feel ambivalent about emotion work. On the one hand, they find it fulfilling, internally rewarding, and sometimes enlightening. On the other hand, they find that it can grow like kudzu to push out institutionally rewarded activities such as scholarship. WPAs feel betrayed when such significant relational work is met by lack of enthusiasm by colleagues, or even hostility on the part of the very individuals for whom it was undertaken. As Phelps notes, for instance, WPAs are unlikely to receive expressions of appreciation for some of their hardest work. Improvements in the conditions of part-timers, she observes, "are always relative and always fall short of the new goals that are quickly set once others are attained" (1995, 317).

For many WPAs emotion work, especially when combined with the other work they are expected to do, leads to sleepless nights and burnout. And for some others there is the cost of feeling like a failure associated with what a male WPA at a research institution described as his messianic complex:

> My really preferred way of handling conflict is to sort of invest more of myself in it. . . . [W]hat I find myself doing a lot of, and I have been increasingly concerned about the personal cost of it, that is to always make the phone call, visit the office, buy somebody coffee, and all of that. And that has its real downsides too. Among them is a kind of a messianic complex that 'If I am only involved enough it would be better' so when it's not resolved, it's probably been some of my failing.

Such feelings of personal failure tend to mask the structural impediments to the smooth functioning of writing programs—obstructions that WPAs feel they must find ways to navigate in order to succeed in their jobs. Indeed, as we have seen, a significant amount of WPAs' emotion work is directed toward overcoming the structural barriers to achieving their official mission. But since few WPAs have many local colleagues from within their disciplinary field, they receive little social validation of this dilemma from within their own institutional settings. It is only when they turn to the national community, or perhaps to feminist communities within their own institutions, that they find support and understanding.

Conclusion

In this chapter we have examined emotion work as it is enacted and experienced in a particular academic role, the combined faculty/administrative role of the writing program administrator. Emotion work reveals relational and gendered aspects of writing program administration that, while vital to the accomplishment of the job, have generally been deemed unworthy of recognition and reward—women's work, invisible work, or at least *not* intellectual work—never mind how intellectually demanding, time-consuming, and draining it may be.

In recent years WPAs have engaged in collective efforts in their major disciplinary organizations to clarify the range of work demands placed on them. The Conference on College Composition and Communication, the Council of Writing Program Administrators, and the Modern Language Association have all produced documents designed to promote a better understanding of the activities that go into effectively running writing programs and to help WPAs get recognition for the various kinds of labor that do not fit traditionally valued categories of academic work. Yet, despite the good intentions and diligent work of their authors, none of the documents produced to date have articulated emotion work. Even WPAs themselves have trouble incorporating these aspects of their work into a vision of the intellectual labor of academic life. Emotion work is typically excluded from our conception of academic labor because it doesn't conform to the ruling relations embedded in academic discourse, which tend to separate intellectual work from more domesticated and gendered or feminized labor, no matter how essential it is to achieving intellectual goals. Those who do emotion work are expected to view it through the medium of ruling relations that render it largely invisible, inconsequential, or of lesser merit than "true intellectual work." It is difficult for WPAs to extricate themselves from this dominant discourse, leading at times to their alienation from their daily academic lives or to their seeing emotion work as keeping them from scholarship. And yet, as our discussion has demonstrated, WPAs' everyday experiences are jarringly discordant with the separation of emotion work from the more valorized "intellectual work" in academic life.

WPAs must articulate emotion work as a central component of their intellectual lives. Jaggar's work suggests that WPAs can use their outlaw emotions to envision alternatives to the discord of the *status quo*. They can do this by taking their own feelings seriously, regardless of the expectation to suppress them. Taking emotions seriously means becoming more—not less—attuned to them, assuming that they may provide a vantage point from which to critique the structure of expectations in academic departments. Many of the WPAs we have talked to do, in fact, see the need for a more balanced and sophisticated emotional milieu in academic life. They argue that emotional literacy should be as much a part of the structure of expectations in academic environments as intellectual development—for their faculty peers as well as for their students.

The changes that would support the incorporation of emotion work into a more sophisticated vision of academic life would include moving away from the notion of the individual scholar toward a more social model of intellectual activity. Western conceptions of knowledge, which have been the bedrock of the academy, have been deeply split since the Enlightenment. On the one hand, we see the notion of education, harking back to Medieval English linguistic roots in the term, *educare*, which meant to *rear* or socialize another—clearly a transmission model of knowledge, but one in which emotion could certainly play a part. On the other hand, the notion of intellect in the Enlightenment emphasized the individual thinker's power of knowing as distinguished from his or her power to feel. The split here is between internal and external notions of knowledge. Each misses the fundamentally dialogic nature of knowledge espoused today by social constructionists, feminists, and other critical social theorists.

A social constructionist view of education requires an emotional environment characterized by dialogue, trust, confidence, and creativity. Such an environment cannot be provided solely, or primarily, by a marginalized segment of the academic workforce. The experience of WPAs calls for a more holistic understanding of social processes and the alignment of joint action in American higher education. We must develop a broader understanding of intellectual labor that acknowledges and rewards "[t]hat kind of disappearing work that you do that's in the people that you worked with."

Earlier we defined emotion work as including attention to personal feelings, the emotional tenor of relationships, empathy and encouragement, mediation of disputes, building emotional solidarity in groups, and using one's own or others' outlaw emotions to interrogate structures. Think for a moment how your workplace might change were a substantial percentage of your colleagues able to perform emotional labor for the benefit of the department. If your mind immediately goes to clichés about Oprah, think Jerry Springer. Pick a recent conflict in your department and study it for a moment. Ask yourself what part of the dispute involved unacknowledged, perhaps unconscious emotional pain. Imagine ways it could have gone better had that pain been addressed—directly or indirectly. Now think of a counterexample, a difficult issue that was resolved well, if imperfectly. Consider the difference in the way the two were handled and who did and did not perform emotional labor. Think about the implications of each case for future situations in the department. Reflect on the sheer productivity, never mind job satisfaction, that a subtle shift in management of difficult issues can lead to. It will take a new vocabulary, an expanded notion of intelligence.

WPAs are teaching emotion work when they ask TAs to role-play confrontations with students. When TAs work in groups and WPAs deal well with the conflict that occurs among them, that's teaching emotion work. It's the move to thinking about this for faculty that stops us short. How do we build emotional literacy into the structure of expectations in academic environments? What would this look like? WPAs, who often become chairs and deans, could set a tone by setting an example. Faculty members who are adept at emotion work could be recognized, asked to serve in such a capacity, and rewarded with merit raises. Even praise or acknowledgement of their skills would be a start. Chairs could take mediation classes, could be encouraged by deans to do so, and instead of ignoring conflicts among faculty members, chairs might in fact address them. It is relatively easy to make a case for recognizing conflict mediation as a valuable skill, since it has been valorized at the national level at Harvard and through the efforts of high-profile politicians such as Jesse Jackson and Jimmy Carter. The recognition of nurturing and outlaw emotional expression as valuable is harder to picture. In beginning to move there, we might explore a vocabulary of emotion that could eventually find its way into job descriptions for chairs and other administrators, in tenure and promotion documents, and in the discourse in our meetings and hallways. It's difficult to move beyond the awkward embarrassment of talking about emotions, but we must do so to move toward recognition and encouragement of emotional intelligence at work.

Note

1. Holt and Anderson collected various kinds of ethnographic and other qualitative data in the course of our study of writing program administration, which was funded by a WPA research grant. First, Holt served as Director of Composition—in

charge of developing and running a university first-year writing program with around sixty instructors who teach a total of approximately 150 sections of First-Year English each year. Holt kept field notes during one year of her tenure as a WPA. Second, Holt and Anderson conducted individual and focus group interviews with more than fifty WPAs from a range of colleges and universities in the United States. A third set of data for this study involves our having downloaded and coded—after receiving permission—four months of conversational strands on the WPA listserv. Our research goal has been to understand the kinds of conflicts that WPAs experience and conflict-management strategies that they have developed. And it quickly became apparent to us that emotion work figures as a central component of WPA labor.

Afterword

Moving Beyond a Sentimental Education

Lynn Worsham

In the afterword to *The Bluest Eye*, written more than twenty years after the novel was first published, Toni Morrison makes a distinction that I think is especially relevant to an appreciation of what is attempted in the essays collected in this volume: the distinction between feeling "touched" and being "moved." She makes this distinction in the context of explaining why she thinks the novel is flawed, why it ultimately does not accomplish what she had hoped it would. The problem, as Morrison sees it, is that too many readers remain touched but are not moved by the story of a little black girl whose impossible wish for blue eyes becomes a window onto the dynamics of racial self-loathing, onto the social and domestic aggression that causes a child "to literally fall apart" (1970, 210). Morrison explains: "One problem was centering: the weight of the novel's inquiry on so delicate and vulnerable a character could smash her and lead readers into the comfort of pitying her rather than into an interrogation of themselves for the smashing" (211). Here, in this provocative statement, Morrison holds herself accountable for failing to produce a narrative that moves readers beyond mere sentimentality. Feeling touched, in other words, goes nowhere and accomplishes nothing except a confirmation of the distance between self and other, between the "blue-eyed" reader (metaphorically if not actually) and the pitiful Pecola. What Morrison reminds us is that pity, despite its apparent other-directedness, is too often a comforting and comfortable sentiment because it is a narcissistic and self-regarding emotion, one that confirms the virtue of the person who feels for the pitiable other ("I feel compassion for the other; therefore, I am a good person"), and, at the same time, reinscribes the qualitative difference between self and other ("There, but for the grace of God, go I"). Pity, in this case, is a sentiment that offers no vehicle for critical consciousness, no way to move beyond the orbit inscribed by the dominant ideologies of race, class, and gender. Pity is not the response Morrison wants.

She wants instead to move readers to the center of the novel's inquiry where we might be induced, through narrative technique, to let the abstractions of difference, distance, and innocence dissolve and thereby put ourselves at risk in an interrogation of our own complicity in what is properly understood as the crime of soul-murder. Indeed, *The Bluest Eye* can be read as an interrogation of how and why soul-murder occurs. What the novel makes all too painfully apparent is that soul-murder takes place most irrevocably through a pervasive and systematic schooling of emotion—in particular, through "the damaging internalization of assumptions of *immutable inferiority* originating in an outside gaze" (210; emphasis added). The novel "pecks away at the gaze" that uses an arbitrary standard of value to condemn a little black girl to *being* ugly, worthless, insignificant, and unlovable. The gaze is white, of course, and historically it has claimed the power to define who is worthy of recognition and dignity by seizing control of ideological state apparatuses (ISAs)—school, religion, the family, the entertainment industry, and communications media, for example. What Morrison shows us in *The Bluest Eye*—and what the essays in *A Way to Move* help us to apprehend more fully—is that ideology and ideological state apparatuses do their work most effectively through a schooling of emotion.

What this means is that the primary work of ideology is more fundamental than the imposition of a dominant framework of meanings. Its primary work is to organize an emotional world, to inculcate patterns of feeling that support the legitimacy of dominant interests, patterns that are deemed especially appropriate to reigning gender, race, and class relations. Ideology locates individuals objectively in a hierarchy of power relations; but also, and more importantly, it organizes their affective relations to those locations, to their own condition of subordination, and to others in that hierarchical structure. Ideology binds each individual to the social world through a complex and often contradictory affective life that too often remains, for the most part, just beyond the horizon of semantic availability, and its success depends on a mystification or misrecognition of this primary work. Ideology works to mystify emotion as purely a personal and private matter; it actively conceals the fact that emotions are prevailing forms of social life, that so-called personal life always takes shape in social and cultural terms. This important work is accomplished, in large part, through therapeutic culture, which in the last thirty-five years has successfully installed itself as a powerful ISA in its own right. Together with popular cultural forms, therapeutic culture works to mystify emotions by making them purely a matter of personal psychology and private psychopathology. Therapeutic culture celebrates a self, as Jean Bethke Elshtain suggests, that "views the world solely through the prism of the self. . . . It's a quivering sentimental self that gets uncomfortable very quickly, because this self has to feel good about itself all the time" (2001, qtd. in "Future" 28). Rather than seeking to understand the political dimension of emotion, this self worries about itself, focusing entirely (and narcissistically) on self-validation, especially the validation of its personal experience and "unique" feelings.

Although we may find comfort in the clarity of abstract terms such as *ISA* and *racism* and *sexism* (we may prefer to speak, for example, of "minority groups" and "racist and sexist institutions"), we must at some point realize that these terms are but euphemisms for multifarious forms of soul-murder, euphemisms for that vast network of shaming practices that ensure that unquestioned forms of *immutable* inferiority take root in the hearts of generations of individuals. We must realize that there are languages that simply offer no way to move. At the end of *The Bluest Eye*, Claudia reflects on what ultimately happens to Pecola, and she speaks from a point of view that must be very close to Morrison's. Her words hold everyone, black and white, responsible for Pecola's destruction: "We honed our egos on her, padded our characters with her frailty, and yawned in the fantasy of our strength. . . . And fantasy it was, for we were not strong, only aggressive; we were not free, merely licensed; we were not compassionate, we were polite; not good, but well behaved" (205). The novel ends with a recognition that it is "much, much, much too late" to save Pecola, to save all the many past generations of Pecolas. However, in the intimate distance between fiction and history, the novel calls on us to smash the thing that smashes Pecola: the white gaze and its subtle and insidious schooling of emotion. If we missed the call that the novel issues, if we were not really listening, Morrison offers us the generous embrace of a second chance by reiterating that call in her afterword to the novel.

In the afterword to this volume of essays—in this space that claims the place and the privilege of "the last word"—I want to refuse that claim and instead provide an opening that links the project of *A Way to Move* to the kind of interrogation called for in *The Bluest Eye*. With the publication of this volume, the first of its kind in Composition Studies, we are called on to center the weight of scholarly inquiry on emotion, to see that all education is sentimental, that all education is an education of sentiment. In other words, we are called on to see that emotion is the primary object of schooling, wherever schooling happens to occur: in the public sphere, in the family, in the classroom, in popular culture, in high culture, in the workplace, in scholarly texts. We are called on to make emotion a critical category—an occasion for interrogation—rather than a comforting warrant for truth and authenticity. It is far too early to predict what such an inquiry will finally produce in the field of Composition Studies. However, it will be a shame if the new interest in the category of emotion is deployed merely to reinforce notions that are already rather securely installed at the center of the field: a largely uninterrogated concept of experience and "the personal" as the ground of and warrant for knowledge; a rather simplistic notion of personal narrative as an instrument of critical reflection; an easy conflation of self-expression with "good" writing; an overinflated sense of just what required composition courses can actually accomplish. It will be a shame if the new interest in emotion as a category of critical *thought* does not move us into a new orbit of social and political possibility.

Works Cited

Abu-Lughod, L. and C. Lutz. 1990. "Introduction: Emotion, Discourse, and the Politics of Everyday Life." In *Language and the Politics of Emotion. See* Lutz and Abu-Lughod 1990, 1–23.

Achtenberg, D. 1996. "Aristotelian Resources for Feminist Thinking." In *Feminism and Ancient Philosophy*, ed. Julia K. Ward, 95–117. New York: Routledge.

Alston, K. 1991. "Teaching, Philosophy, and Eros: Love as a Relation to Truth." *Educational Theory* (Fall): 285–95.

Anderson, C. and M. MacCurdy, eds. 2000. *Writing and Healing: Toward an Informed Practice*. Urbana: National Council of Teachers of English.

Anson, C. 1999. "Tale 135." In *Comp Tales*, eds. R. Haswell and M. Lu, 175–76. New York, Longman.

Anzaldúa, G. 1987. *Borderlands/La Frontera: The New Mestiza*. San Francisco: Aunt Lute Books.

Arendt, H. 1958. *The Human Condition*, 2d ed. Chicago: The University of Chicago Press.

Aristotle. 1991. *Aristotle on Rhetoric: A Theory of Civic Discourse*, trans. G. A. Kennedy. New York: Oxford University Press.

———. 1995. *The Complete Works of Aristotle*, Volumes One and Two, ed. J. Barnes. New Jersey: Princeton University Press.

———. 1962. *Nicomachean Ethics*, trans. M. Ostwald. Englewood Cliffs, NJ: Prentice Hall.

———. 1984. *The Politics*, trans. C. Lord. Chicago: University of Chicago Press.

———. 1984. *Rhetoric*, trans. W. R. Roberts. *The Complete Works of Aristotle: the Revised Oxford Translation*, 2 vols, ed. J. Barnes. Bollingen Series LXXI. New Jersey: Princeton University Press.

———. 1932. *The Rhetoric of Aristotle*, trans. L. Cooper. New Jersey: Prentice–Hall.

———. 1954. *The Rhetoric and Poetics of Aristotle*. New York: Modern Library.

Ashton-Jones, E. 1995. "Collaboration, Conversation, and the Politics of Gender." In *Feminine Principles and Women's Experience in American Composition and Rhetoric*, eds. L. W. Phelps and J. Emig, 5–26. Pittsburgh: University of Pittsburgh Press.

Baldwin, J. 1995. "If Black English Isn't a Language, Then Tell Me, What is?" In *Contemporary Essays*, 3rd ed. D. Hall, 39–43. New York: Bedford/St. Martin's.

———. 1979. "If Black English Isn't a Language, Then Tell Me, What is?" *New York Times*, 29 July, sec. 4, p. 19.

Bar On, B. and A. Ferguson. 1998. *Daring to Be Good: Essays in Feminist Ethico-Politics*. New York: Routledge.

Baron, D. 1982. *Grammar and Good Taste*. New Haven: Yale University Press.

Barr-Ebest, S. 1995. "Gender Differences in Writing Program Administration." *WPA: Writing Program Administration* 18: 53–73.

Bartholomae, D. 1985. "Inventing the University." In *When a Writer Can't Write: Studies in Writer's Block and Other Composing-Process Problems*, ed. M. Rose, 134–65. New York: Guilford.

———. 1995. "Writing with Teachers: A Conversation with Peter Elbow." *College Composition and Communication* 46.1: 62–71.

Bartky, S. L. 1990. "Feeding Egos and Tending Wounds: Deference and Disaffection in Women's Emotional Labor." In *Femininity and Domination: Studies in Phenomenology of Depression*, 99–138. New York: Routledge.

———. 1998, "Skin Deep: Femininity as a Disciplinary Regime." In *Daring to Be Good. See* Bar On and Ferguson, 15–17.

Baugh, J. 2000. *Beyond Ebonics: Linguistic Pride and Racial Prejudice*. New York: Oxford University Press.

Bazerman, C. 1989. "Reading Student Writing: Proteus Grabbing Proteus." In *Encountering Student Texts*, eds. B. Lawson, S. Ryan, and R. Winterowd, 139–46. Urbana: National Council of Teachers of English.

Bell, B., J. Gaventa, and J. Peters, eds. 1990. *We Make the Road by Walking: Conversations on Education and Social Change/Myles Horton and Paulo Freire*. Philadelphia: Temple University Press.

Benedict, R. 1994. *Patterns of Culture*. Boston: Houghton Mifflin.

Bergquist, W. 1993. *The Postmodern Organization: Mastering the Art of Irreversible Change*. San Francisco: Jossey-Bass Publishers.

Berlin, J. 1991. "Composition Studies and Cultural Studies." In *Composition and Resistance*, eds. C. M. Hurlbert and M. Blitz, 47–55. Portsmouth, NH: Boynton/Cook.

———. 1987. *Rhetoric and Reality: Writing Instruction in American Colleges 1900–1985*. Carbondale: Southern Illinois University Press.

Bishop, W. 1993. "Writing Is/And Therapy?: Raising Questions about Writing Classrooms and Writing Program Administration." *JAC: Journal of Advanced Composition* 13: 503–16.

Bishop, W. and G. Crossley. 1996. "How to Tell a Story of Stopping: The Complexities of Narrating a WPA's Experience." *WPA: Writing Program Administration* 19.3: 70–79.

Bizzell, P. 2000. "Feminist Methods of Research in the History of Rhetoric: What Differences do They Make?" *Rhetoric Society Quarterly* 30.4: 5–17.

———. 1991. "Marxist Ideas in Composition Studies." In *Contending with Words. See* Harkin and Schilb 1991, 52–68.

Blair, H. 1965. *Lectures on Rhetoric and Belles Lettres*, ed. H. F. Harding. Carbondale: Southern Illinois University Press.

Bleich, D. 1999. "In Case of Fire, Throw In (What to Do with Textbooks Once You Switch to Sourcebooks)." In *(Re)Visioning Composition Textbooks. See* Gale and Gale 1999, 15–42.

———. 1990. "Literacy and Citizenship: Resisting Social Issues." In *The Right to Literacy*, eds. A. Lunsford, H. Moglen, and J. Slevin, 63–69. New York: Modern Language Association and NCTE.

———. 2001. "The Materiality of Language and the Pedagogy of Exchange." *Pedagogy: Critical Approaches to Teaching Literature, Language, Composition, and Culture* 1.1:117–42.

Bloom, L.1996. "Freshman Composition as A Middleclass Enterprise." *College English* 58: 654–75.

Boler, M. 1999. *Feeling Power: Emotions and Education*. New York: Routledge.

Bourdieu, P. 1991. *Language and Symbolic Power*, trans. G. Raymond and M. Adamson. Cambridge: Harvard University Press.

———. 1977. *Outline of a Theory of Practice*, trans. R. Nice. Cambridge: Cambridge University Press.

Boyd, R. 1995. "'Grammatical Monstrosities' and 'Contemptible Miscreants': Sacrificial Violence in the Late Nineteenth-Century Usage Handbook." In *The Place of Grammar in Writing Instruction: Past, Present, Future*, eds. S. Hunter and R. Wallace, 54–70. Portsmouth, NH: Boynton/Cook.

Boyer, E. 1990. *Scholarship Reconsidered: Priorities of the Professorate*. Princeton, NJ: Carnegie Foundation for the Advancement of Teaching.

Brand, A. 2000. "Healing and the Brain." In *Writing and Healing. See* Anderson and MacCurdy 2000, 201–21.

———. 1985–86. "Hot Cognition: Emotions and Writing Behavior." *JAC: Journal of Advanced Composition* 6: 5–15.

———. 1989. *The Psychology of Writing: The Affective Experience*. Westport, CT: Greenwood.

———. 1991. "Social Cognition, Emotions, and the Psychology of Writing." *JAC: Journal of Advanced Composition* 11: 395–407.

———. 1987. "The Why of Cognition." *College Composition and Communication* 38: 436–443.

———. 1980. *Therapy in Writing: A Psycho-Educational Enterprise*. Lexington, MA: Heath.

Brand, A., and Richard Graves. 1994. "Defining Our Emotional Life." In *Presence of Mind: Writing and the Domain Beyond the Cognitive*, eds. A. Brand and R. L. Graves, 155–78.

Broadie, S. 1991. *Ethics with Aristotle*. Oxford: Oxford University Press.

Brodkey, L. 1994. "Writing on the Bias," *College English* 56: 527–47.

Brooke, R. 1987. "Lacan, Transference, and Writing Instruction." *College English* (49.6): 679–91.

Brown, J. A. 1999. "The Peer Who Isn't a Peer: Authority and the Graduate Student Administrator." In *Kitchen Cooks, Plate Twirlers, and Troubadours. See* George 1999, 120–25.

Bruffee, K. 1999. *Collaborative Learning*. 2nd ed. Baltimore: Johns Hopkins University Press.

Bryant, D. 1994. "Rhetoric: Its Functions and Its Scope." In *Professing the New Rhetoric. See* Enos and Brown 1994, 267–97.

Burch, K. 2000. *Eros as the Educational Principle of Democracy*. New York: Peter Lang.

Burke, K. 1984. *Permanence and Change*. 3rd ed. Berkeley: University of California Press.

———. 1969. *A Rhetoric of Motives*. Berkeley: University of California Press.

Butler, J. 1993. *Bodies That Matter*. New York: Routledge.

Campbell, G. 1968. *The Philosophy of Rhetoric*. New York: Readex Microprint, 1977. Microform.

Cappella, J. N. and K. H. Jamieson. 1994. "Broadcast Adwatch Effects: A Field Experiment." *Communication Research* 21.3: 432–65.

Carson, A. 1986. *Eros the Bittersweet*. New Jersey: Princeton University Press.

Catano, J. 2001. *Ragged Dicks: Masculinity, Steel, and the Rhetoric of the Self-Made Man*. Carbondale: Southern Illinois University Press.

Chappell, D. 1992. "The Stories We Tell: Acknowledging Emotion in the Classroom." *ADE Bulletin* 102: 20–23.

Committee on CCCC Language Statement. 1974. "Students' Right to Their Own Language." Special Issue of *College Composition and Communication* 25.3: 1–32.

Cooper, J. 1999. *Reason and Emotion: Essays on Ancient Moral Psychology and Ethical Theory*. New Jersey: Princeton University Press.

Corder, J. 1994. "Argument as Emergence, Rhetoric as Love." In *Professing the New Rhetorics: A Sourcebook.* See Enos and Brown 1994, 413–28.

Cornelius, R. 1996. *The Science of Emotion: Research and Tradition in the Psychology of Emotion*. Upper Saddle River, NJ: Prentice Hall.

Council of Writing Program Administrators. 1998. "Evaluating the Intellectual Work of Writing Administration." http://www.cas.ilstu.edu/English/Hesse/intellec.htm.

Council of Writing Program Administrators. 1998. "Evaluating the Intellectual Work of Writing Administration." *WPA: Writing Program Administration* 22.1/2: 85–104.

Dalton, H. 2001. "Horatio Alger." In *Rereading America: Cultural Contexts for Critical Thinking and Writing*, 5th ed., eds. G. Colombo, R. Cullen, and B. Lisle, 311–17. Boston: Bedford/St. Martin's.

Damasio, A. R. 1999. *The Feeling of What Happens: Body and Emotion in the Making of Consciousness*. New York: Harcourt Brace.

Daniels, A. 1987. "Invisible Work." *Social Problems* 34: 403–15.

DeCerteau, M. 1984. *The Practice of Everyday Life*. Berkeley: University of California Press.

Dickson, M. 1993. "Directing Without Power: Adventures in Constructing a Model of Feminist Writing Program Administration." In *Writing Ourselves Into the Story*, eds. S. Fontaine and S. Hunter, 140–53. Carbondale, IL: Southern Illinois University Press.

Dixon, K. and W. Archibald. 1998. "Outbursts: The Theory and a Guide to Reading." In *Outbursts in Academe: Multiculturalism and Other Sources of Conflict*, eds. K. Dixon and W. Archibald, ix–xv. Portsmouth, NH: Boynton/Cook.

Duffey, S., B. Feigert, V. Mortimer, J. Phegley, and M. Turnley. 2002. "Conflict, Collaboration, and Authority: Graduate Students and Writing Program Administration." *Rhetoric Review* 21: 41–52.

Durst, R. 1999. *Collision Course: Conflict, Negotiation, and Learning in College Composition*. Urbana: National Council of Teachers of English.

Ede, L. 1994. "Reading the Writing Process." In *Taking Stock: The Writing Process Movement in the 90s,* eds. L. Tobin and T. Newkirk, 31–43. Portsmouth, NH: Boynton/Cook.

Elbow, P. 1973. "The Doubting Game and the Believing Game: An Analysis of the Intellectual Process." In *Writing Without Teachers*, 147–91, Oxford University Press.

———. 1986. "The Pedagogy of the Bamboozled." In *Embracing Contraries: Explorations in Learning and Teaching,* 85–99. New York: Oxford University Press.

Enos, T. 1997. *Gender Roles and Faculty Lives in Rhetoric and Composition*. Carbondale: Southern Illinois University Press.

Enos, T., and S. Brown, eds. 1994. *Professing the New Rhetorics: A Sourcebook*. Englewood Cliffs, NJ: Blair Press.

Faigley, L. 1992. *Fragments of Rationality*. Pittsburgh: University of Pittsburgh Press.

Felman, S. 1995. "Education and Crisis, or the Vicissitudes of Teaching." In *Trauma: Explorations in Memory,* ed. C. Caruth, 13–60. Baltimore: Johns Hopkins University Press.

Firestone, S. 1989. "Love in a Sexist Society." In *Eros, Agape, and Philia. See* Soble 1989, 29–40.

Fishman, S. and L. McCarthy. 1996. "Teaching for Student Change: A Deweyan Alternative to Radical Pedagogy." *College Composition and Communication* 47.3: 342–66.

Fitts, K. and A. France, eds. 1995. *Left Margins: Cultural Studies and Composition Pedagogy*. Albany: SUNY Press.

Flavell, M. 1985. "Kitsch and Propaganda: The Blending of Myth and History in Hedwig Courths—Mahler's Lissa geht ins Gluck" *German Studies Review* 8.1: 65–87.

Fontaine, S. 1998. "Revising Administrative Models and Questioning the Value of Appointing Graduate Student WPAs." In *Foregrounding Ethical Awareness in Composition and English Studies*, eds. S. Fontaine and S. Hunter, 83–92. Portsmouth, NH: Boynton/Cook.

Frede, D. 1996. "Mixed Feelings in Aristotle's *Rhetoric*." In *Essays on Aristotle's* Rhetoric, ed. A. Rorty, 258–85. Berkeley: University of California Press.

Fulkerson, R. 1998. "Call Me Horatio: Negotiating Between Cognition and Affect in Composition." *College Composition and Communication* 50.1: 101–15.

"The Future of the Public Intellectual," *Nation*, February 2001, 25–35.

Gaines, R. 2000. "Aristotle's *Rhetoric* and Contemporary Arts of Practical Discourse." In *Rereading Aristotle's Rhetoric*, eds. A.. Gross and A. Walzer, 3–23. Carbondale: Southern Illinois University Press.

Gale, F., P. Sipiora, and J. Kinneavy. 1999. *Ethical Issues in College Writing*. New York: Peter Lang.

Gale, X. L., and F. G. Gale, eds. 1999. *(Re)Visioning Composition Textbooks: Conflicts of Culture, Ideology, and Pedagogy*. Albany: SUNY.

Gallop, J. 1997. *Feminist Accused of Sexual Harassment*. Durham: Duke University Press.

Garrett, M. 1993. "'Pathos' Reconsidered from the Perspective of Classical Chinese Rhetorical Theories." *Quarterly Journal of Speech* 79.1: 19–39.

Garrison, J. 1997. *Dewey and Eros: Wisdom and Desire in the Art of Teaching*. New York: Teachers College Press.

George, D., ed. 1999. *Kitchen Cooks, Plate Twirlers, and Troubadours: Writing Program Administrators Tell Their Stories*. Portsmouth, NH: Boynton/Cook.

Giddens, A. 1995. *Beyond Right and Left: The Future of Radical Politics*. NY: Cambridge University Press

———. 1993. *The Transformation of Intimacy*. Palo Alto: Stanford University Press.

Gillam, A. 1997. "The Ministration in Administration: Emotional Labor and the Feminist WPA." Conference on College Composition and Communication, Phoenix, AZ.

———. 1999. "Taking It Personally: Redefining the Role and Work of the WPA." In *Kitchen Cooks*. *See* George 1999, 65–72.

Goleman, D. 1995. *Emotional Intelligence*. New York: Bantam Books.

Goodburn, A. and C. Leverenz. 1998. "Feminist Writing Program Administration: Resisting the Bureaucrat Within." In *Feminism and Composition Studies. See* Jarratt and Worsham 1998, 276–90.

Green, L. 1998. "Aspect and Predicate Phrases in African-American Vernacular English." In *African-American English: Structure, History, and Use*, eds. S. Mufwene, J. Rickford, G. Bailey, and J. Baugh. New York: Routledge.

Grimaldi, W. 1972. *Studies in the Philosophy of Aristotle's* Rhetoric. Wiesbaden: Franz Steiner Verlag GMBH.

Groenhout, R. 1998. "The Virtue of Care: Aristotelian Ethics and Contemporary Ethics of Care." In *Feminist Interpretations of Aristotle*, ed. C.. Freeland, 171–200. University Park: The Pennsylvania State University Press.

Gunner, J. 1994. "Decentering the WPA." *WPA: Writing Program Administration* 18.1/2: 8–15.

Hagemann, J. and M.Wininger. 1999. "An Ideological Approach to Grammar Pedagogy in English Education Courses." *English Education* 31: 265–94.

Hall, C. 1998. "Politics, Ethics, and the 'Uses of the Erotic.'" In *Daring to Be Good. See* Bar On and Ferguson 1998, 3–14.

———. 1993. *Uses of the Erotic: Contemporary Feminists and Plato on Eros, Power, and Reason*. Ph.D. dissertation. Princeton University.

Harkin, P. and J. Schilb, eds. 1991. *Contending with Words: Composition and Rhetoric in a Postmodern Age*. New York: Modern Language Association.

Harrington, S., S. Fox, and T. Hogue. 1998. "Power, Partnership, and Negotiations: The Limits of Collaboration." *WPA: Writing Program Administration* 21: 52–64.

Harris, J. 1997. *A Teaching Subject*. Upper Saddle River, N.J.: Prentice Hall.

Haswell, R. and M. Lu, eds. 2000. *Comp Tales: An Introduction to College Composition Through Its Stories*. New York: Longman.

Herrnstein, R. and C. Murray. 1996. *The Bell Curve: Intelligence and Class Structure in American Life*. New York: Touchstone Press.

Hesford, W. 1999. *Framing Identities: Autobiography and the Politics of Pedagogy*. Minneapolis: University of Minnesota Press.

Hesse, D. 1999. "WPA as Father, Husband, Ex." In *Kitchen Cooks*. *See* George 1999, 44–55.

Heyward, C. 1989. *Touching Our Strength: Erotic as Power and the Love of God*. San Francisco: Harper and Row.

Hill, J. 2001. "The Racializing Function of Language Panics." In *Language Ideologies: Critical Perspectives on the Official English Movement. Volume 2: History, Theory and Policy*, eds. R. Gonzales with I. Melis, 245–67. Urbana: National Council of Teachers of English and Mahway, NJ: Lawrence Erlbaum.

Hochschild, A. 1983. *The Managed Heart: Commercialization of Human Feeling*. Berkeley: University of California Press.

Holmes, D. 1999. "Fighting Back by Writing Black: Beyond Racially Reductive Composition Theory." In *Race, Rhetoric, and Composition,* by K. Gilyard 53–66. Portsmouth, NH: Boynton/Cook.

Holt, M. and L. Anderson. 1999. "Emotion Work and Writing Program Administration." Unpublished paper given at the WPA Conference, Purdue University, West Lafayette, Indiana.

Homiak, M. 1993. "Feminism and Aristotle's Rational Ideal." In *A Mind of One's Own,* eds. L. Antony and C. Witt, 1–17. Boulder: Westview.

hooks, b. 1994. *Teaching to Transgress: Education as the Practice of Freedom*. New York: Routledge.

Horner, B. 1999a. "Mapping Errors and Expectations for Basic Writing: From the 'Frontier Field' to 'Border Country.'" In *Representing the "Other": Basic Writers and the Teaching of Basic Writing*, by B. Horner and M. Lu, 117–36. Urbana: National Council of Teachers of English.

———. 1999b. "Re-thinking the 'Sociality' of Error: Teaching Editing as Negotiating." In *Representing the "Other": Basic Writers and the Teaching of Basic Writing*, by B. Horner and M. Lu, 136–65. Urbana: National Council of Teachers of English.

———. 2000. *Terms of Work for Composition: A Materialist Critique*. Albany: SUNY.

Hurlbert, C. M. and M. Blitz, eds. 1991. *Composition and Resistance*. Portsmouth, NH: Boynton/Cook.

Jaggar, A. 1989a. "Love and Knowledge: Emotion in Feminist Epistemology." In *Feminist Reconstructions of Being and Knowing,* eds. A. Jaggar and S. Bordo, 145–71. New Brunswick: Rutgers University Press.

———. 1989b. "Love and Knowledge: Emotion in Feminist Epistemology." In *Women, Knowledge, and Reality: Explorations in Feminist Philosophy,* eds. A. Garry and M. Pearsall, 129–55. Boston: Unwin Hyman.

Jarratt, S. 1991. "Feminism and Composition: The Case for Conflict." In *Contending with Words. See* Harkin and Schilb 1991, 105–23.

———. 2002. "Sappho's Memory." *Rhetoric Society Quarterly* 32.1: 11–43.

Jarratt, S. and N. Reynolds. 1994. "The Splitting Image: Contemporary Feminisms and the Ethics of *Ethos*." In *Ethos: New Essays in Rhetorical and Critical Theory*, eds. J. Baumlin and T. Baumlin, 37–63. Dallas: Southern Methodist University Press.

Jarratt, S. and L. Worsham, eds. 1998. *Feminism and Composition Studies: In Other Words*. New York: MLA.

Johnson, T. R. 2001. "School Sucks." *College Composition and Communication* 52.4: 620–50.

Johnstone, C. 1980. "An Aristotelian Trilogy: Ethics, Rhetoric, Politics, and the Search for Moral Truth." *Philosophy and Rhetoric* 13: 1–24.

Jukuri, S., and W. J. Williamson. 1999. "How to Be a Wishy-Washy Graduate Student WPA, or Undefined but Overdetermined: The Positioning of Graduate Student WPAs." In *Kitchen Cooks. See* George, 105–19.

Karen, R. 1992. "Shame." *The Atlantic Monthly* (February): 40–70.

Kerr, T. 1996. "Eviscerated Discourse: An Interdisciplinary Approach to the Suppression of Pathos and the Ideology of Shame in Academic Discourse and Writing Pedagogy." Ann Arbor: UMI Dissertation Abstracts.

Kosman, L. A. 1980. "Being Properly Affected: Virtues and Feelings in Aristotle's Ethics." In *Essays on Aristotle's Ethics*, ed. A. Rorty, 103–16. Berkeley: University of California Press.

———. 1989. "Platonic Love." In *Eros, Agape, and Philia. See* Soble 1989, 149–64.

———. 1976. "Platonic Love." In *Facets of Plato's Philosophy*, ed. W. H. Werkmeister, 53–69. n.p: Assen.

Koziak, B. 2000. *Retrieving Political Emotion*: Thumos, *Aristotle, and Gender*. University Park: The Pennsylvania State University Press.

Kundera, M. 1988. *The Art of the Novel*, trans. L. Asher. New York: Grove.

———. 1980. *Book of Laughter and Forgetting*, trans. M. Heim. New York: Knopf.

———. 1984. *The Unbearable Lightness of Being*, trans. M. Heim. New York: Harper Row.

Labov, W. 1972. "Is BEV a Separate Linguistic System?" In *Language in the Inner City: Studies in the Black English Vernacular*, by W. Labov, 36–64. Philadelphia: University of Pennsylvania Press.

Lain Entralgo, P. 1970. *The Therapy of the Word in Classical Antiquity*, trans. L. J. Rather and J. Sharp. New Haven: Yale University Press.

Lanham, R. 1975. *Style: An Anti-Textbook.* New Haven: Yale University Press.

Lee, A. 2000. *Composing Critical Pedagogies: Teaching Writing as Revision.* Urbana: National Council of Teachers of English.

LeGuin, Ursula. 1991. Untitled Poem. In *The Writer on Her Work, vol. II: New Essays in New Territory,* ed. Janet Sternberg, 216–17. New York: Norton.

Lord, C. 1996. "Aristotle and the Idea of Liberal Education." In *Demokratia*, eds. J. Ober and C. Hedrick, 271–88. New Jersey: Princeton University Press.

Lorde, A. 1997. *Sister/Outsider*. Freedom, CA: The Crossing Press.

Love, S. and D. Giffels. 1999. *Wheels of Fortune: The Story of Rubber in Akron*. Akron, OH: The University of Akron Press.

Lugg, K. 1999. *Kitsch: From Education to Public Policy*. New York: Garland.

Lutz, C. 1990. "Engendered Emotion: Gender, Power, and the Rhetoric of Emotional Control in American Discourse." In *Language and the Politics of Emotion. See* Lutz and Abu-Lughod 1990, 69–84.

Lutz, C. and L. Abu-Lughod, eds. 1990. *Language and the Politics of Emotion*. Cambridge: Cambridge University Press.

Lyman, P. 1981. "The Politics of Anger: On Silence, Ressentiment, and Political Speech." *Socialist Review* May-June: 55–74.

Lyotard, J. 1988. *The Differend: Phrases in Dispute*, trans. G. Van Den Abbeele. Minneapolis: University of Minnesota Press.

MacIntyre, A. 1984. *After Virtue: A Study in Moral Theory*. Notre Dame: University of Notre Dame Press.

May, R. 1969. *Love and Will*. New York: Norton.

McLaughlin, Thomas. 1996. *Street Smarts and Critical Theory: Listening to the Vernacular*. Madison: University of Wisconsin Press.

McLeod, S. 1997. *Notes on the Heart: Affective Issues in the Writing Classroom.* Carbondale, IL: Southern Illinois University Press.

———. 1987. "Some Thoughts About Feelings: The Affective Domain and the Writing Process." *College Composition and Communication* 38: 426–35.

Micciche, L. 2000. "When Class Equals Crass: A Working-Class Student's Ways with Anger." In *Blundering for a Change: Errors & Expectations in Critical Pedagogy*, eds. J. Tassoni and W. Thelin, 24–36. Portsmouth, NH: Boynton/Cook.

———. 2002. "More Than a Feeling: Disappointment and WPA Work." *College English* 64.4: 432–58.

Miles, L. 2001. "Constructing Composition: Reproduction and WPA Agency in Textbook Publishing." *WPA: Writing Program Administration* 24: 29–53.

Miller, R. 1998. *As if Learning Mattered: Reforming Higher Education*. Ithaca: Cornell University Press.

Miller, S. 1991. *Textual Carnivals: The Politics of Composition*. Carbondale: Southern Illinois University Press.

———. "Writing Theory: :Theory Writing." In *Methods and Methodology in Composition Research*, eds. G. Kirsch and P. Sullivan, 62–83. Carbondale and Edwardsville, IL: Southern Illinois University Press.

MLA Commission on Professional Service. 1996. "Making Faculty Work Visible: Reinterpreting Professional Service, Teaching, and Research in the Fields of Language and Literature." *Profession* 161–216.

Morrison, T. 1970. *The Bluest Eye*. New York: Penguin.

Mountford, R. 2002. "From Labor to Middle Management: Graduate Students in Writing Program Administration" *Rhetoric Review* 21: 41–52.

Mowry, J. 1992. *Way Past Cool*. New York: Farrar, Straus, Giroux.

Mutnick, D. 1996. *Writing in an Alien World: Basic Writing and the Struggle for Equality in Higher Education*. Portsmouth, NH: Boynton/Cook.

Myers, G. 1986. "Reality, Consensus, and Reform in the Rhetoric of Composition Teaching." *College English* 48: 154–71.

New London Group. 1996. "A Pedagogy of Multiliteracies: Designing Social Futures." *Harvard Educational Review* 66.1: 60–92.

Newkirk, T. 1997. *The Performance of Self in Student Writing*. Portsmouth, NH: Boynton/Cook.

Newton-Smith, W. 1989. "A Conceptual Investigation of Love." In *Eros, Agape, and Philia. See* Soble 1989, 199–217.

Nietzsche, F. 1989. "On Truth and Lying in the Extramoral Sense." In *Friedrich Nietzsche on Rhetoric and Language*, eds. S. Gilman, C. Blair, and D. Parent, 246–57. New York: Oxford University Press.

Nussbaum, M. 1994. *The Therapy of Desire: Theory and Practice in Hellenistic Ethics*. New Jersey: Princeton University Press.

———. 2001. *Upheaval of Thought: The Intelligence of Emotion*. Cambridge, UK: Cambridge University Press.

"Oakland Ebonics Resolution." 1998. In *The Real Ebonics Debate. See* Perry and Delpit 1998, 143–45.

Okawa, G. 2000. "From 'Bad Attitudes' to(ward) Linguistic Pluralism: Developing Reflective Language Policy among Preservice Teachers." In *Language Ideologies: Critical Perspectives on the Official English Movement. Vol. 1: Education and the Social Implications of Official Language*, eds. R. Duenas Gonzales with I. Melis, 276–96. Urbana, IL: NCTE and Mahway, NJ: Lawrence Erlbaum.

O'Neil, W. 1998. "If Ebonics Isn't a Language, Then Tell Me, What Is?" In *The Real Ebonics Debate. See* Perry and Delpit 1998, 38–47.

Osborne, C. 1994. *Eros Unveiled: Plato and the God of Love*. Oxford: Clarendon Press.

Paine, C. 1999. *The Resistant Writer: Rhetoric as Immunity, 1850 to the Present*. Albany: SUNY.

Palacas, A. 2001. "Liberating American Ebonics from Euro-English." *College English* 63: 326–52.

Perelman, C., and L. Olbrechts-Tyteca. 1969. *The New Rhetoric: A Treatise on Argumentation*. trans. J. Wilkinson and P. Weaver. Notre Dame: Notre Dame University Press.

Perl, S. 1994, 1981. "Understanding Composing." In *The Writing Teacher's Sourcebook*. 3rd. ed., eds. G. Tate, E. Corbett, and N. Myers, 149–54. New York: Oxford University Press.

Perry, T., and L. Delpit, eds. 1998. *The Real Ebonics Debate: Power, Language, and the Education of African-American Children*. Boston: Beacon.

Pfau, M. and A. Louden. 1994. "Effectiveness of Adwatch Formats in Deflecting Political Attack Ads." *Communication Research* 21.3: 325–41.

Phelps, L. W. 1995. "Becoming a Warrior: Lessons of the Feminist Workplace." In *Feminine Principles and Women's Experience in American Composition and Rhetoric,* eds. L. W. Phelps and J. Emig, 289–339. Pittsburgh: University of Pittsburgh Press.

Pierce, J. 1995. *Gender Trials: Emotional Lives in Contemporary Law Firms*. Berkeley: University of California Press.

Plato. 1914. *Euthyphro, Apology, Crito, Phaedo, Phaedrus*, trans. H. Fowler. London: William Heinemann Ltd.

———. 1952. *Gorgias,* trans. W.C. Heimbold. New York: Macmillan Publishing Co.

———. 1951. *Symposium*, trans. W. Hamilton. London: Penguin Books.

Plutchik, R. and H. Kellerman, eds. 1980. *Theories of Emotion*. Vol. 1, *Emotion: Theory, Research, and Experience*. New York: Academic Press.

Porter, K. 2001. "A Pedagogy of Charity: Donald Davidson and the Student-Negotiated Composition Classroom." *College Composition and Communication* 5.24: 574–611.

Powell, K., P. O'Neill, C. Phillips, and B. Huot. 2002. "Negotiating Resistance and Change: One Composition Program's Struggle Not to Convert." In *Preparing College Teachers of Writing. See* Pytlik and Liggett 2002, 121–32.

Pratt, M. L. 1991. "Arts of the Contact Zone." *Profession* 91: 33–40.

Pytlik, B., and S. Liggett, eds. 2002. *Preparing College Teachers of Writing: Histories, Theories, Programs, Practices*. New York: Oxford University Press.

Reik, T. 1957. *Of Love and Lust*. New York: Farrar, Straus, and Cudahy.

Rickford, J. 1998. "The Creole Origins of African American Vernacular English." In *African American English: Structure, History, and Use*, eds. S. Mufwene, J. Rickford, G. Bailey, and J. Baugh, 154–200. New York: Routledge.

Rickley, R. and S. Harrington. 2002. "Feminist Approaches to Mentoring Teaching Assistants: Conflict, Power, and Collaboration." In *Preparing College Teachers of Writing. See* Pytlik and Liggett 2002, 108–20.

Rodgers, A. April 30, 2001. "A New Brand of Tech Cities." *Newsweek*.

Roediger, D.1991. *The Wages of Whiteness*. London: Verso.

Rorty, A. 1980. *Explaining Emotions*. Berkeley and Los Angeles: University of California Press.

Rose, G. 1996. "As If the Mirrors Had Bled: Masculine Dwelling, Masculinist Theory, and Feminist Masquerade." In *Body Space*, ed. N. Duncan, 56–74. New York: Routledge.

Rose, M. 1981. "Sophisticated, Ineffective Books—The Dismantling of Process in Composition Books." *College Composition and Communcation* 32: 65–74.

———. 1983. "Speculations on Process Knowledge and the Textbook's Static Page." *College Composition and Communication* 34: 298–313.

Rushdie, S. 1996. "How News Becomes Opinion, and Opinion Off-Limits." *Nation* 24 June: 18–20.

Sandoval, C. 1997. "Theorizing White Consciousness for a Post-Empire World: Barthes, Fanon, and the Rhetoric of Love." In *Displacing Whiteness: Essays in Social and Cultural Criticism*, ed. R. Frankenberg, 86–106. Durham: Duke University Press.

Sartre, Jean-Paul. 1948. *The Emotions: Outline of a Theory*, trans. B. Frechtman. New York: The Wisdom Library.

Saunders, F. 1999. *The Cultural Cold War: The CIA and the World of Arts and Letters*. New York: The New Press.

Scarry, E. 1985. *The Body in Pain: The Making and Unmaking of the World*. New York: Oxford University Press.

Schell, E. 1998. "The Costs of Caring: 'Femininism' and Contingent Women Workers in Composition Studies." In *Feminism and Composition Studies. See* Jarratt and Worsham 1998, 74–93.

———. 1998. *Gypsy Academics and Mother Teachers: Gender, Contingent Labor, and Writing Instruction*. Portsmouth, NH: Boynton/Cook.

———. 1998. "Who's the Boss?: The Possibilities and Pitfalls of Collaborative Administration for Untenured WPAs." *WPA: Writing Program Administration* 21.1/2: 65–80.

Schilb, J. 1992. "The Sociological Imagination and the Ethics of Collaboration." In *New Visions of Collaborative Writing*, ed. J. Forman, 15–119. Portsmouth, NH: Boynton/Cook.

Shaughnessy, M. 1977. *Errors and Expectations*. New York: Oxford University Press.

Shor, I. 1987. *Freire for the Classroom*. Portsmouth, N.H.: Boynton/Cook.

Smit, D. 1989. "Some Difficulties with Collaborative Learning." *JAC: Journal of Advanced Composition* 9: 45–58.

Smith, D. 1990. *The Conceptual Practices of Power: A Feminist Sociology of Knowledge*. Boston: Northeastern University Press.

———. 1987. *The Everyday World as Problematic: A Feminist Sociology*. Boston: Northeastern University Press.

———. 1999. *Writing the Social: Critique, Theory, and Investigations*. Toronto: University of Toronto Press.

Smith, E. 1998. "What Is Black English? What Is Ebonics?" In *The Real Ebonics Debate. See* Perry and Delpit 1998, 49–58.

Smitherman, G. 1985. *Talkin and Testifyin: The Language of Black America*. Boston: Houghton Mifflin, 1977. Reprint, Detroit: Wayne State University Press.

Soble, A. ed. 1989. *Eros, Agape, and Philia: Readings in the Philosophy of Love*. New York: Paragon House.

Sommers, N. 1992. "Between the Drafts." *College Composition and Communication* 43: 23–31.

———. 1982. "Responding to Student Writing." *College Composition and Communication* 33: 148–56.

Sommers, S. 1988. "Understanding Emotions: Some Interdisciplinary Considerations." In *Emotion and Social Change: Toward a New Psychohistory*, eds. C. Zisowitz Stearns and P. N. Stearns, 23–38. New York: Holmes & Meier.

Spelman, E. 1989. "Anger and Insubordination." In *Women, Knowledge, and Reality*, eds. A. Garry and M. Pearsall, 263–78. Boston: Unwin Hyman.

Spellmeyer, K. 1998 "Marginal Prospects." *WPA: Writing Program Administration* 21 (Spring): 162–82.

Spigelman, C. 2001. "What Role Virtue?" *JAC: Journal of Advanced Composition* 21.2: 321–348.

Stearns, P. 1986. "Anger and American Work: A Twentieth Century Turning Point." In *Anger: The Struggle for Emotional Control in American History,* by C. Stearns and P. Stearns, 123–48. Chicago: University of Chicago Press..

Stewart, D. 1988. "Collaborative Learning and Composition: Boon or Bane?" *Rhetoric Review* 7: 58–83.

Stuckey, J. E. 1992. *The Violence of Literacy*. Portsmouth, NH: Boynton/Cook.

Stygall, G. 1998. "Women and Language in the Collaborative Writing Classroom." In *Feminism and Composition Studies. See* Jarratt and Worsham 1998, 252–75.

Thompson, J. 1991. Introduction to *Language and Symbolic Power*, by P. Bourdieu. Cambridge: Harvard University Press.

Tompkins, J. 1993. "Me and My Shadow." In *The Intimate Critique*, eds. O. Frey and F. Zaunar, 23–40. Durham: Duke University Press.

Trimbur, J. 1989. "Consensus and Difference in Collaborative Learning." *College English* 51: 602–16.

Turner, B. 1992. *Max Weber: From History to Modernity*. London: Routledge.

Urmson, J. O. 1980. "Aristotle's Doctrine of the Mean." In *Essays on Aristotle's Ethics*, ed. A. Rorty, 157–170. Berkeley: University of California Press.

Walker, J. 1994. "The Body of Persuasion: A Theory of the Enthymeme." *College English* 56.1: 46–65.

———. 2000. "*Pathos* and *Katharsis* in 'Aristotelian' Rhetoric: Some Implications." In *Rereading Aristotle's Rhetoric*, eds. A. Gross and A. Walzer, 74–92. Carbondale: Southern Illinois University Press.

Watson, N. 1999. "The Politics of Middle English Writing." In *The Idea of the Vernacular: An Anthology of Middle English Literary Theory, 1280-1520*, ed. J. Wogan-Browne et al., 331–52. University Park: Pennsylvania State University Press.

Welch, N. 1997. *Getting Restless: Rethinking Revision in Writing Instruction*. Portsmouth, NH: Boynton/Cook.

West, T. 2000. "The Rhetoric of Therapy and the Politics of Anger: From the Safe House to a Praxis of Shelter." *Rhetoric Review* 19.1/2: 42–58.

White, E. 1991. "Use It or Lose It: Power and the WPA." *WPA: Writing Program Administration* 15.1/2: 3–12.

Williams, C. 1995. *Still a Man's World: Men Who Do Women's Work*. Berkeley: University of California Press.

Williams, J. 1981. "The Phenomenology of Error." *College Composition and Communication* 32: 152–68.

Williams, J. 1981. "The Phenomenology of Error." *College Composition and Communication Online*. www.ncte.org/threshold/ccc/1981/3c3202ph.html (1 Nov. 2001). First published in *College Composition and Communication* 32: 152–68.

Williams, R. 1977. *Marxism and Literature*. Oxford: Oxford University Press.

Williams, S. 2001. *Emotion and Social Theory: Corporeal Reflections on the (Ir)Rational*. London: Sage.

Wilson, E. 1978. *On Human Nat*ure. Cambridge: Cambridge University Press.

Wingate, M. 1995. "The Politics of Collaboration: Writing Centers Within Their Institutions." In *Resituating Writing: Constructing and Administering Writing Programs*, eds. J. Janangelo and K. Hansen, 100–107. Portsmouth, NH: Boynton/Cook.

Worsham, L. 2002. "Coming to Terms: Theory, Writing, Politics." In *Rhetoric and Composition as Intellectual Work,* ed. G. Olson, 101–14. Albany: SUNY.

———. 1992–93. "Emotion and Pedagogic Violence." *Discourse: Journal for Theoretical Studies in Media and Culture* 15.2: 119–48.

———. 1998. "Going Postal: Pedagogic Violence and the Schooling of Emotion." *JAC: Journal of Advanced Composition* 18.2: 213–45.

Young, R. E., A. L. Becker, and K. L. Pike. 1970. *Rhetoric: Discovery and Change*. New York: Harcourt.

Contributors

Leon Anderson is Professor and Chair of the Department of Sociology and Anthropology at Ohio University. His research has focused largely on homelessness in the United States. He has also coauthored articles with Mara Holt on academic work practices and the teaching of writing in sociology courses. Currently he is coauthoring (with David Snow, Lyn Lofland, and John Lofland) the fourth edition of a qualitative methods textbook, *Analyzing Social Settings* (Wadsworth, forthcoming).

Janet Bean is Assistant Professor of English at The University of Akron, where she teaches undergraduate and graduate courses in Composition and directs a writing and tutoring program for at-risk urban high school students. Her work has appeared in several edited collections.

Mary Ann Cain is Associate Professor of English at Indiana University Purdue University Fort Wayne where she teaches writing, theory, and pedagogy, as well as Women's Studies. Her book, *Revisioning Writers' Talk: Gender and Culture in Acts of Composing*, was published by SUNY Press in 1995. Her articles have appeared or are forthcoming in *College Composition and Communication*, *College English*, *Dialogue*, *Composition Studies*, *Written Communication*, and others. Her fiction, essays, and prose poetry appears in numerous literary journals.

Ilene Crawford is Assistant Professor of English at Southern Connecticut State University, where she codirects the first-year writing program and teaches basic writing, first-year writing, and graduate courses in rhetoric and composition theory. Her research examines rhetorics of race and emotion.

Peter Elbow is Emeritus Professor of English at the University of Massachusetts at Amherst. He directed the Writing Program there and at SUNY Stony Brook, and taught at M.I.T., Franconia College, Evergreen State College. His recent book, *Everyone Can Write: Essays Toward a Hopeful Theory of Writing and Teaching Writing*, was given the James Britton Award by the Conference on English Education. NCTE recently gave him the James Squire Award "for his transforming influence and lasting intellectual contribution."

Alice Gillam is Associate Professor of English at the University of Wisconsin-Milwaukee. Her published research includes "Writing Center Ecology: A Bakhtinian Perspective," which won an Outstanding Scholarship Award from the National Writing Center Association in 1992. Her essays have appeared in books such as *Intersections*, *Theorizing Composition*, and *Kitchen Cooks, Plate Twirlers, and Troubadours*. Her most recent work includes a coedited collection of essays, *Writing Center Research: Extending the Conversation*; a cowritten first-year writing text,

Reading Rhetorically; and a new research project on rhetoric and the emotions, supported by a year-long fellowship in UWM's Center for 21st Century Studies.

Mara Holt is Associate Professor in the English department at Ohio University. Her work has been published in *JAC*, *College Composition and Communication*, *PRE/TEXT*, and *Profession*. She has published chapters in *Kitchen Cooks, Plate Twirlers, and Troubadours* and in *The Philosophy of Discourse*. She is coauthoring a book on collaborative learning in composition studies with Albert Rouzie.

Dale Jacobs is an Assistant Professor and Director of Composition at the University of Windsor. He is the editor of *The Myles Horton Reader* and his articles have appeared in journals such as *Composition Studies*, *Journal of the Assembly for Expanded Perspectives on Learning, National Writing Project Quarterly*, and *North Carolina English Teacher*. In addition, he is the author of a book of poetry entitled *Beneath the Horse's Eye* and is the editor of *Ice: New Writing on Hockey*. His research interests are in the areas of emotion, critical pedagogies, and literacy.

Tom Kerr is Assistant Professor of Writing and Rhetoric at Ithaca College. His research on the emotions began in his 1996 dissertation, "Eviscerated Discourse: An Interdisciplinary Approach to the Suppression of Pathos and the Ideology of Shame in Academic Discourse and Writing Pedagogy." He has published on various aspects of composition in *Key Words in Composition* and the journal *Pedagogy*. He is currently working on a book that explores the rhetorical foundations of America's prison industrial complex.

Susan Kirtley, Assistant Professor of English at Western Oregon University, teaches a variety of courses in composition and literature. She is currently working on a project investigating how students perceive of new writing technologies and the culture associated with them. Her research interests include medieval women writers, computers and composition, and feminism and Composition Studies.

Laura R. Micciche is Assistant Professor of English at East Carolina University, where she teaches courses in writing, rhetoric, and feminist theory. Her research has appeared in *College English*, *Composition Forum*, *Composition Studies*, and several edited collections. Her research interests focus on rhetorics of difference in relation to pedagogy, professional identity, and academic workplace practices.

Gretchen Flesher Moon is Associate Professor of English and Director of the Writing Center at Willamette University in Salem, Oregon, where she teaches a variety of writing courses, freshman seminars, and Shakespeare courses. She is a founding member of the CCCC special interest group on Composition at the Small College/University and her major administrative work is in faculty development for writing across the curriculum. Her major research interests are in autobiographical writing and the uses of literacy demonstrated in women's overland diaries.

Piper Murray is currently finishing her dissertation, titled "Misfit Emotions," at the University of Wisconsin-Milwaukee. In fall 2003, she will be joining the Program for Writing and Rhetoric at University of Colorado-Boulder, where she will direct the first-year writing program. In addition to her work on the emotions in composition studies, her essays on literature have appeared in *Victorian Literature, Modern Drama*, and *Comparative Literature*.

Brad Peters coordinates the Writing Across the Curriculum program at Northern Illinois University, where he teaches undergraduate and graduate writing courses. Recent publications appear in *Blundering for a Change* and *Questioning Authority: Stories Told in School.*

Ellen Quandahl is Associate Professor of Rhetoric and Writing Studies at San Diego State University, where she directs the Lower Division Writing Program and teaches writing, pedagogy, and rhetorical theory and history. Her publications, including pieces in *College English*, *Rhetoric Society Quarterly* and *Rhetoric Review*, explore interactions of rhetorical theory and pedagogy.

Albert Rouzie is Associate Professor in the English department at Ohio University. His work has been published in *JAC*, *College Composition and Communication*, *Computers and Composition*, and *Kairos*. He is working on a book on serio-ludic discourse in computer-mediated composition classes and is coauthoring a book on collaborative learning in composition studies with Mara Holt.

Wendy Ryden holds a Ph.D. in Composition and Rhetoric from the CUNY Graduate School. Recent publications include the coauthored article "Interrogating the Monologue: Making Whiteness Visible" (*CCC* Dec 2000) and "How Soft is Process? The Feminization of Comp and Pedagogies of Care" (*JBW* Spring 2001). She is currently at work with her coeditor Ian Marshall on a book about whiteness studies and Composition.

Donna Strickland is Assistant Professor of English at Southern Illinois University Carbondale, where she teaches writing, rhetorical theory, and composition pedagogy. She is currently completing a book-length study of the "managerial unconscious" in Composition Studies.

Lynn Worsham is Professor of English at the University of South Florida where she teaches graduate courses in rhetorical theory and undergraduate courses in cultural studies and literature. She is currently editor of *JAC*, a quarterly journal for the interdisciplinary study of rhetoric, writing, and culture. For the last decade, her scholarship has focused on the political dimension of emotion.

William W. Wright is Associate Professor of English at Mesa State College in Grand Junction, Colorado. He has published on rhetorical education, baseball, writing instruction, and discourse conventions, and he is currently at work on a book about baseball and public discourse. His published work appears or is forthcoming in *Advanced Composition: Principles and Practices*, *In Diamond Mines: Baseball and Labor*, *Journal of Teaching Writing*, *Exercise Exchange*, and *Teaching English in the Two-Year College*.